THE ROAD TO WIGAN PIER

GEORGE ORWELL was born Eric Arthur Blair in 1903 in Motihari, in modern Bihar, where his father worked in the Indian Civil Service. He grew up in Oxfordshire and was a King's Scholar at Eton from 1917 to 1921. Between 1922 and 1927, he worked for the Indian Imperial Police; after returning to England, he spent some years living as a tramp and casual manual worker, episodes that informed *Down and Out in Paris and London*, published in 1933 under his newly chosen pseudonym 'George Orwell'. His first novel, *Burmese Days*, which drew on his imperial experience, appeared in 1934. Between 1935 and 1940 he published three more novels and three non-fiction works, including *The Road to Wigan Pier* (1937) and *Homage to Catalonia* (1938), an account of his time fighting in the Spanish Civil War as a Republican volunteer. In 1936 he married Eileen O'Shaughnessy, who died in 1945. At the beginning of the Second World War Orwell, turned down for military service due to ill health, joined the Home Guard. From 1941 to 1943 he worked as a talks producer for the BBC Eastern Service, after which he became literary editor of the left-wing weekly *Tribune* for two years, to which he also contributed a column 'As I Please'. Throughout the war he wrote a large number of occasional articles and periodical essays. Orwell's political satire *Animal Farm*, was completed by the end of February 1944 but not published until August 1945, when it enjoyed enormous success. From 1946 he spent long periods on the isle of Jura in the Inner Hebrides working on the novel that became *Nineteen Eighty-Four* and struggling with worsening tuberculosis; the novel was published in 1949, again to great acclaim. Confined to a sanatorium, he married his second wife, Sonia Brownell, late in 1949; he died of a tubercular haemorrhage in January the following year.

SELINA TODD is Professor of Modern History at Oxford University. She writes about class, inequality, working-class history, feminism, and women's lives in modern Britain. Her book *The People: The Rise and Fall of the Working Class 1910–2010* was a *Sunday Times* bestseller and was described by *The Observer* as 'A book we badly need'.

OXFORD WORLD'S CLASSICS

*For over 100 years Oxford World's Classics have brought
readers closer to the world's great literature. Now with over 700
titles—from the 4,000-year-old myths of Mesopotamia to the
twentieth century's greatest novels—the series makes available
lesser-known as well as celebrated writing.*

*The pocket-sized hardbacks of the early years contained
introductions by Virginia Woolf, T. S. Eliot, Graham Greene,
and other literary figures which enriched the experience of reading.
Today the series is recognized for its fine scholarship and
reliability in texts that span world literature, drama and poetry,
religion, philosophy and politics. Each edition includes perceptive
commentary and essential background information to meet the
changing needs of readers.*

OXFORD WORLD'S CLASSICS

GEORGE ORWELL

The Road to Wigan Pier

Edited with an Introduction and Notes by
SELINA TODD

OXFORD
UNIVERSITY PRESS

OXFORD

UNIVERSITY PRESS

Great Clarendon Street, Oxford, OX2 6DP,
United Kingdom

Oxford University Press is a department of the University of Oxford.
It furthers the University's objective of excellence in research, scholarship,
and education by publishing worldwide. Oxford is a registered trade mark of
Oxford University Press in the UK and in certain other countries

British Library Cataloguing in Publication Data

Data available

ISBN 978-0-19-885090-8

Printed and bound in Great Britain by
Clays Ltd, Elcograf S.p.A.

Links to third party websites are provided by Oxford in good faith and
for information only. Oxford disclaims any responsibility for the materials
contained in any third party website referenced in this work.

CONTENTS

INTRODUCTION

When *The Road to Wigan Pier* was published in 1937, it joined a crowded bookshelf of studies of a changing England. Surveys and travelogues documented the lengthening dole queues and the new assembly lines; decrepit slums and modern council estates; mass democracy and the threat of Fascism. *Wigan Pier* describes George Orwell's account of his journey to Wigan and other northern towns and cities, undertaken between January and March 1936, and his reflections on what to do about the poverty he found there. But unlike the majority of such volumes, *The Road to Wigan Pier* has stood the test of time. It has never been out of print.

Wigan Pier's continued appeal is in part due to the endurance of poverty. In the 1930s, most writers of 'condition of England' books focused on the causes and consequences of unemployment—understandably, for the number of people out of work rose dramatically after the Wall Street Crash in 1929. Throughout the next decade, unemployment was the single most important cause of poverty.[1] But Orwell focused more broadly on the experience of being poor: the hunger, illness, indignity, and despair; the frantic and often fruitless efforts to make ends meet. As long as poverty exists, *Wigan Pier* will resonate.

But Orwell's perspective and tone are also important. This is especially true of Part One of his book, which describes his journey north (in Part Two, Orwell focuses on political solutions to poverty). He is not the detached, omnipotent narrator that many social investigators strived to be. Not for Orwell the statistics and maps of Hubert Llewellyn Smith's *New Survey of London Life and Labour*.[2] Orwell is primarily interested in recording his own responses to what he found. But the result is utterly unlike J. B. Priestley's *English Journey* (1934), whose author took the same approach.[3] This is partly because Orwell is more

---

[1] Selina Todd, *The People: The Rise and Fall of the Working Class, 1910–2010* (London: John Murray, 2014), 61–94.

[2] Hubert Llewellyn Smith, *The New Survey of London Life and Labour*, 9 vols (London: London School of Economics, 1934).

[3] John Boynton Priestley, *English Journey: Being a Rambling but Truthful Account of What One Man Saw and Heard and Felt and Thought During a Journey through England During the Autumn of the Year 1933* (London: W. Heinemann in association with V. Gollancz, 1934).

honest than Priestley about his limitations as a narrator. *Wigan Pier* opens thus: 'The first sound in the mornings was the clumping of the mill-girls' clogs down the cobbled street. Earlier than that, I suppose, there were factory whistles which I was never awake to hear' (p. 3). Life goes on beyond his partial vision: his conclusions and judgements can only ever be partial. The reader is forewarned (and disarmed).

But what life Orwell does observe he documents in rich detail. Few social surveys recorded individual's experiences. Those that did—Priestley's *English Journey*, or Jack Hilton's *English Ways* (1940)—focused on what people said or did.[4] But Orwell is concerned to probe beneath the surface, to work out how people were feeling. In doing so, he provides a vivid account of how poverty starved people of their dignity, as well as of food and shelter. He captures a place or a person in just one pithy, memorable phrase or sentence. Of two salesmen staying at the same Wigan lodging-house, he wrote: 'They used to pay a small sum for their beds and make shamefaced meals in a corner of the kitchen off bacon and bread-and-margarine which they stored in their suit-cases' (p. 7).

Most important to its appeal is that *Wigan Pier* is primarily the story of Orwell's development as a writer, a thinker, and a citizen. He is the central character, as Priestley is in *English Journey* and Hilton in *English Ways*—but unlike them, Orwell consciously learns and changes as a result of what he finds. The first part of *Wigan Pier* is novelistic in this regard: the story of our hero's growth. Orwell captures this best when dealing in relationships between himself and those he meets. In showing us the miner's 'vast achievement', Orwell argues that we can best understand by 'comparing a miner's life with somebody else's', rather than by dealing in statistics or abstract political ideologies. 'If I live to be sixty I shall probably have produced thirty novels, or enough to fill two medium-sized library shelves. In the same period the average miner produces 8400 tons of coal; enough coal to pave Trafalgar Square nearly two feet deep or to supply seven large families with fuel for over a hundred years' (p. 29). And yet many miners' families struggle to make ends meet. He uses the relationship between himself and the miners to capture our interest and draw us into his story. And, by drawing on the landmark of 'Trafalgar Square', his reference to the 'seven families' served by one miner, and his description

---

[4] Jack Hilton, *English Ways: A Walk from the Pennines to Epsom Downs in 1939* (London: Jonathan Cape, 1940).

of 'library shelves', he makes his relationship to the miner as a metaphor for social, economic, and political inequality. The people of Wigan are connected to southern writers and their readers. And their shared humanity is the basis for Orwell's argument that however rich a society is in resources or Gross National Product, it should be judged according to whether all of its people can live in dignity, free of want.

Orwell crafted this moral perspective and tone in *Wigan Pier*; it would characterize almost all his later non-fiction. It unites the two parts of *Wigan Pier*, but at times it could lead to ill-founded and crude judgements. In Part One, his representation of working-class people could become sentimental and partial when he refused to acknowledge facts that challenged his opinions. The second part of the book is an anticlimax after the first. The protagonist has grown to maturity and now he seeks to deliver his political judgement. This can be tedious, and is often naïve and tendentious. Part Two is dominated by Orwell's criticisms of socialism and Socialists and weakened by this. Orwell presented himself as seeking practical solutions to poverty, against the romanticism and condescension (as he saw it) of British Socialists. Orwell powerfully argued against Stalinists, for 'sabotaging democracy' and because, 'their eyes glued to economic facts, they have proceeded on the assumption that man has no soul'. Socialists, argued Orwell, must have 'justice and liberty' as their most important aims (p. 147). These were important criticisms in the mid-1930s; but Orwell overlooked that Stalinism and socialism were not the same. In Britain, William Morris and other nineteenth-century Socialists had argued powerfully for socialism as a moral and humane movement, committed to ending the treatment of people as the possessions of their employers and allowing them to exercise their creative potential. This was the *raison d'être* of many labour movement activists throughout the late nineteenth and early twentieth centuries. Orwell similarly ignored the participation of many working-class people in creating and sustaining socialism.[5]

Orwell's perspective was influenced by his upbringing. He came to renounce much of what he imbibed from his family and schooling, but his distrust of socialism sprang from his upper-middle-class

[5] Edward Palmer Thompson, *William Morris: Romantic to Revolutionary* (London: Lawrence & Wishart, 1955).

background. He was born Eric Blair, in 1903, to a family of the
'lower-upper-middle class' (p. 83) reliant on the British Empire for
their fortunes. Orwell's father, Richard, worked in the Indian Civil
Service, and Eric was born in India. Orwell was brought up in a social
class that prized their own individualism and dismissed the 'lower
classes' as an anonymous, all-too-dependent mass (p. 87).

The family was well off, but acutely aware of their precarity. Orwell
grew up embedded within the ruling class and its institutions—but
not entirely securely, for, as Raymond Williams argues,

> only part of the class was quite wholly in command: able to live on its prop-
> erty and investments, or to move directly into the central metropolitan
> institutions. A much larger part had a harder and humbler function . . . as
> servants of a system . . . these people . . . went out to the edges of the sys-
> tem, facing its realities directly . . . Owning no land or substantial property,
> they were dependent on their professional salaries.[6]

Orwell was brought up in Henley-on-Thames and sent to Eton
College. But Orwell owed his place at the school to a scholarship, and
knew that he would have to earn his living. He left Eton aged 16 to
join the Imperial Police in Burma (then a province of British India).

Orwell became interested in social exploration as a teenager. His
family's connection to India, and his awareness of his family's precar-
ious position on the margins of the ruling class, sparked an interest in
other outsiders. While 'I had . . . no notion that the working class were
human beings . . . through the medium of books—Jack London's *The
People of the Abyss*, for instance—I could agonize over their sufferings' (p. 96). Jack London, an American journalist and social activist,
had published *The People of the Abyss* in 1903, the year of Orwell's
birth.[7] His first-hand account of living in London's East End for several weeks was a highly readable example of what, even by 1903, was
a well-established genre of literary 'slumming'.[8]

Orwell's experience in the Imperial Police deepened his feeling for
the underdog. 'I had been part of an oppressive system, and it had left
me with a bad conscience', he wrote in *Wigan Pier*. 'I felt that I had
got to escape not merely from imperialism but from every form of

---

[6] Raymond Williams, *Orwell* (London: Fontana, 1971), 18–19.
[7] Jack London, *The People of the Abyss* (London: Macmillan, 1903).
[8] Seth Koven, *Slumming: Sexual and Social Politics in Victorian London* (Princeton:
Princeton University Press, 2004).

man's dominion over man' (p. 101). In 1928 he returned to England determined to write about social conditions. He invented the pseudonym 'George Orwell', a sign of his determination to embark on a new life. His first non-fiction book, *Down and Out in Paris and London* (1933), was part of this project: Orwell lived as a tramp for several months.

Orwell's sense of himself as an outsider informed a critical detachment from the situations in which he found himself. This helped him to become a great writer. But by 1936 he acknowledged that having 'to think everything out in solitude' meant he did not have to hone his arguments in debate, and risked idealizing those he sought to champion. 'I had reduced everything to the simple theory that the oppressed are always right and the oppressors are always wrong' (p. 101).

Orwell became critical of *Down and Out* for focusing on 'social outcasts: tramps, beggars, criminals, prostitutes' (p. 102). Writing in *Wigan Pier* about his earlier book, Orwell disparaged his forays into this life as a dilettante expedition. '[D]own there in the squalid and, as a matter of fact, horribly boring sub-world of the tramp I had a feeling of release, of adventure, which seems absurd when I look back, but which was sufficiently vivid at the time' (p. 105). By 1936, he no longer saw poverty as the 'brute starvation' (p. 102) of a small distinct group. He now treated it as a symptom of a deeper division in society, between the many who were exploited, and the few who benefited from their labour. 'Foreign oppression is a much more obvious, understandable evil than economic oppression', he wrote in *Wigan Pier*. 'Thus in England we tamely admit to being robbed in order to keep half a million worthless idlers in luxury, but we would fight to the last man sooner than be ruled by Chinamen' (p. 99).

Orwell's understanding of poverty was influenced by unemployment, and by his introduction to Socialists. At any time between 1921 and 1933, more than one million people were out of work. The situation worsened after the Wall Street Crash and the global recession it precipitated. In Britain, unemployment was particularly high in those regions that relied on heavy industries: steel, iron, cotton, and mining. These included South Wales, Clydeside, Tyneside, the Yorkshire coalfield, and Lancashire's textile and mining towns. In 1932, more than 22 per cent of the workforce in Wigan were unemployed. By

1936, unemployment was falling but 13 per cent of workers were claiming unemployment benefit and far more in northern England. Those who remained in work, but relied on heavy industry for their livelihood, found it hard to live on their low wages.[9]

Among the unemployed were those skilled workers who, before the First World War, had formed the backbone of the labour movement. Their possession of a craft that employers needed had offered them a degree of bargaining power. They were able to establish trade unions, friendly societies, and the co-operative movement. After the war, recession, and the government's punitive approach to the unemployed, jeopardized not just these workers' livelihoods but their ability to organize collectively and exercise political power.

Orwell knew about this because of his increased involvement in the British Left. In the early 1930s, the British Left—Communists, Labour Party activists, trade unionists, and non-aligned Socialists—was an important force in cultural life. Orwell wrote for left-wing periodicals like *The Adelphi*. He knew the publisher Victor Gollancz, who was to found the Left Book Club in 1936, and Jack Common and Jack Hilton, two of those working-class writers who got into print thanks to their involvement in left-wing politics.[10]

In January 1936, Victor Gollancz invited Orwell to write a book about the unemployed in northern England. By the mid-1930s, Socialists like Gollancz looked nervously at the rise of Fascism in continental European countries and wondered if the same might happen in Britain. Politicians' responses to unemployment did not inspire much hope. Labour had won the general election of 1929 but in the following year the prime minister, Ramsay MacDonald, decided a 'government of all parties' must address the economic crisis. His National Government was a Conservative-dominated administration committed to swingeing public spending cuts. In 1931, the government introduced a household means test for anyone seeking to claim unemployment benefit. Claimants had to submit to having their home and the income of all household members means tested. Members of the local Public Assistance Committee

[9] John Stevenson and Chris Cook, *The Slump* (London: Routledge, 2013), 66–8.

[10] For an excellent analysis of Orwell's connections with this group and their influence on him, see Ben Clarke, 'George Orwell, Jack Hilton, and the Working Class', *Review of English Studies*, 67 (2016), 764–85.

(PAC) were responsible for deciding whether claimants were 'deserving' of any help. The only time Orwell met outright hostility in his research for *Wigan Pier* was when he was mistaken for a 'Means Test nark' (p. 50).

Orwell accepted Gollancz's commission and set about planning his trip north. He relied heavily on Jack Common, Jack Hilton, and other *Adelphi* acquaintances for advice and contacts. Orwell had originally intended to find lodgings in Rochdale, but Hilton recommended Wigan, because the town relied on mining as well as cotton and he thought that Orwell would get ' "good stuff" ' from the miners there.[11] *Wigan Pier* would help to create an enduring representation of the 'traditional' British working class to which miners were central.

On 31 January 1936, Orwell travelled to Coventry. He wanted to travel in much the same way as an unemployed man seeking work might do. He spent four days travelling to Manchester by bus and on foot, staying in lodging-houses and hostels. He was armed with letters of introduction from Middleton Murry, the editor of *The Adelphi*, and from members of the Independent Labour Party (ILP). Formed in 1893, the ILP had helped establish the Labour Party, but opposed MacDonald's formation of a National Government and fielded its own MPs and councillors through the 1930s. It was a vibrant political and intellectual force.

In *Down and Out in Paris and London* Orwell had travelled incognito. But by 1936, his views on social class, and how to address class inequality, had changed. Once, he had believed that bridging the class divide would bring mutual understanding, leading to the end of enmity and suspicion on both sides. By 1936, he had decided that 'unfortunately you do not solve the class problem by making friends with tramps' (p. 106). And while it had been possible to disguise himself as a tramp simply 'by putting on the right clothes . . . you can't become a navvy or a coal-miner' in this way (p. 107). Aside from the physical demands of manual work, Orwell knew that the life of those he intended to study in northern England was quite different from the itinerant existence of tramps. In settled communities like Wigan, people would know immediately that 'I was not one of them' (p. 107).

---

[11] Quoted in Clarke, 'George Orwell, Jack Hilton, and the Working Class', 765.

Nevertheless, in an important respect Orwell's approach was similar to that he had adopted for *Down and Out*. '[Y]ou can only mingle with the working class by staying in their houses as a lodger', he wrote; and while he noted that this 'has a dangerous resemblance to "slumming"' (p. 107), it was nevertheless what he did on his travels in 1936.

Orwell's most valuable contacts were labour movement activists. In Manchester, he stayed with Mr and Mrs Meade—Mr Meade was a trade union official and both were Socialists. They introduced Orwell to Joe Kennan, an electrician who lived in Wigan and a member of the ILP and the National Unemployed Workers' Movement (NUWM). Communists had founded the NUWM in 1921, but by the 1930s members came from across the Left. Kennan found Orwell lodgings in Wigan and, during February 1936, his NUWM contacts took Orwell to visit unemployed households around the town.

Kennan also arranged for Orwell to take a trip down Crippen's mine on 23 February. Two days later Orwell left Wigan for Liverpool, apparently suffering from exhaustion caused by this trip, and possibly from bronchitis. He turned up at the home of John and May Deiner, ILP members and supporters of *The Adelphi*. The Deiners nursed Orwell for three days, and then spent a day showing him around Liverpool's slums and new housing estates. Orwell returned briefly to Wigan before taking the train to Yorkshire—he had arrived in Sheffield by 2 March. He was met by William Brown, an unemployed Communist, who found Orwell lodgings with a miner's family and showed him round the city's working-class districts. On 5 March Orwell left for his sister's home in the genteel Leeds suburb of Headingley, where he stayed for almost a week. On 11 March he travelled to Barnsley and, thanks to an introduction from William Brown, was given lodgings with the Gray family and shown round by a local Communist, Tommy Degnan. Orwell left Barnsley on 26 March and, after a long weekend with his sister in Leeds, returned to London.

On his arrival back home, Orwell became preoccupied with moving to the village of Wallington in Surrey. He had taken over the tenancy of a cottage from his aunt, and was keen to establish a small shop there. Letters to friends make clear that by May he had begun writing *Wigan Pier*, but, typically, was busy with several other projects, including finishing his novel *Keep the Aspidistra Flying*, and running his shop, which he opened each afternoon. In June he married Eileen

O'Shaughnessy. By September he had begun to prepare to go to Spain, in order to fight with the Republican forces. This experience would lead him to write *Homage to Catalonia*.

Only in the autumn of 1936 did Orwell decide that *Wigan Pier* would be 'a sort of book of essays'—and the phrase suggests a lingering uncertainty about its form.[12] He struggled to reconcile two aims: to depict poverty and to suggest solutions to it. As late as 29 October, Gollancz didn't know what Orwell was writing.[13] Eventually, Orwell divided *Wigan Pier* into two. The first part relied on personal recollections and a wealth of data on housing, unemployment, and rents, to describe and examine life in northern industrial districts. The second part focused on political solutions, and particularly on what Orwell saw as the Left's failure to address working-class people's experiences and aspirations.

Orwell was aware that his criticisms of Socialists would anger left-wing readers. In May 1936, Gollancz, Stafford Cripps, and John Strachey had founded the Left Book Club (LBC) to 'help in the struggle for world peace and against fascism'.[14] LBC members received a book each month; these distinctive orange paperbacks and red hardbacks, published by Gollancz, were not offered for sale to the general public. By 1937 the LBC had surpassed its founders' wildest expectations: it had more than 40,000 members, and 300 reading groups across Britain. Orwell was well aware that an LBC book was guaranteed good sales and publicity. But when he sent the manuscript to his agent, Leonard Moore, on 15 December 1936 he was pessimistic about *Wigan Pier*'s prospects. 'I should think the chances of Gollancz choosing it as a Left Book Club selection are small, as it is too fragmentary and, on the surface, not very left-wing.'[15]

Moore sent Orwell's manuscript to Gollancz, who read it immediately. Orwell was half right about his editor's reaction. Gollancz privately described Part Two of *Wigan Pier* as ' "repugnant" '.[16]

---

[12] George Orwell, letter to Jack Common, 5 October 1936; quoted in *A Kind of Compulsion, 1903–1936*, vol. x of *The Complete Works of George Orwell*, ed. Peter Davison (London: Secker & Warburg, 1998), 507.

[13] David John Taylor, *Orwell* (London: Chatto & Windus, 2003), 175.

[14] Quoted in Ruth Dudley Edwards, *Victor Gollancz: A Biography* (London: Faber & Faber, 2012), n.p. (electronic resource).

[15] Letter from Orwell to Leonard Moore, 15 December 1936; repr. in *A Kind of Compulsion, 1903–1936*, 528.

[16] Quoted in Dudley Edwards, *Victor Gollancz: A Biography*, n.p.

Nevertheless, he considered it an important book and was keen to publish quickly. On 19 December, he telegraphed Orwell asking to meet as soon as possible and announcing: ' "I think we can make it a Left Book Club choice" '.[17] The two men met on 21 December 1936. Also present was Clough Williams Ellis, an architect with an interest in social problems. The trio agreed that photographs would be included in the book: a sign that Gollancz and Orwell wanted *Wigan Pier* to be read as a documentary study. The following day, Gollancz's fellow director, Norman Collins, wrote to a number of likely sources, probably recommended by Williams Ellis.[18]

Orwell left for Spain almost immediately, and was there when Gollancz published *Wigan Pier* in March 1937. By this time, Orwell had moved on, mentally and emotionally, to the project that would become *Homage to Catalonia*.

While Orwell travelled to Spain, Gollancz swiftly prepared for production. He asked Moore to consider a small edition of both halves for the general public, alongside a larger LBC edition that would simply include the first part. But when Moore and Orwell's wife, Eileen (to whom Orwell had entrusted his affairs while he was in Spain), refused to countenance this, Gollancz acquiesced. The LBC edition included both parts of *Wigan Pier*, albeit with an introduction written by Gollancz himself which was critical of Part Two.

Wigan Pier quickly reached a large audience. The first edition numbered 43,690 and it was twice reissued.[19] By November 1939 Orwell had royalties of £604.57, far exceeding what he'd received for earlier books.[20] *Wigan Pier* has remained in print ever since.

The Road to Wigan Pier was a milestone in the history of social studies. Jack London's *The People of the Abyss*, and the 'slumming' genre of which it was part, continued to influence Orwell. But other kinds of social survey shaped his project, too: statistical surveys of

---

[17] *Orwell's England:* The Road to Wigan Pier *in the Context of Essays, Reviews, Letters and Poems Selected from the Complete Works of George Orwell*, ed. Peter Davison (London: Penguin, 2001), 331.

[18] On the inclusion of illustrations, see Orwell, *The Collected Non-Fiction*, ed. Peter Davison (London: Penguin, 2017), 341.

[19] Quoted in Bernard Crick, *George Orwell: A Life* (London: Secker & Warburg, 1980), 311.

[20] *The Orwell Diaries*, ed. Peter Davison (London: Penguin, 2010), 72.

working-class life, pioneered by Charles Booth's *Survey of London Life and Labour*, undertaken in the late nineteenth century, and with recent additions like Hubert Llewellyn Smith's ten-volume *New Survey of London Life and Labour*, published between 1929 and 1932, and David Caradog Jones's *Social Survey of Merseyside*.[21] During his travels, Orwell collected statistics on employment, rents, and wages. In the first week of March 1936 he 'went to Sheffield Town Hall to ask for certain statistics' on housing: these would inform Chapter 3 of *Wigan Pier*.[22] Later that month, he decided to leave Barnsley earlier than expected, in part because he could not get the statistics he wanted: 'the public library is no good. There is no proper reference library.'[23] Orwell believed his argument would be more robust if supported with statistics that showed his subjects were representative of a larger group.

But Orwell did not strive for the 'objective' tone of these social surveys. He condemned the 'hopeless idleness' of the unemployed, and the punitive benefits system to which they were subjected (p. 57). 'It is disgraceful that men who are expected to keep alive on the P.A.C. should not even have the chance to grow vegetables for their families', he wrote (p. 57). He described the desperate efforts that the unemployed made to get hold of food and fuel. 'In Wigan the competition among unemployed people for the waste coal has become so fierce that it has led to an extraordinary custom called 'scrambling for the coal', he wrote (p. 70). He described families scrambling to the slap heaps, 'kneeling, swiftly scrabbling with their hands in the damp dirt and picking out lumps of coal the size of an egg or smaller' (p. 70). He showed that moral judgement need not mean hyperbole or sentimentality, if it sprang from astute observation. Neat juxtapositions between how he and his readers knew life *ought* to be, and how it was in reality, reinforced his point. '[E]ven the snow was black', is how he described the effect of pollution in Sheffield (p. 75).

Orwell wanted to move his readers, and persuade them of his point of view. Statistics helped; so too did juxtaposing life in Wigan with life among the southern middle class. But he also wanted to hold his readers' attention. To this end, he followed Jack London in amalgamating

[21] Smith, *New Survey of London Life and Labour*, 1934; David Caradog Jones, *The Social Survey of Merseyside*, 3 vols. (Liverpool: Liverpool University Press, 1934).
[22] *Orwell Diaries*, ed. Davison, 55.   [23] *Orwell Diaries*, ed. Davison, 58.

situations (such as his several visits to mines) and creating characters who were composites of several people he had met, to make these more vivid and powerful. And while he had changed his view on 'slumming' since *Down and Out*, Orwell believed that his study would have greater credibility if he could claim to have first-hand experience of what he witnessed. He exaggerated the length of his stay in the North, writing that 'For some months I lived entirely in coal-miners' houses. I ate my meals with the family, I washed at the kitchen sink, I shared bedrooms with miners, drank beer with them, played darts with them, talked to them by the hour together' (p. 107). Notably, he omitted his visit to his sister in Headingley from the book. In the diary he kept during his journey, Orwell describes this six-day sojourn as an important period of rest and recuperation: 'The essential difference is that here there is *elbow-room* . . . if you definitely want to be alone you can be so.'[24] But readers of *Wigan Pier* are encouraged to believe that Orwell was entirely immersed in the lives and events he portrays for several months.

This approach had precedent. E. Wight Bakke, an American academic who lived among the unemployed in Greenwich, London, for several months in order to write *The Unemployed Man*, published in 1933, used a similar method.[25] A year later, J. B. Priestley, who made his living from journalism, wrote his *English Journey* as a seamless travelogue that took readers from Southampton to Lancashire, when in reality he had undertaken several shorter trips, interspersed with periods at home. Both Bakke and Priestley, in different ways, saw themselves as advocates for those they encountered on their travels. All these writers believed that immersion in their subject would give them a special authority.

But the Orwell of *Wigan Pier* was different from these other social investigators. He did not seek to absent himself from the story, like the omnipotent narrator in Bakke's study of *The Unemployed Man*. Nor did he present himself as an intermediary, secure in his social position and world-view, as Priestley did. Instead, Orwell presented himself as a lonely traveller on a journey of self-exploration. 'Before I had been down a mine I had vaguely

---

[24] *The Collected Essays, Journalism and Letters of George Orwell*, ed. Sonia Orwell and Ian Angus, vol. i (London: Secker & Warburg, 1968), 196.
[25] Edward Wight Bakke, *The Unemployed Man* (London: Nisbet, 1933).

imagined the miner stepping out of the cage and getting to work on a ledge of coal a few yards away', he wrote of his visit to a pit. He emerged 'more exhausted than you would be by a twenty-five-mile walk above ground' (pp. 16, 19). He invites his readers to learn alongside him.

Orwell's approach was strikingly similar to Priestley's in one significant way. For all his criticisms of capitalism, Orwell shared Priestley's belief that social class was natural to British society, and wasn't an impediment to national unity and social harmony. Like Priestley, Orwell believed that an educated observer might help foster this. A writer could demonstrate to the different groups he encountered where their common interests lay. In *Wigan Pier* Orwell connected working-class life with national stability. He thought the best of British life was epitomized by the 'sane and comely' working-class family: 'on winter evenings after tea, when the fire glows in the open range and dances mirrored in the steel fender, Father, in shirt-sleeves, sits in the rocking chair at one side of the fire reading the racing finals, and Mother sits on the other with her sewing, and the children are happy with a pennorth of mint humbugs' (p. 81). He did not argue for a classless society, but against the destruction of this working class by unemployment and poverty.

Orwell declared that he had gone to Wigan in search of the 'typical' working class (p. 83). But he wrote about an idealized working class, epitomized by miners. While Jack Hilton suggested he visit a mining area, the idea may already have been in Orwell's mind—in 1947 he claimed that 'studying the conditions of miners in the north of England' was his chief objective in accepting Gollancz's commission.[26] 'More than anyone else, perhaps, the miner can stand as the type of the manual worker', he wrote in the first chapter of *Wigan Pier*, 'not only because his work is so exaggeratedly awful, but also because it is so vitally necessary and yet so remote from our experience' (p. 23).

Mining was not men's largest employer—more found work in transport and engineering, also tough and 'vitally necessary' jobs. They too suffered hardship and unemployment. But for the British Left, miners were heroes. They had a long history as staunch trade

---

[26] Quoted in Clarke, 'George Orwell, Jack Hilton, and the Working Class', 765.

unionists and, as recently as 1926, had fought a long and ultimately unsuccessful battle against their employers for better wages and greater bargaining rights. It was in support of their struggle that the Trades Union Congress (TUC) had called a general strike. Four per cent of the population walked out of work to support the strike on 4 May 1926, and while it ended in ignominious failure just nine days later, it remains one of the largest industrial and political disputes that Britain has ever experienced.[27]

Orwell, however, was less concerned with miners' political activism than with their manliness. He praised their 'noble bodies; wide shoulders tapering to slender supple waists, and small pronounced buttocks and sinewy thighs, with not an ounce of waste flesh' (p. 15). Orwell comes uncomfortably close to depicting his working-class heroes as animals (a criticism that has also been made of some of his later works of fiction, notably *Animal Farm* where all the workers are literally animals, and the 'proles' in *Nineteen Eighty-Four*). Elsewhere in *Wigan Pier* he describes 'decent young miners and cotton workers' made unemployed as 'gazing at their destiny with the same sort of dumb amazement as an animal in a trap' (p. 58).

Orwell believed the virtues of working-class life were found in people's bodies and homes rather than politics or trade unionism. His positive descriptions of working-class life focused on home and hearth, without reflecting that the wages to pay the rent, or the existence of council housing, were the results of long struggles by trade unionists and Labour Party members. As Richard Hoggart would later write, some of Orwell's depictions of working-class people had more in common with 'music hall' caricatures than reality.[28]

Orwell's relationship with the British Left was not straightforward. He was chary of joining groups or signing up to ideologies, and refused to call himself a Socialist at this point (though he began to do so after fighting on the Republican side in the Spanish Civil War in 1937). His criticisms of socialism studded the second part of *Wigan Pier*. Like many left-wingers before and since, he was caught between the desire for purity in action and thought, and the need for realism. Orwell could not resolve this dilemma. He was cynical about

---

[27] For more on the strike, see Todd, *The People*, ch. 3.
[28] Richard Hoggart, 'Introduction to *The Road to Wigan Pier*', in Raymond Williams (ed.), *George Orwell: A Collection of Critical Essays* (Englewood Cliffs, NJ: Prentice-Hall, 1974), 41 and 42.

revolution, but despised those Socialists who were not revolutionaries. 'Socialism, at least in this island, does not smell any longer of revolution and the overthrow of tyrants; it smells of crankishness, machine-worship, and the stupid cult of Russia' (p. 149). He disliked what he saw as the romanticism of 'bourgeois' Socialists, far removed from ordinary workers. Socialism was, he argued, the doctrine of 'every fruit-juice drinker, nudist, sandal-wearer, sex-maniac, Quaker, "Nature Cure" quack, pacifist, and feminist in England . . . that is, a person out of touch with common humanity' (p. 119). He was equally disenchanted by the prosaic and pragmatic approach of political strategists, condemning 'Labour Party backstairs-crawlers' (p. 149).

Orwell craved a place for himself in an England he mythologized: among the 'beer-drinking English' and the 'cricket crowds' that 'assemble at Lord's' (p. 22).[29] Running a small village shop may seem a curious distraction for a successful and productive writer, especially since Orwell chose to embark on this venture while struggling with the shape and structure of *Wigan Pier*. He knew that he probably wouldn't make any money: 'there couldn't be much profit in a village of 50–100 inhabitants', he wrote to Jack Common in April 1936.[30] He hoped that the shop would cover the low rent; another attraction was that he could keep hens and goats and grow vegetables.[31] This new venture marked Orwell's attempt to live the world-view he expressed in *Wigan Pier*. As he wrote in the book, he believed the 'beautiful village' (p. 77) of rural England epitomized the community and continuity that he saw endangered by industrialization and poverty in the North. This was a hierarchical England, not one of social, economic, or political equality. But it was one where everyone had a valued role.[32]

Orwell did not believe that community was confined to southern rural England. He lovingly described the 'working-class family sitting round the coal fire after kippers and strong tea' (p. 81). In writing *Wigan Pier*, he sought to arouse readers' desire to re-establish this peaceable working class, which he believed had existed 'before the war' (p. 81).

[29] See Williams, *Orwell* (1971), 19–20.
[30] Orwell to Jack Common, 3 April 1936; repr. in *The Collected Essays, Journalism and Letters*, ed. Orwell and Angus, i. 214.
[31] *Orwell's England*, ed. Davison, 300.   [32] Williams, *Orwell* (1971), 19–20.

But Orwell represented an idealized working class, devoid of history or politics. His critique of industry and capitalism bordered on the romantic. 'The typical post-war factory is not a gaunt barrack or an awful chaos of blackness and belching chimneys; it is a glittering white structure of concrete, glass, and steel, surrounded by green lawns and beds of tulips', he acknowledged. 'But . . . though the ugliness of industrialism is the most obvious thing about it . . . I doubt whether it is centrally important' (p. 75). Orwell recognized that assembly-line production could bring its own problems. But in suggesting that 'perhaps it is not even desirable, industrialism being what it is, that it should learn to disguise itself as something else' (p. 75), Orwell overlooked some significant improvements in industry, and that these were the achievements of the labour movement. In writing that 'it is *not* the triumphs of modern engineering, nor the radio, nor the cinematograph, nor the five thousand novels which are published yearly . . . but the memory of working-class interiors—especially as I sometimes saw them in my childhood before the war, when England was still prosperous—that reminds me that our age has not been altogether a bad one to live in' (p. 82), Orwell dismissed the contribution that working people had made to these developments, and the benefits they had reaped from them. It was as if there had been an authentic England once, now corrupted by both industrialization and socialism—'an *urban* creed' (p. 129).

These corrupting influences threatened Orwell's imagined working class, who were simultaneously 'comely' (p. 81) and revolutionary. '[T]he working class are submissive where they used to be openly hostile', Orwell regretfully concluded (p. 90), overlooking that struggles for more political and workplace rights continued, albeit in different forms from a century earlier, and in different places.

Orwell criticized British Socialists for prioritizing idealism over action. Yet in the mid-1930s the Labour Party and the labour movement were responsible for important reforms. In 1935 the Labour Party had increased its number of Parliamentary seats under the leadership of Clement Attlee, partly because of the welfare programmes energetically established by large Labour-controlled local authorities, and helped by increasing trade union membership. The campaign for Holidays with Pay (eventually won in 1938) was a victory for members of the Transport and General Workers' Union, many of them workers in the 'glittering' factories Orwell despised (p. 75).

Orwell's idealized working class acted from instinct, unencumbered by either socialism or the 'sickly and debilitating' pretensions of middle-class life (p. 81). 'To the working class, the notion of staying at school till you are nearly grown-up seems merely contemptible and unmanly', he declared. '[T]here is not one working-class boy in a thousand who does not pine for the day when he will leave school. He wants to be doing real work, not wasting his time on ridiculous rubbish like history and geography' (p. 80). In fact, many working-class people had long campaigned for greater education. Pressure from miners' unions had helped bring about the 1870 Education Act, which made school compulsory for five- to twelve-year-olds. The Workers' Educational Association (WEA), founded in 1903 to provide adult education, had a strong base in Lancashire. Jack Hilton was a former student of Ruskin College, one of a network of colleges funded by the trade union movement. '[S]ociety has too much of its bias weighted on the side of working, or making things', he wrote in his 1937 travelogue *English Ways*. Oxford, wrote Hilton, was 'a great place . . . for the students who are fortunate to be there': the pity was that so few people could experience it.[33]

The activists who sustained the WEA and Ruskin played no part in Orwell's working class. He saw politics as something separate from, even foreign to, working-class life. 'Via Socialist politics you can get in touch with the working-class intelligentsia, but they are hardly more typical than tramps or burglars', he declared (p. 107). Despite admitting that prior to 1936 he 'knew nothing' of working-class life (p. 102), he delineated the 'typical' working class with astonishing confidence. In his diary, Orwell dismissed his Manchester hosts, Mr and Mrs Meade, as 'bourgeois' because of their corporation house and love of political debate: 'as soon as a working man gets an official post in the Trade Union or goes into Labour politics, he becomes middle-class'.[34] He caricatured ILP members as eccentric utopian cranks, epitomized by 'dreadful-looking' hikers, with 'khaki shorts into which their huge bottoms were crammed so tightly that you could study every dimple' (p. 120). But he depended on ILP members in Manchester and Lancashire for contacts and research.[35] Orwell confessed himself

---

[33] Hilton, *English Ways*, 181. [34] Quoted in *Orwell's England*, ed. Davison, 27.
[35] Crick, *George Orwell*, 279. Crick also provides an excellent summary of Orwell's journey between 31 January and 30 March 1936.

'surprised' at the size of NUWM meetings in Wigan—about 200 people at one he attended—and at 'the amount of Communist feeling here'.[36] Yet these meetings did not feature in *Wigan Pier*.

The NUWM was pivotal in Orwell's development as a non-fiction writer. Orwell's diary reveals that his writing and perspective changed on 15 February 1936. Prior to this, his diary entries are detached, factual observations, albeit enlivened by sharp description: 'board and lodging 25s a week'; 'bargemen were muffled to the eyes in sacks'.[37] Then, on 15 February, Orwell joined NUWM activists on their rounds to collect subscriptions, 'with a view to collecting facts about housing conditions'. Orwell visited many houses that day, chiefly meeting women. 'What chiefly struck me was the expression of some of the women's faces', he wrote in his diary. 'One woman had a face like a death's head . . . I gathered that she felt as I would feel if I were coated all over with dung.' For the first time, Orwell reflected on his subjects' responses to their circumstances, and realized that these were no different from how he would react.[38] This humanism lifted *Wigan Pier* above most other social surveys of the early and mid-twentieth century, valuable though they were.

He began to reflect on the relationship between himself and those he encountered. It was on 15 February that, 'Passing up a horrible squalid side-alley', he 'saw a woman, youngish but very pale and with the usual draggled exhausted look, kneeling by the gutter outside a house and poking a stick up the leaden waste-pipe, which was blocked. I thought how dreadful a destiny it was . . . At that moment she looked up and caught my eye, and her expression was as desolate as I have ever seen; it struck me that she was thinking just the same thing as I was.'[39]

While these episodes appeared in *Wigan Pier*, they were afforded less time and significance than Orwell's meetings with miners. He rewrote his encounter with the young woman unblocking a drain as a sighting from a train in which he 'was almost near enough to catch her eye' (p. 12). This distanced her from the authority of the male narrator, and objectified her. In his diary, the point is the fleeting connection they forge, the mutual recognition of humanity and their shared sense that no one should endure such desolation. She is not

---

[36] *Orwell Diaries*, ed. Davison, 33.

[37] *Orwell Diaries*, ed. Davison, 31, 33, and 35.

[38] *Orwell Diaries*, ed. Davison, 35.

[39] *Orwell Diaries*, ed. Davison, 35.

just the subject of inquiry, but an agent in her own life, with the potential to recognize and challenge her destiny.

Orwell's treatment of these incidents was shaped by his perspective on women. He could not regard women as his equals, nor as heroic like the miners. He ignored women's significance as breadwinners, despite acknowledging in his diaries that Wigan's unemployed included many female former mill-workers. He also overlooked women's role in local politics. Most working-class women had won the vote just eight years before Orwell visited Wigan, and Lancashire had long been a centre of female suffrage activism. There were dozens of Labour Party women's sections, an active Co-operative Women's Guild, and many women were active trade unionists. Women's centrality to Socialist politics and NUWM activism helps explain Orwell's dismissive attitude towards both. In his diaries he observed that most participants at NUWM socials were female— 'gaping girls and shapeless middle-aged women dozing over their knitting' as he described them.[40] These were not the heroic miners Orwell hoped to find.

For some writers, young working-class women provided portents of a brighter future. Before the Second World War, domestic service was women's largest employer, though in Lancashire and parts of Yorkshire the mills had long provided many with work. But by the mid 1930s, young women in southern England and the Midlands were able to get relatively well-paid work on the assembly lines in light manufacturing industries or as office clerks. They were the chief clientele of new cinemas and dance halls. They were more likely to get a secondary education than ever before—the school leaving age had been raised to 14 in 1921. And they were the first generation to grow up expecting the vote. In 1933, J. B. Priestley saw the relatively well-paid 'hundreds of girls' at a Leicester factory as heralding a newly-affluent working class.[41] Jack Hilton described 'clean, well-dressed, apparently happy, young women' on the assembly lines, and 'big, lusty lasses of fourteen', who he saw 'leaving school and riding to dinner on their bikes', going home to new council houses. 'I have never seen such a crowd of hefty young women.' Mary, his wife, 'wished we could dwell there'.[42] Hilton's observation was grounded in

---

[40] *Orwell Diaries*, ed. Davison, 39.   [41] Priestley, *English Journey*, 148–9.
[42] Hilton, *English Ways*, 48.

his recognition that the working conditions, wages, and education of the younger generation owed much to the struggles of labour movement activists.

By contrast, Orwell suspected that women's gains were won at the expense of men. He described approvingly that unemployment 'has not altered the relative status of the sexes. In a working-class home it is the man who is the master and not, as in a middle-class home, the woman or the baby . . . the women do not protest' (p. 55). Any alteration in this division of labour incurred his disapproval. Mrs Brooker, the landlady of his second lodging-house in Wigan, was an invalid with a weak heart who relied on her husband's help around the home. 'I suspect that her only real trouble was over-eating', wrote Orwell (p. 4). Whereas Hilton approved of 'hefty' young women, Orwell pilloried women's greed. In Coventry, he was served by a 'half-witted servant girl with huge body, tiny head and rolls of fat at back of neck curiously recalling ham-fat'.[43]

Orwell could have chosen to write differently about women. In March 1936 Winifred Holtby's novel *South Riding* was published to widespread acclaim. Based in Holtby's native Yorkshire, *South Riding* follows Sarah Burton, a woman from a working-class background who returns to her native county to become headmistress of a girls' high school, determined to expand girls' opportunities, regardless of their class. Holtby traced the terrible consequences of the sexual double standard and women's limited rights at work, in education, and in politics. *South Riding* was widely reviewed; Orwell could not fail to know about it. Holtby's characters, and Jack Hilton's writing, provide portents of the women who would go on to be war workers and swell the trade unions between 1939 and 1945, and vote for a progressive Labour government at the end of the war. By contrast, Orwell's 'gaping' women are allowed no potential to be agents of change.

Orwell's views of women prevented him from grasping significant clues to progressive change. He dismissed feminism, as well as 'Pacifism, internationalism, humanitarianism of all kinds, . . . free love, divorce-reform, atheism [and] birth-control' as fads that, in the turbulent years after 1918, received 'a better hearing than they would

---

[43] *Orwell Diaries*, ed. Davison, 26.

get in normal times' (p. 95). Orwell was writing at a time when feminists within and beyond the labour movement were campaigning for the right to divorce (at this point limited to wealthy women who could prove spousal adultery or harm) and for birth control.[44] In his introduction to the first edition of *Wigan Pier*, Victor Gollancz suggested that it was Orwell who was divorced from the realities of working-class life, not these women: 'there is no more "commonsensical" work than that which is being done at the present time by the birth control clinics up and down the country'.[45] Over the next half-century, many of the campaigns Orwell derided were to score notable successes: divorce became easier, birth control was made freely available on the National Health Service, and both internationalism and humanitarianism informed the Campaign for Nuclear Disarmament.

Victor Gollancz knew that Part Two of *Wigan Pier* would attract criticism from the British Left. There was, however, no question that it would be excluded from the Left Book Club. Gollancz (and many of his readers) were more tolerant to debate and discussion than Orwell presumed. Many of Orwell's fellow writers and artists inherited the view that socialism must be built on vigorous debate; this was one reason why expanding access to education was important to so many activists. Gollancz used his introduction to the LBC edition of *Wigan Pier* to justify the inclusion of Part Two. Orwell's book, he wrote, embodied

the whole meaning and purpose of the Club. On the one hand we have to go out and rouse the apathetic by showing them the utter vileness which Mr Orwell lays bare in the first part of the book, and by appealing to the decency which is in them; on the other hand we have so to equip ourselves by thought and study that we run no danger, having once mobilized all this good will, of seeing it dispersed for lack of trained leaders.[46]

He urged readers to see the second part of *Wigan Pier* as a provocation, which encouraged them to debate and hone the arguments with which they could confront their opponents.

---

[44] Deirdre Beddoe, 'Hindrances and Help-Meets: Women in the Writings of George Orwell', in Christopher Norris (ed.), *Inside the Myth: Orwell: Views from the Left* (London: Lawrence & Wishart, 1984), 153.

[45] Victor Gollancz, 'Foreword' to Orwell, *The Road to Wigan Pier* (London: Victor Gollancz, 1937), p. xvii.

[46] Gollancz, 'Foreword', pp. xxiii–xiv.

Gollancz was less concerned by what became one of Orwell's most infamous lines: '*The lower classes smell*' (p. 87). As Gollancz anticipated, some of his readers strongly objected to this, including Harry Pollitt, the leader of the Communist Party of Great Britain, who singled out this line for particular criticism in his hostile review of *Wigan Pier*.[47] But in his introduction, Gollancz wrote that 'I know of no other book in which a member of the middle class exposes with such complete frankness the shameful way in which he was brought up to think of large numbers of his fellow men.'[48]

Orwell believed that a 'European of bourgeois upbringing, even when he calls himself a Communist, cannot without a hard effort think of a working man as his equal' (p. 87). How to overcome such prejudice was a moot point for Orwell. He dismissed attempts to foster brotherly love through university settlements—those Christian missions established in the inner cities during the late nineteenth and early twentieth centuries, where students sought to enlighten their poorer brethren. Yet he could not shake his own conviction that without he and his class kindling their affection, even love, for the 'great sweaty navvy', socialism must fail (p. 88). Orwell was thinking of himself when he wrote that a middle-class person's socialism 'is actuated by a love of the working class. He [*sic*] is endeavouring to shed his bourgeois status and fight on the side of the proletariat' (p. 123).

Orwell implied that class was defined by accent, appearance, and taste. As Gollancz gently pointed out, this reflected Orwell's ignorance of socialist and Marxist thought. 'Mr Orwell does not once define what he *means* by Socialism (though he likens it to USSR); nor does he explain *how* the oppressors oppress', he observed.[49] In Raymond Williams's words:

it is true that if class means only these differences in private social behaviour, differences that are often little more than external and trivial, a certain 'classlessness' is inevitable in conditions of growing prosperity and extended education and communications . . . But . . . another set of facts, in which class is a powerful and continuing economic relationship—as between the owners of property and capital and the owners only of labour and skill—is effectively masked.[50]

---

[47] See *Orwell's England*, ed. Davison, 331.   [48] Gollancz, 'Foreword', p. xv.
[49] Gollancz, 'Foreword', p. xxiii.   [50] Williams, *Orwell* (1971), 24.

Because of his emphasis on class-as-culture, and his ignorance or neglect of the history of class struggle, Orwell concluded that class was natural to British life. His vision was of a community where everyone could fulfil their different social role without fear of poverty. But this ignored the exploitation—both of resources and of people—on which capitalist societies depended, as Orwell himself acknowledged.

Left-wing reviewers praised the first part of the book but disliked the second part. Ethel Mannin, a left-wing popular novelist, reviewed it for the ILP's *New Leader*. It was, she thought, ' "a great pity . . . he did not confine himself to facts and figures" '.[51] Others pointed out that the lack of Socialist success in Britain was hardly due to ILP ramblers. As Arthur Calder-Marshall wrote in *Time and Tide,* the Labour Party leadership's willingness to enter coalition with the Conservatives might have been a worthier matter for discussion.[52]

These reasonable criticisms were shared by a broader spectrum of commentators. The Liberal *Manchester Guardian* judged Part One 'clear and lively . . . an effective check to complacency, and . . . stirring'. Part Two, by contrast, was 'spoilt by reckless generalisations'.[53] Leonora Eyles, reviewing the book for *The Times Literary Supplement*, praised the 'sense of shock' generated by Orwell's 'word-pictures of the conditions under which about twenty million of our fellow country men and women are living today'. As she observed, 'We have grown used to hearing the words "two million unemployed" '—Orwell's achievement was to make that statistic into a human story. But she denounced Part Two as 'propaganda' for socialism—while noting that Orwell's 'sweeping denunciations on purely personal grounds' did nothing to help his cause.[54]

The people of Wigan and those who had assisted Orwell with his research were also critical of the finished product. Their concerns focused on distortions and omissions that were not always obvious to newspaper reviewers. Many of Wigan's residents thought that Orwell's depiction of poverty invited shock and disgust rather than understanding of people's struggle or anger at the conditions described. While Orwell wrote that his lodgings above the tripe shop

---

[51] Quoted in Crick, *George Orwell*, 343.

[52] Quoted in Crick, *George Orwell*, 343.

[53] Untitled review of *The Road to Wigan Pier*, *Manchester Guardian*, 9 April 1937, p. 7.

[54] 'Those Who Live Poorly', *Times Literary Supplement*, 27 March 1937, p. 238.

were 'fairly normal as lodging-houses in the industrial areas go' (p. 10), neighbours recalled it as an exceptionally ' "filthy hole" '.[55] Many agreed with Jim Hammond, a National Union of Mineworkers official, that Orwell had set out to ' "go right down into muck and start muckraking" '.[56] Ernie Benson, a Communist Party member from Leeds who spent much of the 1930s on the dole, heard similar stories about Orwell from comrades in Wigan. 'How little people with such ideas knew about us of the working class . . . of our desire and ability to climb from the filth, poverty, wars and starvation which capitalism creates for us, and of our endeavours to create a more just and humane society', he wrote of Orwell.[57] While Orwell criticized Socialists for misrepresenting working-class people, some of those he wrote about condemned his assumption that poverty inevitably produced hopelessness and apathy.

In 1959, the historian E. P. Thompson criticized current scholarship and journalism for

a tendency to view working people as the *subjects* of history, as pliant *recipients* of the imprint of the mass media, as *victims* of alienation, as *data* for sociological enquiry: a tendency to underestimate the tensions and conflicts of working-class life . . . and a shame-faced evasion of that impolite historical concept—the class struggle.[58]

He was speaking of a tradition which sprang from *Wigan Pier*. Orwell's book had a lasting influence on the investigation of society, political ideas about class, and especially the representation of the working class.

In the 1950s, full employment, the welfare state, and slum clearance provoked more writers to explore the changing conditions of working-class life. In 1957 Richard Hoggart drew on his own upbringing in interwar Leeds to write *The Uses of Literacy: Aspects of Working-Class Life, with Special Reference to Publications and Entertainments*.[59] Hoggart acknowledged his debt to Orwell, who had

---

[55] Quoted in Crick, *George Orwell*, 281.

[56] Quoted in Crick, *George Orwell*, 282.

[57] Ernie Benson, *To Struggle is to Live: A Working Class Autobiography*, ii. *Starve or Rebel, 1927–1971* (Newcastle-upon-Tyne: People's Publications, 1980), 159.

[58] Edward Palmer Thompson, 'Commitment in Politics', *Universities and Left Review*, 6 (Spring 1959), 52.

[59] (London: Chatto & Windus, 1957).

suggested that working-class people's experiences were worthy of consideration, and as a result told Hoggart his own experience was part of a bigger story. 'This is the thirties all right,' wrote Hoggart of *Wigan Pier*; 'for many in the working-classes a long-drawn-out waste and misery.'[60]

But as Thompson hinted, Orwell's work also fed an ahistorical and depoliticized representation of working-class life. *The Uses of Literacy* and Orwell's *Wigan Pier* helped to create an influential image of working-class life: close-knit families, packed northern streets, and cohesive communities. Hoggart called Orwell's focus on the home and neighbourhood 'sensible and humane'; neither writer spent much time on the workplace and even less on the labour movement.[61] Their focus on home and community characterized the spate of studies of working-class life that appeared in the 1950s and early 1960s.[62] In a groundbreaking examination of the impact of affluence on working-class life, John Goldthorpe's team of sociologists explicitly compared life in 1960s Luton with the vision of working-class life evoked by Richard Hoggart.[63] Orwell's working class of self-sacrificial women and heroic male manual workers, devoid of political engagement or intellectual ambition, had, by the 1960s, become the 'traditional' working class.

This tradition has continued into the twenty-first century. In 2009, the writer Andrew O'Hagan delivered the annual George Orwell Memorial Lecture, lamenting the appearance of a 'working class [who] were no longer a working class . . . people who craved not values but designer labels and satellite dishes' and formed 'the most conservative force in Britain'.[64] Like Orwell and Hoggart, O'Hagan was unable to offer any solution, instead lamenting that affluence had corrupted 'my own people'.[65] In 2019, the journalist John Harris

---

[60] Hoggart, 'Introduction', 41 and 42.   [61] Hoggart, 'Introduction', 42.

[62] Michael D. Young and Peter Willmott, *Family and Kinship in East London* (London: Routledge and Kegan Paul, 1957); Brian Jackson, *Working Class Community* (Harmondsworth: Penguin, 1968); John H. Goldthorpe et al., *The Affluent Worker in the Class Structure* (Cambridge: Cambridge University Press, 1969).

[63] Goldthorpe et al., *The Affluent Worker*, 92.

[64] Andrew O'Hagan, 'The Age of Indifference', *The Guardian*, 10 January 2009, https://www.theguardian.com/books/2009/jan/10/andrew-ohagan-george-orwell-memoriallecture.

[65] O'Hagan, 'The Age of Indifference'.

undertook his own journey across Britain to discover 'people . . . desperate to be heard', experiencing 'poverty' and 'social decay'.[66]

These commentators' solutions to Britain's ills echo Orwell's stress on culture rather than politics. Orwell thought that increasing affluence might erode class divisions—failing to address the bigger division between those who own capital and those who rely on their labour power. By the twenty-first century writers like O'Hagan argued that, somehow, affluence had corrupted 'my own people'. Frequently, these writers shared Orwell's belief that the job of the Left was to create a sense of national unity. For Orwell, that moment came during the Second World War. But that war produced an exceptional and transient sense of social cohesion. And even wartime unity was always fragile and never overcame inequalities of power between the social classes or between men and women.[67]

The most searing critiques of this tradition have come from feminist writers. In 1984, Beatrix Campbell's *Wigan Pier Revisited* challenged Orwell's romanticized image of miners and neglect of women's work.[68] Campbell highlighted Orwell's ignorance of how women, as a sex, were exploited because of their actual and potential role as mothers. Instead of evoking nostalgic versions of community, she argued, Britain needed to recognize the centrality of women's paid and unpaid work to sustaining capitalism—not least as reproducers of labour power. Since then, feminist memoirists and historians have interrogated the image of the selfless working-class 'mam' evoked by Orwell and later by Hoggart, showing that women's dreams and ambitions were often sacrificed, and that they played a key role in fighting for better housing and education so their daughters would not face the same hardships. They transmitted their aspirations to daughters who grew up with the security of the welfare state, some of whom instigated second-wave feminism in the 1970s.[69]

[66] John Harris et al., 'Anywhere but Westminster', *The Guardian*, 21 March 2019, https://www.theguardian.com/commentisfree/video/2019/mar/21/brexit-breakdown-anywhere-but-westminster-a-big-day-in-the-north-video; 9 April 2019, https://www.theguardian.com/commentisfree/video/2019/apr/09/brexit-breakdown-affluence-decay-and-fury-in-the-tory-heartlands-video.

[67] Todd, *The People*, 119–48; Angus Calder, *The Myth of the Blitz* (London: Jonathan Cape, 1991).

[68] Beatrix Campbell, *Wigan Pier Revisited: Poverty and Politics in the Eighties* (London: Virago, 1984).

[69] Annette Kuhn, *Family Secrets: Acts of Memory and Imagination* (London: Verso, 1995); Pat Mahony and Christine Zmroczek (eds), *Class Matters: 'Working-Class*

Less than five years after Orwell visited Wigan, some of those he met fought in a world war against Fascism. Less than ten years after the book's publication, Wigan's voters helped to achieve a Labour landslide victory in the 1945 general election. That Labour government didn't create a classless society, or even eradicate poverty—but the establishment of full employment and a welfare state would have been viewed as utopian by many just a decade earlier. Those who dared to dream of a brighter future helped to make some of their vision into a reality. They are at the margins of Orwell's Wigan, but without the book would not exist, and we would all be the poorer for that.

Orwell did recognize that it isn't only history's apparent victors who merit our attention. He suggested the poverty he documented needed to be tackled not because it affects a majority, nor for short-term political gain, but because, morally, it is wrong for people to live this way. In his hands, social investigation becomes a dynamic web of personal perspective, careful and compassionate observation, and critical evaluation of the relationship between what he sees and the wider political and economic context. 'It is a great mistake to think of a miner's working day as being only seven and a half hours', he wrote. 'In another house where I stayed a boy of fifteen was working on the night shift. He left for work at nine at night and got back at eight in the morning, had his breakfast, and then promptly went to bed and slept till six in the evening; so that his leisure time amounted to about four hours a day—actually a good deal less, if you take off the time for washing, eating, and dressing' (p. 26). In such dispassionate, lucid prose, Orwell made his point: this boy's youth was wasted in dark tunnels and exhausted sleep; his only alternative was the dole queue. Orwell showed that 'class' and 'poverty' were, unlike the 'celebrated Wigan Pier', vividly real (p. 50). And far from separating the people of Wigan from the southern writer, they were important connections; both because the latter depended on the former's labour in myriad ways, and because all could unite in agreeing that life should not be this way.

Women's Perspectives on Social Class (London: Taylor & Francis, 1997); Diane Reay, *Miseducation: Inequality, Education and the Working Classes* (Bristol: Policy Press, 2017); Carolyn Steedman, *Landscape for a Good Woman* (London: Virago, 1986); Selina Todd, *Tastes of Honey: The Making of Shelagh Delaney and a Cultural Revolution* (London: Chatto & Windus, 2019).

NOTE ON THE TEXT

THIS volume aims to provide a usable and authoritative text of *The Road to Wigan Pier*. The version of the text is that from the first edition, published on 8 March 1937. Orwell submitted the manuscript to his author, Victor Gollancz, in December 1936. Gollancz was keen to publish quickly. As a result, neither Orwell (who went to fight in the Spanish Civil War in January 1937) nor his wife, Eileen Blair, were able to proofread the text. But Orwell sent Eileen a message asking for one amendment. He had described 'rooks copulating'. Gollancz changed this to 'courting'. Orwell asked for it to be altered to 'treading', and the text was accordingly revised. That amendment is included in this volume.

Gollancz had some criticisms of the second part of the book, but was happy to let the text stand as Orwell had written it. He asked Orwell's literary agent, Leonard Moore, to consider a small edition of both halves for the general public, alongside a larger Left Book Club edition that would simply include the first part. When Moore, and Eileen Blair (who Orwell had entrusted with his affairs while he was in Spain), refused to countenance this, Gollancz acquiesced. On 8 March a Left Book Club edition appeared simultaneously with a more expensive trade edition. These were identical except that the Left Book Club edition was prefaced by an introduction written by Gollancz himself. Gollancz also produced a much smaller edition that only included Part One, but fewer than 900 of these were distributed. In all subsequent editions, both Parts One and Two have appeared.

The original edition of *The Road to Wigan Pier* was illustrated with a section of thirty-two plates, twenty-eight of which are reproduced in this volume. The quality is compromised because they have had to be reproduced from the plates used in the original edition. Nevertheless, the photographs are worthy of inclusion because they were a highly significant feature of the first edition, and noted as such by several reviewers. They shaped readers' understanding of the book's intention and conclusions. Four illustrations are not included due to high resolution files not being available.

The illustrations appear to have been the idea of Victor Gollancz and the architect Clough Williams Ellis. On 21 December 1936 they met George Orwell and agreed to have forty-eight plates in the book. Williams Ellis appears to have suggested names of those who might provide them. Ultimately only thirty-two plates were included. Victor Gollancz was keen to ensure that the book was published as quickly as possible, so the search for photographs was limited.

The thirty-two plates depict Welsh coal miners and poor housing across Britain. Their geographic range supports the point Orwell made repeatedly in *The Road to Wigan Pier*: that the problems he examined were endemic to working-class life, not confined to particular neighbourhoods or to the poorest regions. The importance of housing conditions in shaping people's lives was emphasized in the photographs of London as well as in Orwell's text.

In several important ways the photographs echo Orwell's own narrative and perspective. The significance of the photographs in giving a human face to unemployment and poverty was remarked upon by reviewers in the *Times Literary Supplement* and the *Manchester Guardian*. The photographic sequence offers no sense of progression; neither does Orwell's prose (except with regard to his own development). Most of the figures in the photographs are static: they bear witness to their conditions but cannot change them. Only rarely do they face the camera lens. The viewer is invited to observe and judge their conditions, while those in the photograph simply bear them. We are encouraged to admire but also to pity their stoicism. The photographs suggest that only the actions of those behind the camera—such as the viewers and readers themselves—can enact reform.

The conspicuousness of miners in the photographs emphasizes their iconic place in Orwell's version of working-class life. Missing are those elements of working-class life that were neglected by Orwell's text but were significant in the 1930s. These include the signs of new affluence in south-east England, where the Depression was coming to an end: cinema queues and production lines in new factories were beyond the remit of Orwell's book. But the photographs also miss the NUWM rallies, hunger marches, and Workers' Educational Association classes that were part of working-class life in northern England. Orwell conspicuously avoided evidence that his subjects were hungry to change their own circumstances and had ideas about how to do so.

In other respects, the photographs differ from Orwell's authorial intention. The photographs corroborate Gollancz's conviction that

the first part of *Wigan Pier*—Orwell's representation of the facts, figures, and human face of working-class life—was the most powerful
part of the book. In this way, the inclusion of the photographs subtly
shifts the balance of the book towards Part One, although in fact Part
Two is just as long and, for Orwell, at least as significant.

SELECT BIBLIOGRAPHY

Editions

The Collected Essays, Journalism and Letters of George Orwell, ed. Sonia Orwell and Ian Angus, vol. i (London: Secker & Warburg, 1968).

The Collected Non-Fiction, ed. Peter Davison (London: Penguin, 2017).

A Kind of Compulsion, 1903–1936, vol. x of *The Complete Works of George Orwell*, ed. Peter Davison (London: Secker & Warburg, 1998).

The Orwell Diaries, ed. Peter Davison (London: Penguin, 2010).

Orwell's England: The Road to Wigan Pier in the Context of Essays, Reviews, Letters and Poems Selected from the Complete Works of George Orwell, ed. Peter Davison (London: Penguin, 2001).

The Road to Wigan Pier (London: Victor Gollancz, 1937).

Biography

Crick, Bernard, *George Orwell: A Life* (London: Secker & Warburg, 1980).

Davison, Peter, *George Orwell: A Literary Life* (London: Macmillan, 1996).

Taylor, D. J., *Orwell: The Life* (London: Chatto & Windus, 2003).

Critical Studies

Clarke, Ben, 'George Orwell, Jack Hilton, and the Working Class', *Review of English Studies*, 67 (2016), 764–85.

Colls, Robert, *George Orwell: English Rebel* (Oxford: Oxford University Press, 2013).

Norris, Christopher (ed.), *Inside the Myth: Orwell, Views from the Left* (London: Lawrence & Wishart, 1984).

Rai, Alok, *Orwell and the Politics of Despair: A Critical Study of the Writings of George Orwell* (Cambridge: Cambridge University Press, 1988).

Rodden, John (ed.), *The Cambridge Companion to George Orwell* (Cambridge: Cambridge University Press, 2007).

Williams, Raymond, *Orwell* (London: Fontana, 1971).

Williams, Raymond (ed.), *George Orwell: A Collection of Critical Essays* (Englewood Cliffs, NJ: Prentice-Hall, 1974).

Historical and Contextual Studies

Armstrong, Stephen, *The Road to Wigan Pier Re-visited* (London: Verso, 2012).

Bakke, Edward Wight, *The Unemployed Man* (London: Nisbet, 1933).

Beales, Hugh Lancelot, and Richard Stanton Lambert, *Memoirs of the Unemployed* (London: Victor Gollancz, 1934).

Campbell, Beatrix, *Wigan Pier Revisited: Poverty and Politics in the Eighties* (London: Virago, 1984).

Collini, Stefan, *Absent Minds: Intellectuals in Britain* (Oxford: Oxford University Press, 2006).

Dudley Edwards, Ruth, *Victor Gollancz: A Biography* (London: Faber & Faber, 2012).

Good, Graham, *The Observing Self: Rediscovering the Essay* (London: Routledge, 1988).

Hilton, Jack, *English Ways: A Walk from the Pennines to Epsom Downs in 1939* (London: Jonathan Cape, 1940).

Jones, David Caradog, *The Social Survey of Merseyside*, 3 vols (Liverpool: Liverpool University Press, 1934).

London, Jack, *The People of the Abyss* (London: Macmillan, 1903).

Priestley, John Boynton, *English Journey: Being a Rambling but Truthful Account of What One Man Saw and Heard and Felt and Thought During a Journey through England during the Autumn of the Year 1933* (London: W. Heinemann in association with V. Gollancz, 1934).

Smith, Hubert Llewellyn, *The New Survey of London Life and Labour*, 9 vols (London: London School of Economics, 1934).

Stevenson, John, and Chris Cook, *The Slump* (London: Routledge, 2013).

Further Reading in Oxford World's Classics

Orwell, George, *A Clergyman's Daughter*, ed. Nathan Waddell.

Orwell, George, *Animal Farm*, ed. David Dwan.

Orwell, George, *Burmese Days*, ed. Rosinka Chaudhuri.

Orwell, George, *Coming Up for Air*, ed. Marina MacKay.

Orwell, George, *Down and Out in Paris and London*, ed. John Brannigan.

Orwell, George, *Homage to Catalonia*, ed. Lisa Mullen.

Orwell, George, *Keep the Aspidistra Flying*, ed. Benjamin Kohlmann.

Orwell, George, *Nineteen Eighty-Four*, ed. John Bowen.

Orwell, George, *Selected Essays*, ed. Stefan Collini.

A CHRONOLOGY OF GEORGE ORWELL

1903 (25 June) Eric Arthur Blair born to Richard Walmesley Blair and Ida Mabel Blair (née Limouzin) in Motihari, in modern Bihar, where Richard Blair works in the Opium Department of the Indian Civil Service.

1904 Ida Blair returns to England with Eric and his elder sister, Marjorie (b. 1898), and settles at Henley-on-Thames, Oxfordshire.

1908 (April) Eric's younger sister, Avril, is born.

1911 Goes as a boarder to St Cyprian's, a private preparatory school near Eastbourne, Sussex.

1912 On Richard Blair's retirement, the family moves to the village of Shiplake, Oxfordshire.

1917 Goes to Eton College as a King's Scholar.

1921 Leaves Eton. Richard and Ida Blair move to Southwold, on the Suffolk coast.

1922 Joins the Indian Imperial Police and serves in Burma for five years.

1927 Returns to England and resigns from his position in the Indian Imperial Police.

1927–9 Spends periods as a casual manual labourer and living as a tramp in London and Paris.

1930 Begins to write the book that becomes *Down and Out in Paris and London*.

1932 Engages Leonard Moore as his literary agent. After several rejections, *Down and Out in Paris and London* is accepted by Victor Gollancz. Decides to use a pseudonym and selects 'George Orwell'.

1932–3 Teaches at boys' private schools in Middlesex.

1933 (January) *Down and Out in Paris and London* published by Gollancz.

1934 Lives in Southwold with his parents. (October) *Burmese Days* published in New York by Harper & Brothers (published by Gollancz in the UK in 1935).

1934–6 Works part-time at Booklovers' Corner, a bookshop in Hampstead.

1935 (March) *A Clergyman's Daughter* published by Gollancz.

1936 (February–March) Spends two months visiting the north of England. (April) *Keep the Aspidistra Flying* published by Gollancz; moves to The Stores (a small village general shop) at Wallington, Hertfordshire. (June) Marries Eileen O'Shaughnessy. (December) Goes to Spain to fight on the Republican side in the Civil War.

1937 (March) *The Road to Wigan Pier* published by Gollancz. (May) Wounded in the throat. (July) Returns to England.

1938 (April) *Homage to Catalonia* published by Secker & Warburg (after rejection by Gollancz).

1938–9 Recovers from tuberculosis in Morocco, where he writes *Coming Up for Air*.

1939 (March) Returns to England. (June) *Coming Up for Air* published by Gollancz; Richard Blair dies.

1940 (March) *Inside the Whale and Other Essays* published by Gollancz. (May) Turned down for military service on health grounds; enrols in the Home Guard.

1941 (February) *The Lion and the Unicorn* published by Gollancz.

1941–3 Works as a talks producer in the Indian Section of the BBC Eastern Service.

1943 (March) Ada Blair dies.

1943–4 (November–February) Writes *Animal Farm*.

1943–5 Works as literary editor of *Tribune*, a left-wing weekly.

1944 (June) Adopts a son, Richard Horatio Blair.

1945 (February–March) Goes to Europe as a war correspondent. (March) Eileen Blair dies. (August) After many rejections, *Animal Farm* published by Secker & Warburg.

1946 (February) *Critical Essays* published by Secker & Warburg. (May–October) Lives on the Isle of Jura, writing what becomes *Nineteen Eighty-Four*.

1947 (April–December) Returns to Jura. (November) Completes the first draft of *Nineteen Eighty-Four*.

1948 (July–December) Again living on Jura; revises *Nineteen Eighty-Four*; becomes increasingly ill with tuberculosis. (December) Sends off the completed typescript of *Nineteen Eighty-Four* to Secker & Warburg.

1949 (January–September) Largely confined to a sanatorium in Gloucestershire. (June) *Nineteen Eighty-Four* published by Secker & Warburg; plans a further book, consisting of reprinted essays. (September) Transferred to University College Hospital, London. (October) Marries Sonia Brownell.

1950 (21 January) Dies, aged 46, after a lung haemorrhage. (October) *Shooting an Elephant and Other Essays* published by Secker & Warburg.

THE ROAD TO WIGAN PIER

PART ONE

I

THE first sound in the mornings was the clumping of the mill-girls' clogs down the cobbled street.* Earlier than that, I suppose, there were factory whistles which I was never awake to hear.

There were generally four of us in the bedroom, and a beastly place it was, with that defiled impermanent look of rooms that are not serving their rightful purpose. Years earlier the house had been an ordinary dwelling-house, and when the Brookers had taken it and fitted it out as a tripe-shop and lodging-house,* they had inherited some of the more useless pieces of furniture and had never had the energy to remove them. We were therefore sleeping in what was still recognizably a drawing-room. Hanging from the ceiling there was a heavy glass chandelier on which the dust was so thick that it was like fur. And covering most of one wall there was a huge hideous piece of junk, something between a sideboard and a hall-stand, with lots of carving and little drawers and strips of looking-glass, and there was a once-gaudy carpet ringed by the slop-pails of years, and two gilt chairs with burst seats, and one of those old-fashioned horsehair armchairs which you slide off when you try to sit on them. The room had been turned into a bedroom by thrusting four squalid beds in among this other wreckage.

My bed was in the right-hand corner on the side nearest the door. There was another bed across the foot of it and jammed hard against it (it had to be in that position to allow the door to open) so that I had to sleep with my legs doubled up; if I straightened them out I kicked the occupant of the other bed in the small of the back. He was an elderly man named Mr Reilly, a mechanic of sorts and employed 'on top' at one of the coal pits. Luckily he had to go to work at five in the morning, so I could uncoil my legs and have a couple of hours' proper sleep after he was gone. In the bed opposite there was a Scotch miner who had been injured in a pit accident (a huge chunk of stone pinned him to the ground and it was a couple of hours before they could lever it off), and had received five hundred pounds compensation. He was

a big handsome man of forty, with grizzled hair and a clipped mous-
tache, more like a sergeant-major than a miner, and he would
lie in bed till late in the day, smoking a short pipe. The other bed
was occupied by a succession of commercial travellers, newspaper-
canvassers, and hire-purchase touts who generally stayed for a couple
of nights. It was a double bed and much the best in the room. I had
slept in it myself my first night there, but had been manoeuvred out
of it to make room for another lodger. I believe all newcomers spent
their first night in the double bed, which was used, so to speak, as bait.
All the windows were kept tight shut, with a red sand-bag jammed in
the bottom, and in the morning the room stank like a ferret's cage.
You did not notice it when you got up, but if you went out of the room
and came back, the smell hit you in the face with a smack.

I never discovered how many bedrooms the house contained, but
strange to say there was a bathroom, dating from before the Brookers'
time. Downstairs there was the usual kitchen living-room with its
huge open range burning night and day. It was lighted only by a sky-
light, for on one side of it was the shop and on the other the larder,
which opened into some dark subterranean place where the tripe was
stored. Partly blocking the door of the larder there was a shapeless
sofa upon which Mrs Brooker, our landlady, lay permanently ill, fes-
tooned in grimy blankets. She had a big, pale yellow, anxious face. No
one knew for certain what was the matter with her; I suspect that her
only real trouble was over-eating. In front of the fire there was almost
always a line of damp washing, and in the middle of the room was the
big kitchen table at which the family and all the lodgers ate. I never
saw this table completely uncovered, but I saw its various wrappings
at different times. At the bottom there was a layer of old newspaper
stained by Worcester Sauce; above that a sheet of sticky white oilcloth; above that a green serge cloth; above that a coarse linen cloth,
never changed and seldom taken off. Generally the crumbs from
breakfast were still on the table at supper. I used to get to know individual crumbs by sight and watch their progress up and down the
table from day to day.

The shop was a narrow, cold sort of room. On the outside of the
window a few white letters, relics of ancient chocolate advertisements,
were scattered like stars. Inside there was a slab upon which lay the
great white folds of tripe, and the grey flocculent stuff known as
'black tripe', and the ghostly translucent feet of pigs, ready boiled.

It was the ordinary 'tripe and pea' shop, and not much else was stocked except bread, cigarettes, and tinned stuff. 'Teas' were advertised in the window, but if a customer demanded a cup of tea he was usually put off with excuses. Mr Brooker, though out of work for two years, was a miner by trade, but he and his wife had been keeping shops of various kinds as a side-line all their lives. At one time they had had a pub, but they had lost their licence for allowing gambling on the premises. I doubt whether any of their businesses had ever paid; they were the kind of people who run a business chiefly in order to have something to grumble about. Mr Brooker was a dark, small-boned, sour, Irish-looking man, and astonishingly dirty. I don't think I ever once saw his hands clean. As Mrs Brooker was now an invalid he prepared most of the food, and like all people with permanently dirty hands he had a peculiarly intimate, lingering manner of handling things. If he gave you a slice of bread-and-butter there was always a black thumb-print on it. Even in the early morning when he descended into the mysterious den behind Mrs Brooker's sofa and fished out the tripe, his hands were already black. I heard dreadful stories from the other lodgers about the place where the tripe was kept. Blackbeetles were said to swarm there. I do not know how often fresh consignments of tripe were ordered, but it was at long intervals, for Mrs Brooker used to date events by it. 'Let me see now, I've had in three lots of froze (frozen tripe) since that happened,' etc. We lodgers were never given tripe to eat. At the time I imagined that this was because tripe was too expensive; I have since thought that it was merely because we knew too much about it. The Brookers never ate tripe themselves, I noticed.

The only permanent lodgers were the Scotch miner, Mr Reilly, two old-age pensioners, and an unemployed man on the P.A.C. named Joe—he was the kind of person who has no surname. The Scotch miner was a bore when you got to know him. Like so many unemployed men he spent too much time reading newspapers, and if you did not head him off he would discourse for hours about such things as the Yellow Peril, trunk murders, astrology, and the conflict between religion and science. The old-age pensioners had, as usual, been driven from their homes by the Means Test.* They handed their weekly ten shillings over to the Brookers and in return got the kind of accommodation you would expect for ten shillings; that is, a bed in the attic and meals chiefly of bread-and-butter. One of them was of 'superior' type and was dying of some malignant disease—cancer, I believe. He only got out of bed on the days when he went to draw his pension. The other, called by everyone Old Jack, was an ex-miner aged seventy-eight who had worked well over fifty years in the pits. He was alert and intelligent, but curiously enough he seemed only to remember his boyhood experiences and to have forgotten all about the modern mining machinery and improvements. He used to tell me tales of fights with savage horses in the narrow galleries underground. When he heard that I was arranging to go down several coal-mines he was contemptuous and declared that a man of my size (six feet two and a half) would never manage the 'travelling'; it was no use telling him that the 'travelling' was better than it used to be. But he was friendly to everyone and used to give us all a fine shout of 'Good night, boys!' as he crawled up the stairs to his bed somewhere under the rafters. What I most admired about Old Jack was that he never cadged; he was generally out of tobacco towards the end of the week, but he always refused to smoke anyone else's. The Brookers had insured the lives of both old-age pensioners with one of the tanner-a-week companies. It was said that they were overheard anxiously asking the insurance-tout 'how long people lives when they've got cancer'.

Joe, like the Scotchman, was a great reader of newspapers and spent almost his entire day in the public library. He was the typical unmarried unemployed man, a derelict-looking, frankly ragged creature with a round, almost childish face on which there was a naïvely naughty expression. He looked more like a neglected little boy than a grown-up man. I suppose it is the complete lack of responsibility that makes so many of these men look younger than their ages. From Joe's appearance I took him to be about twenty-eight, and was amazed to learn that he was forty-three. He had a love of resounding phrases and was very proud of the astuteness with which he had avoided getting married. He often said to me, 'Matrimonial chains is a big item,' evidently feeling this to be a very subtle and portentous remark. His total income was fifteen shillings a week, and he paid out six or seven to the Brookers for his bed. I sometimes used to see him making himself a cup of tea over the kitchen fire, but for the rest he got his meals somewhere out of doors; it was mostly slices of bread-and-marg and packets of fish and chips, I suppose.

Besides these there was a floating clientele of commercial travellers of the poorer sort, travelling actors—always common in the North because most of the larger pubs hire variety artists at the week-ends—and newspaper-canvassers. The newspaper-canvassers were a type I had never met before. Their job seemed to me so hopeless, so appalling that I wondered how anyone could put up with such a thing when prison was a possible alternative. They were employed mostly by weekly or Sunday papers, and they were sent from town to town, provided with maps and given a list of streets which they had to 'work' each day. If they failed to secure a minimum of twenty orders a day, they got the sack. So long as they kept up their twenty orders a day they received a small salary—two pounds a week, I think; on any order over the twenty they drew a tiny commission. The thing is not so impossible as it sounds, because in working-class districts every family takes in a twopenny weekly paper and changes it every few weeks; but I doubt whether anyone keeps a job of that kind long. The newspapers engage poor desperate wretches, out-of-work clerks and commercial travellers and the like, who for a while make frantic efforts and keep their sales up to the minimum; then as the deadly work wears them down they are sacked and fresh men are taken on. I got to know two who were employed by one of the more notorious weeklies. Both of them were middle-aged men with families to support, and one of them was a grandfather. They were on their feet ten hours a day, 'working' their appointed streets, and then busy late into the night filling in blank forms for some swindle their paper was running—one of those schemes by which you are 'given' a set of crockery if you take out a six weeks' subscription and send a two-shilling postal order as well. The fat one, the grandfather, used to fall asleep with his head on a pile of forms. Neither of them could afford the pound a week which the Brookers charged for full board. They used to pay a small sum for their beds and make shamefaced meals in a corner of the kitchen off bacon and bread-and-margarine which they stored in their suit-cases.

The Brookers had large numbers of sons and daughters, most of whom had long since fled from home. Some were in Canada 'at Canada', as Mrs Brooker used to put it. There was only one son living near by, a large pig-like young man employed in a garage, who frequently came to the house for his meals. His wife was there all day with the two children, and most of the cooking and laundering was done by her and by Emmie, the fiancée of another son who was in London. Emmie was a fair-haired, sharp-nosed, unhappy-looking girl who

worked at one of the mills for some starvation wage, but nevertheless
spent all her evenings in bondage at the Brookers' house. I gathered
that the marriage was constantly being postponed and would probably
never take place, but Mrs Brooker had already appropriated Emmie as
a daughter-in-law, and nagged her in that peculiar watchful, loving
way that invalids have. The rest of the housework was done, or not
done, by Mr Brooker. Mrs Brooker seldom rose from her sofa in the
kitchen (she spent the night there as well as the day) and was too ill to
do anything except eat stupendous meals. It was Mr Brooker who
attended to the shop, gave the lodgers their food, and 'did out' the
bedrooms. He was always moving with incredible slowness from
one hated job to another. Often the beds were still unmade at six in the
evening, and at any hour of the day you were liable to meet Mr Brooker
on the stairs, carrying a full chamber-pot which he gripped with his
thumb well over the rim. In the mornings he sat by the fire with a tub
of filthy water, peeling potatoes at the speed of a slow-motion picture.
I never saw anyone who could peel potatoes with quite such an air of
brooding resentment. You could see the hatred of this 'bloody woman's work', as he called it, fermenting inside him, a kind of bitter juice.
He was one of those people who can chew their grievances like a cud.

Of course, as I was indoors a good deal, I heard all about the
Brookers' woes, and how everyone swindled them and was ungrateful
to them, and how the shop did not pay and the lodging-house hardly
paid. By local standards they were not so badly off, for, in some way
I did not understand, Mr Brooker was dodging the Means Test and
drawing an allowance from the P.A.C.,* but their chief pleasure was
talking about their grievances to anyone who would listen. Mrs Brooker
used to lament by the hour, lying on her sofa, a soft mound of fat and
self-pity, saying the same things over and over again. 'We don't seem
to get no customers nowadays. I don't know 'ow it is. The tripe's just
a-laying there day after day—such beautiful tripe it is, too! It does
seem 'ard, don't it now?' etc., etc., etc. All Mrs Brooker's laments
ended with 'It does seem 'ard, don't it now?' like the refrain of a bal-
lade. Certainly it was true that the shop did not pay. The whole place
had the unmistakable dusty, flyblown air of a business that is going
down. But it would have been quite useless to explain to them *why*
nobody came to the shop, even if one had had the face to do it; neither
was capable of understanding that last year's dead bluebottles supine
in the shop window are not good for trade.

But the thing that really tormented them was the thought of those two old-age pensioners living in their house, usurping floor-space, devouring food, and paying only ten shillings a week. I doubt whether they were really losing money over the old-age pensioners, though certainly the profit on ten shillings a week must have been very small. But in their eyes the two old men were a kind of dreadful parasite who had fastened on them and were living on their charity. Old Jack they could just tolerate, because he kept out-of-doors most of the day, but they really hated the bedridden one, Hooker by name. Mr Brooker had a queer way of pronouncing his name, without the H and with a long U—'Uker'. What tales I heard about old Hooker and his fractiousness, the nuisance of making his bed, the way he 'wouldn't eat' this and 'wouldn't eat' that, his endless ingratitude and, above all, the selfish obstinacy with which he refused to die! The Brookers were quite openly pining for him to die. When that happened they could at least draw the insurance money. They seemed to feel him there, eating their substance day after day, as though he had been a living worm in their bowels. Sometimes Mr Brooker would look up from his potato-peeling, catch my eye, and jerk his head with a look of inexpressible bitterness towards the ceiling, towards old Hooker's room. 'It's a b——, ain't it?' he would say. There was no need to say more; I had heard all about old Hooker's ways already. But the Brookers had grievances of one kind and another against all their lodgers, myself included, no doubt. Joe, being on the P.A.C., was practically in the same category as the old-age pensioners. The Scotchman paid a pound a week, but he was indoors most of the day and they 'didn't like him always hanging round the place', as they put it. The newspaper-canvassers were out all day, but the Brookers bore them a grudge for bringing in their own food, and even Mr Reilly, their best lodger, was in disgrace because Mrs Brooker said that he woke her up when he came downstairs in the mornings. They couldn't, they complained perpetually, get the kind of lodgers they wanted—good-class 'commercial gentlemen' who paid full board and were out all day. Their ideal lodger would have been somebody who paid thirty shillings a week and never came indoors except to sleep. I have noticed that people who let lodgings nearly always hate their lodgers. They want their money but they look on them as intruders and have a curiously watchful, jealous attitude which at bottom is a determination not to let the lodger make himself too much at home. It is an inevitable result of the bad system by which the lodger has to live in somebody else's house without being one of the family.

The meals at the Brookers' house were uniformly disgusting. For breakfast you got two rashers of bacon and a pale fried egg, and bread-and-butter which had often been cut overnight and always had thumb-marks on it. However tactfully I tried, I could never induce Mr Brooker to let me cut my own bread-and-butter; he *would* hand it to me slice by slice, each slice gripped firmly under that broad black thumb. For dinner there were generally those threepenny steak puddings which are sold ready-made in tins—these were part of the stock of the shop, I think—and boiled potatoes and rice pudding. For tea there was more bread-and-butter and frayed-looking sweet cakes which were probably bought as 'stales' from the baker. For supper there was the pale flabby Lancashire cheese and biscuits. The Brookers never called these biscuits biscuits. They always referred to them reverently as 'cream crackers'—'Have another cream cracker, Mr Reilly. You'll like a cream cracker with your cheese'—thus glozing over the fact that there was only cheese for supper. Several bottles of Worcester Sauce and a half-full jar of marmalade lived permanently on the table. It was usual to souse everything, even a piece of cheese, with Worcester Sauce, but I never saw anyone brave the marmalade jar, which was an unspeakable mass of stickiness and dust. Mrs Brooker had her meals separately but also took snacks from any meal that happened to be going, and manoeuvred with great skill for what she called 'the bottom of the pot', meaning the strongest cup of tea. She had a habit of constantly wiping her mouth on one of her blankets. Towards the end of my stay she took to tearing off strips of newspaper for this purpose, and in the morning the floor was often littered with crumpled-up balls of slimy paper which lay there for hours. The smell of the kitchen was dreadful, but, as with that of the bedroom, you ceased to notice it after a while.

It struck me that this place must be fairly normal as lodging-houses in the industrial areas go, for on the whole the lodgers did not complain. The only one who ever did so to my knowledge was a little black-haired, sharp-nosed Cockney, a traveller for a cigarette firm. He had never been in the North before, and I think that till recently he had been in better employ and was used to staying in commercial hotels. This was his first glimpse of really low-class lodgings, the kind of place in which the poor tribe of touts and canvassers have to shelter upon their endless journeys. In the morning as we were dressing (he had slept in the double bed, of course) I saw him look round the desolate room with a sort of wondering aversion. He caught my eye and suddenly divined that I was a fellow-Southerner.

'The filthy bloody bastards!' he said feelingly.

After that he packed his suit-case, went downstairs and, with great strength of mind, told the Brookers that this was not the kind of house he was accustomed to and that he was leaving immediately. The Brookers could never understand why. They were astonished and hurt. The ingratitude of it! Leaving them like that for no reason after a single night! Afterwards they discussed it over and over again, in all its bearings. It was added to their store of grievances.

On the day when there was a full chamber-pot under the breakfast table I decided to leave. The place was beginning to depress me. It was not only the dirt, the smells, and the vile food, but the feeling of stagnant meaningless decay, of having got down into some subterranean place where people go creeping round and round, just like blackbeetles, in an endless muddle of slovened jobs and mean grievances. The most dreadful thing about people like the Brookers is the way they say the same things over and over again. It gives you the feeling that they are not real people at all, but a kind of ghost for ever rehearsing the same futile rigmarole. In the end Mrs Brooker's self-pitying talk—always the same complaints, over and over, and always ending with the tremulous whine of 'It does seem 'ard, don't it now?'—revolted me even more than her habit of wiping her mouth with bits of newspaper. But it is no use saying that people like the Brookers are just disgusting and trying to put them out of mind. For they exist in tens and hundreds of thousands; they are one of the characteristic by-products of the modern world. You cannot disregard them if you accept the civilization that produced them. For this is part at least of what industrialism has done for us. Columbus sailed the Atlantic, the first steam engines tottered into motion, the British squares stood firm under the French guns at Waterloo, the one-eyed scoundrels of the nineteenth century praised God and filled their pockets; and this is where it all led—to labyrinthine slums and dark back kitchens with sickly, ageing people creeping round and round them like blackbeetles. It is a kind of duty to see and smell such places now and again, especially smell them, lest you should forget that they exist; though perhaps it is better not to stay there too long.

The train bore me away, through the monstrous scenery of slag-heaps, chimneys, piled scrap-iron, foul canals, paths of cindery mud criss-crossed by the prints of clogs. This was March, but the weather had been horribly cold and everywhere there were mounds of blackened snow. As we moved slowly through the outskirts of the town we passed row after row of little grey slum houses running at right angles to the embankment. At the back of one of the houses a young woman was kneeling on the stones, poking a stick up the leaden waste-pipe which ran from the sink inside and which I suppose was blocked. I had time to see everything about her—her sacking apron, her clumsy clogs, her arms reddened by the cold. She looked up as the train passed, and I was almost near enough to catch her eye. She had a round pale face, the usual exhausted face of the slum girl who is twenty-five and looks forty, thanks to miscarriages and drudgery; and it wore, for the second in which I saw it, the most desolate, hopeless expression I have ever seen. It struck me then that we are mistaken when we say that 'It isn't the same for them as it would be for us,' and that people bred in the slums can imagine nothing but the slums. For what I saw in her face was not the ignorant suffering of an animal. She knew well enough what was happening to her—understood as well as I did how dreadful a destiny it was to be kneeling there in the bitter cold, on the slimy stones of a slum backyard, poking a stick up a foul drain-pipe.*

But quite soon the train drew away into open country, and that seemed strange, almost unnatural, as though the open country had been a kind of park; for in the industrial areas one always feels that the smoke and filth must go on for ever and that no part of the earth's surface can escape them. In a crowded, dirty little country like ours one takes defilement almost for granted. Slag-heaps and chimneys seem a more normal, probable landscape than grass and trees, and even in the depths of the country when you drive your fork into the ground you half expect to lever up a broken bottle or a rusty can. But out here the snow was untrodden and lay so deep that only the tops of the stone boundary-walls were showing, winding over the hills like black paths. I remembered that D. H. Lawrence, writing of this same landscape or another near by, said that the snow-covered hills rippled away into the distance 'like muscle'. It was not the simile that would have occurred to me. To my eye the snow and the black walls were more like a white dress with black piping running across it.

Although the snow was hardly broken the sun was shining brightly, and behind the shut windows of the carriage it seemed warm. According to the almanac this was spring, and a few of the birds seemed to believe it. For the first time in my life, in a bare patch beside the line, I saw rooks treading.* They did it on the ground and not, as I should have expected, in a tree. The manner of courtship was curious. The female stood with her beak open and the male walked round her and appeared to be feeding her. I had hardly been in the train half an hour, but it seemed a very long way from the Brookers' back-kitchen to the empty slopes of snow, the bright sunshine, and the big gleaming birds.

The whole of the industrial districts are really one enormous town, of about the same population as Greater London but, fortunately, of much larger area; so that even in the middle of them there is still room for patches of cleanness and decency. That is an encouraging thought. In spite of hard trying, man has not yet succeeded in doing his dirt everywhere. The earth is so vast and still so empty that even in the filthy heart of civilization you find fields where the grass is green instead of grey; perhaps if you looked for them you might even find streams with live fish in them instead of salmon tins. For quite a long time, perhaps another twenty minutes, the train was rolling through open country before the villa-civilization began to close in upon us again, and then the outer slums, and then the slag-heaps, belching chimneys, blast-furnaces, canals, and gasometers of another industrial town.

II

OUR civilization, *pace* Chesterton,* *is* founded on coal, more completely than one realizes until one stops to think about it. The machines that keep us alive, and the machines that make the machines, are all directly or indirectly dependent upon coal. In the metabolism of the Western world the coal-miner is second in importance only to the man who ploughs the soil. He is a sort of grimy caryatid upon whose shoulders nearly everything that is *not* grimy is supported. For this reason the actual process by which coal is extracted is well worth watching, if you get the chance and are willing to take the trouble.

When you go down a coal-mine it is important to try and get to the coal face when the 'fillers' are at work. This is not easy, because when the mine is working visitors are a nuisance and are not encouraged, but if you go at any other time, it is possible to come away with a totally wrong impression. On a Sunday, for instance, a mine seems almost peaceful. The time to go there is when the machines are roaring and the air is black with coal dust, and when you can actually see what the miners have to do. At those times the place is like hell, or at any rate like my own mental picture of hell. Most of the things one imagines in hell are there—heat, noise, confusion, darkness, foul air, and, above all, unbearably cramped space. Everything except the fire, for there is no fire down there except the feeble beams of Davy lamps and electric torches which scarcely penetrate the clouds of coal dust.

When you have finally got there—and getting there is a job in itself: I will explain that in a moment—you crawl through the last line of pit props and see opposite you a shiny black wall three or four feet high. This is the coal face. Overhead is the smooth ceiling made by the rock from which the coal has been cut; underneath is the rock again, so that the gallery you are in is only as high as the ledge of coal itself, probably not much more than a yard. The first impression of all, overmastering everything else for a while, is the frightful, deafening din from the conveyor belt which carries the coal away. You cannot see very far, because the fog of coal dust throws back the beam of your lamp, but you can see on either side of you the line of half-naked kneeling men, one to every four or five yards, driving their shovels under the fallen coal and flinging it swiftly over their left shoulders.

They are feeding it on to the conveyor belt, a moving rubber belt a couple of feet wide which runs a yard or two behind them. Down this belt a glittering river of coal races constantly. In a big mine it is carrying away several tons of coal every minute. It bears it off to some place in the main roads where it is shot into tubs holding half a ton, and thence dragged to the cages and hoisted to the outer air.

It is impossible to watch the 'fillers' at work without feeling a pang of envy for their toughness. It is a dreadful job that they do, an almost superhuman job by the standards of an ordinary person. For they are not only shifting monstrous quantities of coal, they are also doing it in a position that doubles or trebles the work. They have got to remain kneeling all the while—they could hardly rise from their knees without hitting the ceiling—and you can easily see by trying it what a tremendous effort this means. Shovelling is comparatively easy when you are standing up, because you can use your knee and thigh to drive the shovel along; kneeling down, the whole of the strain is thrown upon your arm and belly muscles. And the other conditions do not exactly make things easier. There is the heat—it varies, but in some mines it is suffocating—and the coal dust that stuffs up your throat and nostrils and collects along your eyelids, and the unending rattle of the conveyor belt, which in that confined space is rather like the rattle of a machine-gun. But the fillers look and work as though they were made of iron. They really do look like iron—hammered iron statues—under the smooth coat of coal dust which clings to them from head to foot. It is only when you see miners down the mine and naked that you realize what splendid men they are. Most of them are small (big men are at a disadvantage in that job) but nearly all of them have the most noble bodies; wide shoulders tapering to slender supple waists, and small pronounced buttocks and sinewy thighs, with not an ounce of waste flesh anywhere. In the hotter mines they wear only a pair of thin drawers, clogs, and knee-pads; in the hottest mines of all, only the clogs and knee-pads. You can hardly tell by the look of them whether they are young or old. They may be any age up to sixty or even sixty-five, but when they are black and naked they all look alike. No one could do their work who had not a young man's body, and a figure fit for a guardsman at that; just a few pounds of extra flesh on the waist-line, and the constant bending would be impossible. You can never forget that spectacle once you have seen it—the line of bowed, kneeling figures, sooty black all over, driving their huge shovels under the coal with stupendous force and speed. They are on the job for seven and a half hours, theoretically without a break, for there is no time 'off'. Actually they snatch a quarter of an hour or so at some time during the shift to eat the food they have brought with them, usually a hunk of bread and dripping and a bottle of cold tea. The first time I was watching the 'fillers' at work I put my hand upon some dreadful slimy thing among the coal dust. It was a chewed quid of tobacco. Nearly all the miners chew tobacco, which is said to be good against thirst.

Probably you have to go down several coal-mines* before you can get much grasp of the processes that are going on round you. This is chiefly because the mere effort of getting from place to place makes it difficult to notice anything else. In some ways it is even disappointing, or at least is unlike what you have expected. You get into the cage, which is a steel box about as wide as a telephone box and two or three times as long. It holds ten men, but they pack like pilchards in a tin, and a tall man cannot stand upright in it. The steel door shuts upon you, and somebody working the winding gear above drops you into the void. You have the usual momentary qualm in your belly and a bursting sensation in the ears, but not much sensation of movement till you get near the bottom, when the cage slows down so abruptly that you could swear it is going upwards again. In the middle of the run the cage probably touches sixty miles an hour; in some of the deeper mines it touches even more. When you crawl out at the bottom you are perhaps four hundred yards under ground. That is to say you have a tolerable-sized mountain on top of you; hundreds of yards of solid rock, bones of extinct beasts, subsoil, flints, roots of growing things, green grass, and cows grazing on it—all this suspended over your head and held back only by wooden props as thick as the calf of your leg. But because of the speed at which the cage has brought you down, and the complete blackness through which you have travelled, you hardly feel yourself deeper down than you would at the bottom of the Piccadilly Tube.

What *is* surprising, on the other hand, is the immense horizontal distances that have to be travelled underground. Before I had been down a mine I had vaguely imagined the miner stepping out of the cage and getting to work on a ledge of coal a few yards away. I had not realized that before he even gets to his work he may have to creep through passages as long as from London Bridge to Oxford Circus.

In the beginning, of course, a mine shaft is sunk somewhere near a seam of coal. But as that seam is worked out and fresh seams are followed up, the workings get further and further from the pit bottom. If it is a mile from the pit bottom to the coal face, that is probably an average distance; three miles is a fairly normal one; there are even said to be a few mines where it is as much as five miles. But these distances bear no relation to distances above ground. For in all that mile or three miles as it may be, there is hardly anywhere outside the main road, and not many places even there, where a man can stand upright.

You do not notice the effect of this till you have gone a few hundred yards. You start off, stooping slightly, down the dim-lit gallery, eight or ten feet wide and about five high, with the walls built up with slabs of shale, like the stone walls in Derbyshire. Every yard or two there are wooden props holding up the beams and girders; some of the girders have buckled into fantastic curves under which you have to duck. Usually it is bad going underfoot—thick dust or jagged chunks of shale, and in some places where there is water it is mucky as a farm-yard. Also there is the track for the coal tubs, like a miniature railway track with sleepers a foot to two apart, which is tiresome to walk on. Everything is grey with shale dust; there is a dusty fiery smell which seems to be the same in all mines. You see mysterious machines of which you never learn the purpose, and bundles of tools slung together on wires, and sometimes mice darting away from the beam of the lamps. They are surprisingly common, especially in mines where there are or have been horses. It would be interesting to know how they got there in the first place; possibly by falling down the shaft—for they say a mouse can fall any distance uninjured, owing to its surface area being so large relative to its weight. You press yourself against the wall to make way for lines of tubs jolting slowly towards the shaft, drawn by an endless steel cable operated from the surface. You creep through sacking curtains and thick wooden doors which, when they are opened, let out fierce blasts of air. These doors are an important part of the ventilation system. The exhausted air is sucked out of one shaft by means of fans, and the fresh air enters the other of its own accord. But if left to itself the air will take the shortest way round, leaving the deeper workings unventilated; so all short cuts have to be partitioned off.

At the start to walk stooping is rather a joke, but it is a joke that soon wears off. I am handicapped by being exceptionally tall, but when the roof falls to four feet or less it is a tough job for anybody except a dwarf or a child. You have not only got to bend double, you have also got to keep your head up all the while so as to see the beams and girders and dodge them when they come. You have, therefore, a constant crick in the neck, but this is nothing to the pain in your knees and thighs. After half a mile it becomes (I am not exaggerating) an unbeatable agony. You begin to wonder whether you will ever get to the end—still more, how on earth you are going to get back. Your pace grows slower and slower. You come to a stretch of a couple of hundred yards where it is all exceptionally low and you have to work yourself along in a squatting position. Then suddenly the roof opens out to a mysterious height—scene of an old fall of rock, probably— and for twenty whole yards you can stand upright. The relief is overwhelming. But after this there is another low stretch of a hundred yards and then a succession of beams which you have to crawl under. You go down on all fours; even this is a relief after the squatting business. But when you come to the end of the beams and try to get up again, you find that your knees have temporarily struck work and refuse to lift you. You call a halt, ignominiously, and say that you would like to rest for a minute or two. Your guide (a miner) is sympathetic. He knows that your muscles are not the same as his. 'Only another four hundred yards,' he says encouragingly; you feel that he might as well say another four hundred miles. But finally you do somehow creep as far as the coal face. You have gone a mile and taken the best part of an hour; a miner would do it in not much more than twenty minutes. Having got there, you have to sprawl in the coal dust and get your strength back for several minutes before you can even watch the work in progress with any kind of intelligence.

Coming back is worse than going, not only because you are already tired out but because the journey back to the shaft is probably slightly uphill. You get through the low places at the speed of a tortoise, and you have no shame now about calling a halt when your knees give way. Even the lamp you are carrying becomes a nuisance and probably when you stumble you drop it; whereupon, if it is a Davy lamp, it goes out. Ducking the beams becomes more and more of an effort, and sometimes you forget to duck. You try walking head down as the miners do, and then you bang your backbone. Even the miners bang their backbones fairly often. This is the reason why in very hot mines, where it is necessary to go about half naked, most of the miners have what they call 'buttons down the back'—that is, a permanent scab on each vertebra. When the track is downhill the miners sometimes fit their clogs, which are hollow underneath, on to the trolley rails and slide down. In mines where the 'travelling' is very bad all the miners carry sticks about two and a half feet long, hollowed out below the handle. In normal places you keep your hand on top of the stick and in the low places you slide your hand down into the hollow. These sticks are a great help, and the wooden crash-helmets—a comparatively recent invention—are a godsend. They look like a French or Italian steel helmet, but they are made of some kind of pith and very light, and so strong that you can take a violent blow on the head without feeling it. When finally you get back to the surface you have been perhaps three hours underground and travelled two miles, and you are more exhausted than you would be by a twenty-five-mile walk above ground. For a week afterwards your thighs are so stiff that coming downstairs is quite a difficult feat; you have to work your way down in a peculiar sidelong manner, without bending the knees. Your miner friends notice the stiffness of your walk and chaff you about it. ('How'd ta like to work down pit, eh?' etc.) Yet even a miner who has been long away from work—from illness, for instance—when he comes back to the pit, suffers badly for the first few days.

It may seem that I am exaggerating, though no one who has been down an old-fashioned pit (most of the pits in England are old-fashioned) and actually gone as far as the coal face, is likely to say so. But what I want to emphasize is this. Here is this frightful business of crawling to and fro, which to any normal person is a hard day's work in itself; and it is not part of the miner's work at all, it is merely an extra, like the City man's daily ride in the Tube. The miner does that journey to and fro, and sandwiched in between there are seven and a half hours of savage work. I have never travelled much more than a mile to the coal face; but often it is three miles, in which case I and most people other than coal-miners would never get there at all. This is the kind of point that one is always liable to miss. When you think of a coal-mine you think of depth, heat, darkness, blackened figures hacking at walls of coal; you don't think, necessarily, of those miles of creeping to and fro. There is the question of time, also. A miner's working shift of seven and a half hours does not sound very long, but one has got to add on to it at least an hour a day for 'travelling', more often two hours and sometimes three. Of course, the 'travelling' is

not technically work and the miner is not paid for it; but it is as like
work as makes no difference. It is easy to say that miners don't mind
all this. Certainly, it is not the same for them as it would be for you or
me. They have done it since childhood, they have the right muscles
hardened, and they can move to and fro underground with a startling
and rather horrible agility. A miner puts his head down and *runs*, with
a long swinging stride, through places where I can only stagger. At the
workings you see them on all fours, skipping round the pit props
almost like dogs. But it is quite a mistake to think that they enjoy it.
I have talked about this to scores of miners and they all admit that the
'travelling' is hard work; in any case when you hear them discussing
a pit among themselves the 'travelling' is always one of the things
they discuss. It is said that a shift always returns from work faster
than it goes; nevertheless the miners all say that it is the coming away,
after a hard day's work, that is especially irksome. It is part of their
work and they are equal to it, but certainly it is an effort. It is comparable, perhaps, to climbing a smallish mountain before and after your
day's work.

When you have been down two or three pits you begin to get some
grasp of the processes that are going on underground. (I ought to say,
by the way, that I know nothing whatever about the technical side of
mining: I am merely describing what I have seen.) Coal lies in thin
seams between enormous layers of rock, so that essentially the process
of getting it out is like scooping the central layer from a Neapolitan ice.
In the old days the miners used to cut straight into the coal with pick
and crowbar—a very slow job because coal, when lying in its virgin
state, is almost as hard as rock. Nowadays the preliminary work is done
by an electrically-driven coal-cutter, which in principle is an immensely
tough and powerful band-saw, running horizontally instead of verti-
cally, with teeth a couple of inches long and half an inch or an inch
thick. It can move backwards or forwards on its own power, and the
men operating it can rotate it this way and that. Incidentally it makes
one of the most awful noises I have ever heard, and sends forth clouds
of coal dust which make it impossible to see more than two or three
feet and almost impossible to breathe. The machine travels along the
coal face cutting into the base of the coal and undermining it to the
depth of five feet or five feet and a half; after this it is comparatively
easy to extract the coal to the depth to which it has been undermined.
Where it is 'difficult getting', however, it has also to be loosened with

explosives. A man with an electric drill, like a rather smaller version of the drills used in street-mending, bores holes at intervals in the coal, inserts blasting powder, plugs it with clay, goes round the corner if there is one handy (he is supposed to retire to twenty-five yards distance) and touches off the charge with an electric current. This is not intended to bring the coal out, only to loosen it. Occasionally, of course, the charge is too powerful, and then it not only brings the coal out but brings the roof down as well.

After the blasting has been done the 'fillers' can tumble the coal out, break it up, and shovel it on to the conveyor belt. It comes out at first in monstrous boulders which may weigh anything up to twenty tons. The conveyor belt shoots it on to tubs, and the tubs are shoved into the main road and hitched on to an endlessly revolving steel cable which drags them to the cage. Then they are hoisted, and at the surface the coal is sorted by being run over screens, and if necessary is washed as well. As far as possible the 'dirt'—the shale, that is—is used for making the roads below. All that cannot be used is sent to the surface and dumped; hence the monstrous 'dirt-heaps', like hideous grey mountains, which are the characteristic scenery of the coal areas. When the coal has been extracted to the depth to which the machine has cut, the coal face has advanced by five feet. Fresh props are put in to hold up the newly exposed roof, and during the next shift the conveyor belt is taken to pieces, moved five feet forward, and re-assembled. As far as possible the three operations of cutting, blasting, and extraction are done in three separate shifts, the cutting in the afternoon, the blasting at night (there is a law, not always kept, that forbids its being done when there are other men working near by), and the 'filling' in the morning shift, which lasts from six in the morning until half past one.

Even when you watch the process of coal-extraction you probably only watch it for a short time, and it is not until you begin making a few calculations that you realize what a stupendous task the 'fillers' are performing. Normally each man has to clear a space four or five yards wide. The cutter has undermined the coal to the depth of five feet, so that if the seam of coal is three or four feet high, each man has to cut out, break up, and load on to the belt something between seven and twelve cubic yards of coal. This is to say, taking a cubic yard as weighing twenty-seven hundredweight, that each man is shifting coal at a speed approaching two tons an hour. I have just enough experience of pick and shovel work to be able to grasp what this means. When I am digging trenches in my garden, if I shift two tons of earth during the afternoon, I feel that I have earned my tea. But earth is tractable stuff compared with coal, and I don't have to work kneeling down, a thousand feet underground, in suffocating heat and swallowing coal dust with every breath I take; nor do I have to walk a mile bent double before I begin. The miner's job would be as much beyond my power as it would be to perform on the flying trapeze or to win the Grand National. I am not a manual labourer and please God I never shall be one, but there are some kinds of manual work that I could do if I had to. At a pinch I could be a tolerable road-sweeper or an inefficient gardener or even a tenth-rate farm hand. But by no conceivable amount of effort or training could I become a coal-miner; the work would kill me in a few weeks.

Watching coal-miners at work, you realize momentarily what different universes different people inhabit. Down there where coal is dug it is a sort of world apart which one can quite easily go through life without ever hearing about. Probably a majority of people would even prefer not to hear about it. Yet it is the absolutely necessary counterpart of our world above. Practically everything we do, from eating an ice to crossing the Atlantic, and from baking a loaf to writing a novel, involves the use of coal, directly or indirectly. For all the arts of peace coal is needed; if war breaks out it is needed all the more. In time of revolution the miner must go on working or the revolution must stop, for revolution as much as reaction needs coal. Whatever may be happening on the surface, the hacking and shovelling have got to continue without a pause, or at any rate without pausing for more than a few weeks at the most. In order that Hitler may march the goosestep, that the Pope may denounce Bolshevism, that the cricket crowds may assemble at Lord's, that the Nancy poets may scratch one another's backs, coal has got to be forthcoming. But on the whole we are not aware of it; we all know that we 'must have coal', but we seldom or never remember what coal getting involves. Here am I, sitting writing in front of my comfortable coal fire. It is April but I still need a fire. Once a fortnight the coal cart drives up to the door and men in leather jerkins carry the coal indoors in stout sacks smelling of tar and shoot it clanking into the coal-hole under the stairs. It is only very rarely, when I make a definite mental effort, that I connect this coal with that far-off labour in the mines. It is just 'coal'—something that

I have got to have; black stuff that arrives mysteriously from nowhere in particular, like manna except that you have to pay for it. You could quite easily drive a car right across the north of England and never once remember that hundreds of feet below the road you are on the miners are hacking at the coal. Yet in a sense it is the miners who are driving your car forward. Their lamp-lit world down there is as necessary to the daylight world above as the root is to the flower.

It is not long since conditions in the mines were worse than they are now. There are still living a few very old women who in their youth have worked underground, with a harness round their waists and a chain that passed between their legs, crawling on all fours and dragging tubs of coal. They used to go on doing this even when they were pregnant. And even now, if coal could not be produced without pregnant women dragging it to and fro, I fancy we should let them do it rather than deprive ourselves of coal. But most of the time, of course, we should prefer to forget that they were doing it. It is so with all types of manual work; it keeps us alive, and we are oblivious of its existence. More than anyone else, perhaps, the miner can stand as the type of the manual worker, not only because his work is so exaggeratedly awful, but also because it is so vitally necessary and yet so remote from our experience, so invisible, as it were, that we are capable of forgetting it as we forget the blood in our veins. In a way it is even humiliating to watch coal-miners working. It raises in you a momentary doubt about your own status as an 'intellectual' and a superior person generally. For it is brought home to you, at least while you are watching, that it is only because miners sweat their guts out that superior persons can remain superior. You and I and the editor of the *Times Lit. Supp.*, and the Nancy poets and the Archbishop of Canterbury and Comrade X, author of *Marxism for Infants*—all of us *really* owe the comparative decency of our lives to poor drudges underground, blackened to the eyes, with their throats full of coal dust, driving their shovels forward with arms and belly muscles of steel.

III

WHEN the miner comes up from the pit his face is so pale that it is noticeable even through the mask of coal dust. This is due to the foul air that he has been breathing, and will wear off presently. To a Southerner, new to the mining districts, the spectacle of a shift of several hundred miners streaming out of the pit is strange and slightly sinister. Their exhausted faces, with the grime clinging in all the hollows, have a fierce, wild look. At other times, when their faces are clean, there is not much to distinguish them from the rest of the population. They have a very upright square-shouldered walk, a reaction from the constant bending underground, but most of them are shortish men and their thick ill-fitting clothes hide the splendour of their bodies. The most definitely distinctive thing about them is the blue scars on their noses. Every miner has blue scars on his nose and forehead, and will carry them to his death. The coal dust of which the air underground is full enters every cut, and then the skin grows over it and forms a blue stain like tattooing, which in fact it is. Some of the older men have their foreheads veined like Roquefort cheeses from this cause.

As soon as the miner comes above ground he gargles a little water to get the worst of the coal dust out of his throat and nostrils, and then goes home and either washes or does not wash according to his temperament. From what I have seen I should say that a majority of miners prefer to eat their meal first and wash afterwards, as I should do in their circumstances. It is the normal thing to see a miner sitting down to his tea with a Christy-minstrel face, completely black except for very red lips which become clean by eating. After his meal he takes a largish basin of water and washes very methodically, first his hands, then his chest, neck, and armpits, then his forearms, then his face and scalp (it is on the scalp that the grime clings thickest), and then his wife takes the flannel and washes his back. He has only washed the top half of his body and probably his navel is still a nest of coal dust, but even so it takes some skill to get passably clean in a single basin of water. For my own part I found I needed two complete baths after going down a coal-mine. Getting the dirt out of one's eyelids is a ten minutes' job in itself.

At some of the larger and better appointed collieries there are pithead baths. This is an enormous advantage, for not only can the miner wash himself all over every day, in comfort and even luxury, but at the baths he has two lockers where he can keep his pit clothes separate from his day clothes, so that within twenty minutes of emerging as black as a Negro he can be riding off to a football match dressed up to the nines. But it is only comparatively seldom because a seam of coal does not last for ever, so that it is not necessarily worth building a bath every time a shaft is sunk. I cannot get hold of exact figures, but it seems likely that rather less than one miner in three has access to a pithead bath. Probably a large majority of miners are completely black from the waist down for at least six days a week. It is almost impossible for them to wash all over in their own homes. Every drop of water has got to be heated up, and in a tiny living-room which contains, apart from the kitchen range and a quantity of furniture, a wife, some children, and probably a dog, there is simply not room to have a proper bath. Even with a basin one is bound to splash the furniture. Middle-class people are fond of saying that the miners would not wash themselves properly even if they could, but this is nonsense, as is shown by the fact that where pithead baths exist practically all the men use them. Only among the very old men does the belief still linger that washing one's legs 'causes lumbago'. Moreover the pithead baths, where they exist, are paid for wholly or partly by the miners themselves, out of the Miners' Welfare Fund.* Sometimes the colliery company subscribes, sometimes the Fund bears the whole cost. But doubtless even at this late date the old ladies in Brighton boarding-houses are saying that 'if you give those miners baths they only use them to keep coal in'.

As a matter of fact it is surprising that miners wash as regularly as they do, seeing how little time they have between work and sleep. It is a great mistake to think of a miner's working day as being only seven and a half hours. Seven and a half hours is the time spent actually on the job, but, as I have already explained, one has got to add on to this time taken up in 'travelling', which is seldom less than an hour and may often be three hours. In addition most miners have to spend a considerable time in getting to and from the pit. Throughout the industrial districts there is an acute shortage of houses, and it is only in the small mining villages, where the village is grouped round the pit, that the men can be certain of living near their work. In the larger mining towns where I have stayed, nearly everyone went to work by bus; half a crown a week seemed to be the normal amount to spend on fares. One miner I stayed with was working on the morning shift, which was from six in the morning till half past one. He had to be out of bed at a quarter to four and got back somewhere after three in the afternoon. In another house where I stayed a boy of fifteen was working on the night shift. He left for work at nine at night and got back at eight in the morning, had his breakfast, and then promptly went to bed and slept till six in the evening; so that his leisure time amounted to about four hours a day—actually a good deal less, if you take off the time for washing, eating, and dressing.

The adjustments a miner's family have to make when he is changed from one shift to another must be tiresome in the extreme. If he is on the night shift he gets home in time for breakfast, on the morning shift he gets home in the middle of the afternoon, and on the afternoon shift he gets home in the middle of the night; and in each case, of course, he wants his principal meal of the day as soon as he returns. I notice that the Rev. W. R. Inge, in his book *England*, accuses the miners of gluttony. From my own observation I should say that they eat astonishingly little. Most of the miners I stayed with ate slightly less than I did. Many of them declare that they cannot do their day's work if they have had a heavy meal beforehand, and the food they take with them is only a snack, usually bread-and-dripping and cold tea. They carry it in a flat tin called a snap-can which they strap to their belts. When a miner gets back late at night his wife waits up for him, but when he is on the morning shift it seems to be the custom for him to get his breakfast for himself. Apparently the old superstition that it is bad luck to see a woman before going to work on the morning shift is not quite extinct. In the old days, it is said, a miner who happened to meet a woman in the early morning would often turn back and do no work that day.

Before I had been in the coal areas I shared the widespread illusion that miners are comparatively well paid. One hears it loosely stated that a miner is paid ten or eleven shillings a shift, and one does a small multiplication sum and concludes that every miner is earning round about £2 a week or £150 a year. But the statement that a miner receives ten or eleven shillings a shift is very misleading. To begin with, it is only the actual coal 'getter' who is paid at this rate; a 'dataller', for instance, who attends to the roofing, is paid at a lower rate, usually eight or nine shillings a shift. Again, when the coal 'getter' is paid piecework, so much per ton extracted, as is the case in many mines, he is dependent on the quality of the coal; a breakdown in the machinery or a 'fault'—that is, a streak of rock running through the coal seam—may rob him of his earnings for a day or two at a time. But in any case one ought not to think of the miner as working six days a week, fifty-two weeks a year. Almost certainly there will be a number of days when he is 'laid off'. The average earning per shift worked for every mine-worker, of all ages and both sexes, in Great Britain in 1934, was 9s.[1] If everyone were in work all the time, this would mean that the mine-worker was earning a little over £142 a year, or nearly £2 15s. a week. His real income, however, is far lower than this, for the 9s. 1¾d. is merely an average calculation on shifts actually worked and takes no account of blank days.

I have before me five pay-checks belonging to a Yorkshire miner, for five weeks (not consecutive) at the beginning of 1936. Averaging them up, the gross weekly wages they represent is £2 15s. 2d.; this is an average of nearly 9s. 2½d. a shift. But these pay-checks are for the winter, when nearly all mines are running full time. As spring advances the coal trade slacks off and more and more men are 'temporarily stopped', while others still technically in work are laid off for a day or two in every week. It is obvious therefore that £150 or even £142 is an immense over-estimate for the mine-worker's yearly income. As a matter of fact, for the year 1934 the average gross earnings of all miners throughout Great Britain was only £115 11s. 6d. It varied considerably from district to district, rising as high as £133 2s. 8d. in Scotland, while in Durham it was a little under £105 or barely more than £2 a week. I take these figures from *The Coal Scuttle*, by Mr Joseph Jones, Mayor of Barnsley, Yorkshire. Mr Jones adds:

These figures cover the earnings of youths as well as adults and of the higher- as well as the lower-paid grades...any particularly high earning would be included in these figures, as would the earnings of certain officials and other higher-paid men as well as the higher amounts paid for overtime work.

The figures, being averages, fail... to reveal the position of thousands of adult workers whose earnings were substantially below the average and who received only 30s. to 40s. or less per week.

[1] From the *Colliery Year Book and Coal Trades Directory* for 1935.

Mr Jones's italics. But please notice that even these wretched earnings are *gross* earnings. On top of this there are all kinds of stoppages which are deducted from the miner's wages every week. Here is a list of weekly stoppages which was given me as typical in one Lancashire district:

	s.	d.
Insurance (unemployment and health)	1	5
Hire of lamp		6
For sharpening tools		6
Check-weighman		9
Infirmary		2
Hospital		1
Benevolent Fund		6
Union fees		6
Total	4	5

Some of these stoppages, such as the Benevolent Fund and the union fees, are, so to speak, the miner's own responsibility, others are imposed by the colliery company. They are not the same in all districts. For instance, the iniquitous swindle of making the miner pay for the hire of his lamp (at sixpence a week he buys the lamp several times over in a single year) does not obtain everywhere. But the stoppages always seem to total up to about the same amount. On the Yorkshire miner's five pay-checks, the average gross earning per week is £2 15s. 2d.; the average net earning, after the stoppages have come off, is only £2 11s. 4d.—a reduction of 3s. 10d. a week. But the pay-check, naturally, only mentions stoppages which are imposed or paid through the colliery company; one has got to add the union fees, bringing the total reduction up to something over four shillings. Probably it is safe to say that stoppages of one kind and another cut four shillings or thereabouts from *every* adult miner's weekly wage. So that the £115 11s. 6d. which was the mine-worker's average earning throughout Great Britain in 1934 should really be something nearer £105. As against this, most miners receive allowances in kind, being able to purchase coal for their own use at a reduced rate, usually eight or nine shillings a ton. But according to Mr Jones, quoted above, 'the average value of all allowances in kind for the country as a whole is only fourpence a day'. And this fourpence a day is offset, in many cases, by the amount the miner has to spend on fares in getting to and from the pit. So, taking the industry as a whole, the sum the miner can actually bring home and call his own does not average more, perhaps slightly less, than two pounds a week.

Meanwhile, how much coal is the average miner producing?

The tonnage of coal raised yearly per person employed in mining rises steadily though rather slowly. In 1914 every mine-worker produced, on average, 253 tons of coal; in 1934 he produced 280 tons.[1] This of course is an average figure for mine-workers of all kinds; those actually working at the coal face extract an enormously greater amount—in many cases, probably, well over a thousand tons each. But taking 280 tons as a representative figure, it is worth noticing what a vast achievement this is. One gets the best idea of it by comparing a miner's life with somebody else's. If I live to be sixty I shall probably have produced thirty novels, or enough to fill two medium-sized library shelves. In the same period the average miner produces 8400 tons of coal; enough coal to pave Trafalgar Square nearly two feet deep or to supply seven large families with fuel for over a hundred years.

Of the five pay-checks I mentioned above, no less than three are rubber-stamped with the words 'death stoppage'. When a miner is killed at work it is usual for the other miners to make up a subscription, generally of a shilling each, for his widow, and this is collected by the colliery company and automatically deducted from their wages. The significant detail here is the *rubber stamp*. The rate of accidents among miners is so high, compared with that in other trades, that casualties are taken for granted almost as they would be in a minor war. Every year one miner in about nine hundred is killed and one in about six is injured; most of these injuries, of course, are petty ones, but a fair number amount to total disablement. This means that if a miner's working life is forty years the chances are nearly seven to one against his escaping injury and not much more than twenty to one against his being killed outright. No other trade approaches this in dangerousness; the next most dangerous is the shipping trade, one sailor in a little under 1300 being killed every year. The figures I have given apply, of course, to mine-workers as a whole; for those actually working underground the proportion of injuries would be very much higher. Every miner of long standing that I have talked to had either

[1] *The Coal Scuttle.* The *Colliery Year Book and Coal Trades Directory* gives a slightly higher figure.

been in a fairly serious accident himself or had seen some of his mates killed, and in every mining family they tell you tales of fathers, brothers, or uncles killed at work. ('And he fell seven hundred feet, and they wouldn't never have collected t'pieces only he were wearing a new suit of oil-skins,' etc., etc., etc.) Some of these tales are appalling in the extreme. One miner, for instance, described to me how a mate of his, a 'dataller', was buried by a fall of rock. They rushed to him and managed to uncover his head and shoulders so that he could breathe, and he was alive and spoke to them. Then they saw that the roof was coming down again and had to run to save themselves; the 'dataller' was buried a second time. Once again they rushed to him and got his head and shoulders free, and again he was alive and spoke to them. Then the roof came down a third time, and this time they could not uncover him for several hours, after which, of course, he was dead. But the miner who told me the story (he had been buried himself on one occasion, but he was lucky enough to have his head jammed between his legs so that there was a small space in which he could breathe) did not think it was a particularly appalling one. Its significance, for him, was that the 'dataller' had known perfectly well that the place where he was working was unsafe, and had gone there in daily expectation of an accident. 'And it worked on his mind to that extent that he got to kissing his wife before he went to work. And she told me afterwards that it were over twenty years since he'd kissed her.'

The most obviously understandable cause of accidents is explosions of gas, which is always more or less present in the atmosphere of the pit. There is a special lamp which is used to test the air for gas, and when it is present in at all large quantities it can be detected by the flame of an ordinary Davy lamp burning blue. If the wick can be turned up to its full extent and the flame is still blue, the proportion of gas is dangerously high; it is, nevertheless, difficult to detect, because it does not distribute itself evenly throughout the atmosphere but hangs about in cracks and crevices. Before starting work a miner often tests for gas by poking his lamp into all the corners. The gas may be touched off by a spark during blasting operations, or by a pick striking a spark from a stone, or by a defective lamp, or by 'gob fires'—spontaneously generated fires which smoulder in the coal dust and are very hard to put out. The great mining disasters which happen from time to time, in which several hundred men are killed, are usually caused by explosions; hence one tends to think of explosions as the chief danger of mining. Actually, the great majority of accidents are due to the normal every-day dangers of the pit; in particular, to falls of roof. There are, for instance, 'pot-holes'—circular holes from which a lump of stone big enough to kill a man shoots out with the promptitude of a bullet. With, so far as I can remember, only one exception, all the miners I have talked to declared that the new machinery, and 'speeding up' generally, have made the work more dangerous. This may be partly due to conservatism, but they can give plenty of reasons. To begin with, the speed at which the coal is now extracted means that for hours at a time a dangerously large stretch of roof remains unpropped. Then there is the vibration, which tends to shake everything loose, and the noise, which makes it harder to detect signs of danger. One must remember that a miner's safety underground depends largely on his own care and skill. An experienced miner claims to know by a sort of instinct when the roof is unsafe; the way he puts it is that he 'can feel the weight on him'. He can, for instance, hear the faint creaking of the props. The reason why wooden props are still generally preferred to iron girders is that a wooden prop which is about to collapse gives warning by creaking, whereas a girder flies out unexpectedly. The devastating noise of the machines makes it impossible to hear anything else, and thus the danger is increased.

When a miner is hurt it is of course impossible to attend to him immediately. He lies crushed under several hundredweight of stone in some dreadful cranny underground, and even after he has been extricated it is necessary to drag his body a mile or more, perhaps, through galleries where nobody can stand upright. Usually when you talk to a man who has been injured you find that it was a couple of hours or so before they got him to the surface. Sometimes, of course, there are accidents to the cage. The cage is shooting several yards up or down at the speed of an express train, and it is operated by somebody on the surface who cannot see what is happening. He has very delicate indicators to tell him how far the cage has got, but it is possible for him to make a mistake, and there have been cases of the cage crashing into the pit-bottom at its very maximum speed. This seems to me a dreadful way to die. For as that tiny steel box whizzes through the blackness there must come a moment when the ten men who are locked inside it *know* that something has gone wrong; and the remaining seconds before they are smashed to pieces hardly bear thinking about. A miner told me he was once in a cage in which something went wrong. It did not slow up when it should have done, and they thought the cable must have snapped. As it happened they got to the bottom safely, but when he stepped out he found that he had broken a tooth; he had been clenching his teeth so hard in expectation of that frightful crash.

Apart from accidents miners seem to be healthy, as obviously they have got to be, considering the muscular efforts demanded of them. They are liable to rheumatism and a man with defective lungs does not last long in that dust-impregnated air, but the most characteristic industrial disease is nystagmus. This is a disease of the eyes which makes the eyeballs oscillate in a strange manner when they come near a light. It is due presumably to working in half-darkness, and sometimes results in total blindness. Miners who are disabled in this way or any other way are compensated by the colliery company, sometimes with a lump sum, sometimes with a weekly pension. This pension never amounts to more than twenty-nine shillings a week; if it falls below fifteen shillings the disabled man can also get something from the dole or the P.A.C. If I were a disabled miner I should very much prefer the lump sum, for then at any rate I should know that I had got my money. Disability pensions are not guaranteed by any centralized fund, so that if the colliery company goes bankrupt that is the end of the disabled miner's pension, though he does figure among the other creditors.

In Wigan I stayed for a while with a miner who was suffering from nystagmus. He could see across the room but not much further. He had been drawing compensation of twenty-nine shillings a week for the past nine months, but the colliery company were now talking of putting him on 'partial compensation' of fourteen shillings a week. It all depended on whether the doctor passed him as fit for light work 'on top'. Even if the doctor did pass him there would, needless to say, be no light work available, but he could draw the dole and the company would have saved itself fifteen shillings a week. Watching this man go to the colliery to draw his compensation, I was struck by the profound differences that are still made by *status*. Here was a man who had been half blinded in one of the most useful of all jobs and was drawing a pension to which he had a perfect right, if anybody has a right to anything. Yet he could not, so to speak, *demand* this pension— he could not, for instance, draw it when and how he wanted it. He had to go to the colliery once a week at a time named by the company, and when he got there he was kept waiting about for hours in the cold wind. For all I know he was also expected to touch his cap and show gratitude to whoever paid him; at any rate he had to waste an afternoon and spend sixpence in bus fares. It is very different for a member of the bourgeoisie, even such a down-at-heel member as I am. Even when I am on the verge of starvation I have certain rights attaching to my bourgeois status. I do not earn much more than a miner earns, but I do at least get it paid into my bank in a gentlemanly manner and can draw it out when I choose. And even when my account is exhausted the bank people are passably polite.

This business of petty inconvenience and indignity, of being kept waiting about, of having to do everything at other people's convenience, is inherent in working-class life. A thousand influences constantly press a working man down into a *passive* role. He does not act, he is acted upon. He feels himself the slave of mysterious authority and has a firm conviction that 'they' will never allow him to do this, that, and the other. Once when I was hop-picking I asked the sweated pickers (they earn something under sixpence an hour) why they did not form a union. I was told immediately that 'they' would never allow it. Who were 'they'? I asked. Nobody seemed to know; but evidently 'they' were omnipotent.

A person of bourgeois origin goes through life with some expectation of getting what he wants, within reasonable limits. Hence the fact that in times of stress 'educated' people tend to come to the front; they are no more gifted than the others and their 'education' is generally quite useless in itself, but they are accustomed to a certain amount of deference and consequently have the cheek necessary to a commander. That they *will* come to the front seems to be taken for granted, always and everywhere. In Lissagaray's *History of the Commune* there is an interesting passage describing the shootings that took place after the Commune had been suppressed. The authorities were shooting the ringleaders, and as they did not know who the ringleaders were, they were picking them out on the principle that those of better class would be the ringleaders. An officer walked down a line of prisoners, picking out likely-looking types. One man was shot because he was wearing a watch, another because he 'had an intelligent face'. I should not like to be shot for having an intelligent face, but I do agree that in almost any revolt the leaders would tend to be people who could pronounce their aitches.

IV

As you walk through the industrial towns you lose yourself in laby-
rinths of little brick houses blackened by smoke, festering in planless
chaos round miry alleys and little cindered yards where there are stinking dust-bins and lines of grimy washing and half-ruinous W.C.s. The
interiors of these houses are always very much the same, though the
number of rooms varies between two or five. All have an almost exactly
similar living-room, ten or fifteen feet square, with an open kitchen
range; in the larger ones there is a scullery as well, in the smaller ones
the sink and copper are in the living-room. At the back there is the yard,
or part of a yard shared by a number of houses, just big enough for the
dustbin and the W.C. Not a single one has hot water laid on. You might
walk, I suppose, through literally hundreds of miles of streets inhabited
by miners, every one of whom, when he is in work, gets black from head
to foot every day, without ever passing a house in which one could have
a bath. It would have been very simple to install a hot-water system
working from the kitchen range, but the builder saved perhaps ten
pounds on each house by not doing so, and at the time when these
houses were built no one imagined that miners wanted baths.

For it is to be noted that the majority of these houses are old, fifty
or sixty years old at least, and great numbers of them are by any
ordinary standard not fit for human habitation. They go on being
tenanted simply because there are no others to be had. And that is the
central fact about housing in the industrial areas: not that the houses
are poky and ugly, and insanitary and comfortless, or that they are
distributed in incredibly filthy slums round belching foundries and
stinking canals and slag-heaps that deluge them with sulphurous
smoke—though all this is perfectly true—but simply that there are
not enough houses to go round.

'Housing shortage' is a phrase that has been bandied about pretty
freely since the war, but it means very little to anyone with an income of
more than £10 a week, or even £5 a week for that matter. Where rents
are high the difficulty is not to find houses but to find tenants. Walk
down any street in Mayfair and you will see 'To Let' boards in half the
windows. But in the industrial areas the mere difficulty of getting hold
of a house is one of the worst aggravations of poverty. It means that

people will put up with anything—any hole and corner slum, any misery of bugs and rotting floors and cracking walls, any extortion of skin-flint landlords and blackmailing agents—simply to get a roof over their heads. I have been into appalling houses, houses in which I would not live a week if you paid me, and found that the tenants had been there twenty and thirty years and only hoped they might have the luck to die there. In general these conditions are taken as a matter of course, though not always. Some people hardly seem to realize that such things as decent houses exist and look on bugs and leaking roofs as acts of God; others rail bitterly against their landlords; but all cling desperately to their houses lest worse should befall. So long as the housing shortage continues the local authorities cannot do much to make existing houses more livable. They can 'condemn' a house, but they cannot order it to be pulled down till the tenant has another house to go to; and so the condemned houses remain standing and are all the worse for being condemned, because naturally the landlord will not spend more than he can help on a house which is going to be demolished sooner or later. In a town like Wigan, for instance, there are over two thousand houses standing which have been condemned for years, and whole sections of the town would be condemned *en bloc* if there were any hope of other houses being built to replace them. Towns like Leeds and Sheffield have scores of thousands of 'back to back' houses which are all of a condemned type but will remain standing for decades.

I have inspected great numbers of houses in various mining towns and villages and made notes on their essential points. I think I can best give an idea of what conditions are like by transcribing a few extracts from my notebook, taken more or less at random. They are only brief notes and they will need certain explanations which I will give afterwards. Here are a few from Wigan:

1. House in Wallgate quarter. Blind back type. One up, one down. Living-room measures 12 ft by 10 ft, room upstairs the same. Alcove under stairs measuring 5 ft by 5 ft and serving as larder, scullery, and coal-hole. Windows will open. Distance to lavatory 50 yards. Rent 4s. 9d., rates 2s. 6d., total 7s. 3d.

2. Another near by. Measurements as above, but no alcove under stairs, merely a recess two feet deep containing the sink—no room for larder, etc. Rent 3s. 2d., rates 2s., total 5s. 2d.

3. House in Scholes quarter. Condemned house. One up, one down. Rooms 15 ft by 15 ft. Sink and copper in living-room, coal-hole under

stairs. Floor subsiding. No windows will open. House decently dry. Landlord good. Rent 3s. 8d., rates 2s. 6d., total 6s. 2d.

4. Another near by. Two up, two down, and coal-hole. Walls falling absolutely to pieces. Water comes into upstairs rooms in quantities. Floor lopsided. Downstairs windows will not open. Landlord bad. Rent 6s., rates 3s. 6d., total 9s. 6d.

5. House in Greenough's Row. One up, two down. Living-room 13 ft by 8 ft. Walls coming apart and water comes in. Back windows will not open, front ones will. Ten in family with eight children very near together in age. Corporations are trying to evict them for overcrowding but cannot find another house to send them to. Landlord bad. Rent 4s., rates 2s. 3d., total 6s. 3d.

So much for Wigan. I have pages more of the same type. Here is one from Sheffield—a typical specimen of Sheffield's several score thousand 'back to back' houses:

House in Thomas Street. Back to back, two up, one down (i.e. a three-storey house with one room on each storey). Cellar below. Living-room 14 ft by 10 ft, and rooms above corresponding. Sink in living-room. Top floor has no door but gives on open stairs. Walls in living-room slightly damp, walls in top rooms coming to pieces and oozing damp on all sides. House is so dark that light has to be kept burning all day. Electricity estimated at 6d. a day (probably an exaggeration). Six in family, parents and four children. Husband (on P.A.C.) is tuberculous. One child in hospital, the others appear healthy. Tenants have been seven years in this house. Would move, but no other house available. Rent 6s. 6d., rates included.

Here are one or two from Barnsley:

1. House in Wortley Street. Two up, one down. Living-room 12 ft by 10 ft. Sink and copper in living-room, coal-hole under stairs. Sink worn almost flat and constantly overflowing. Walls not too sound. Penny in slot gaslight. House very dark and gaslight estimated 4d. a day. Upstairs rooms are really one large room partitioned into two. Walls very bad—wall of back room cracked right through. Window-frames coming to pieces and have to be stuffed with wood. Rain comes through in several places. Sewer runs under house and stinks in summer but Corporation 'says they can't do nowt'. Six people in house, two adults and four children, the eldest aged fifteen. Youngest but one attending hospital—tuberculosis suspected. House infested by bugs. Rent 5s. 3d., including rates.

2. House in Peel Street. Back to back, two up, two down and large cellar. Living-room 10 ft square with copper and sink. The other downstairs

room the same size, probably intended as parlour but used as bedroom. Upstairs rooms the same size as those below. Living-room very dark. Gas-light estimated at 4½d. a day. Distance to lavatory 70 yards. Four beds in house for eight people—two old parents, two adult girls (the eldest aged twenty-seven), one young man, and three children. Parents have one bed, eldest son another, and remaining five people share the other two. Bugs very bad—'You can't keep 'em down when it's 'ot.' Indescribable squalor in downstairs room and smell upstairs almost unbearable. Rent 5s. 7½d., including rates.

3. House in Mapplewell (small mining village near Barnsley). Two up, one down. Living-room 14 ft by 12 ft. Sink in living-room. Plaster crack-ing and coming off walls. No shelves in oven. Gas leaking slightly. The upstairs rooms each 10 ft by 8 ft. Four beds (for six persons, all adult), but 'one bed does nowt', presumably for lack of bedclothes. Room nearest stairs has no door and stairs have no banister, so that when you step out of bed your foot hangs in vacancy and you may fall ten feet on to stones. Dry rot so bad that one can see through the floor into the room below. Bugs, but 'I keeps 'em down with sheep dip'. Earth road past these cottages is like a muck-heap and said to be almost impassable in winter. Stone lavatories at ends of gardens in semi-ruinous condition. Tenants have been twenty-two years in this house. Are £11 in arrears with rent, and have been paying an extra 1s. a week to pay this off. Landlord now refuses this and has served orders to quit. Rent 5s., including rates.

And so on and so on and so on. I could multiply examples by the score—they could be multiplied by the hundred thousand if anyone chose to make a house-to-house inspection throughout the industrial districts. Meanwhile some of the expressions I have used need explaining. 'One up, one down' means one room on each storey—i.e. a two-roomed house. 'Back to back' houses are two houses built in one, each side of the house being somebody's front door, so that if you walk down a row of what is apparently twelve houses you are in reality seeing not twelve houses but twenty-four. The front houses give on the street and the back ones on the yard, and there is only one way out of each house. The effect of this is obvious. The lavatories are in the yard at the back, so that if you live on the side facing the street, to get to the lavatory or the dust-bin you have to go out of the front door and walk round the end of the block—a distance that may be as much as two hundred yards; if you live at the back, on the other hand, your outlook is on to a row of lavatories. There are also houses of what is called the 'blind back' type, which are single houses, but in which the builder has omitted to put in a back door—from pure spite, apparently. The windows which refuse to open are a peculiarity of old mining towns. Some of these towns are so undermined by ancient workings that the ground is constantly subsiding and the houses above slip sideways. In Wigan you pass whole rows of houses which have slid to startling angles, their windows being ten or twenty degrees out of the horizontal. Sometimes the front wall bellies outward till it looks as though the house were seven months gone in pregnancy. It can be refaced, but the new facing soon begins to bulge again. When a house sinks at all suddenly its windows are jammed for ever and the door has to be refitted. This excites no surprise locally. The story of the miner who comes home from work and finds that he can only get indoors by smashing down the front door with an axe is considered humorous. In some cases I have noted 'Landlord good' or 'Landlord bad', because there is great variation in what the slum-dwellers say about their landlords. I found—one might expect it, perhaps—that the small landlords are usually the worst. It goes against the grain to say this, but one can see why it should be so. Ideally, the worst type of slum landlord is a fat wicked man, preferably a bishop, who is drawing an immense income from extortionate rents. Actually, it is a poor old woman who has invested her life's savings in three slum houses, inhabits one of them, and tries to live on the rent of the other two—never, in consequence, having any money for repairs.

But mere notes like these are only valuable as reminders to myself. To me as I read them they bring back what I have seen, but they cannot in themselves give much idea of what conditions are like in those fearful northern slums. Words are such feeble things. What is the use of a brief phrase like 'roof leaks' or 'four beds for eight people'? It is the kind of thing your eye slides over, registering nothing. And yet what a wealth of misery it can cover! Take the question of overcrowding, for instance. Quite often you have eight or even ten people living in a three-roomed house. One of these rooms is a living-room, and as it probably measures about a dozen feet square and contains, besides the kitchen range and the sink, a table, some chairs, and a dresser, there is no room in it for a bed. So there are eight or ten people sleeping in two small rooms, probably in at most four beds. If some of these people are adults and have to go to work, so much the worse. In one house, I remember, three grown-up girls shared the same bed and all went to work at different hours, each disturbing the others when she got up or came in; in another house a young miner working on the night shift slept by day in a narrow bed in which another member of the family slept by night. There is an added difficulty when there are grown-up children, in that you cannot let adolescent youths and girls sleep in the same bed. In one family I visited there were a father and mother and a son and daughter aged round about seventeen, and only two beds for the lot of them. The father slept with the son and the mother with the daughter; it was the only arrangement that ruled out the danger of incest. Then there is the misery of leaking roofs and oozing walls, which in winter makes some rooms almost uninhabitable. Then there are bugs. Once bugs get into a house they are in it till the crack of doom; there is no sure way of exterminating them. Then there are the windows that will not open. I need not point out what this must mean, in summer, in a tiny stuffy living-room where the fire, on which all the cooking is done, has to be kept burning more or less constantly. And there are the special miseries attendant upon back to back houses. A fifty yards' walk to the lavatory or the dust-bin is not exactly an inducement to be clean. In the front houses—at any rate in a side-street where the Corporation don't interfere—the women get into the habit of throwing their refuse out of the front door, so that the gutter is always littered with tea-leaves and bread crusts. And it is worth considering what it is like for a child to grow up in one of the back alleys where its gaze is bounded by a row of lavatories and a wall.

In such places as these a woman is only a poor drudge muddling among an infinity of jobs. She may keep up her spirits, but she cannot keep up her standards of cleanliness and tidiness. There is always something to be done, and no conveniences and almost literally not room to turn round. No sooner have you washed one child's face than another's is dirty; before you have washed the crocks from one meal the next is due to be cooked. I found great variation in the houses I visited. Some were as decent as one could possibly expect in the circumstances, some were so appalling that I have no hope of describing them adequately. To begin with, the smell, the dominant and essential thing, is indescribable. But the squalor and the confusion! A tub full of filthy water here, a basin full of unwashed crocks there, more crocks piled in any odd corner, torn newspaper littered everywhere, and in the middle always the same dreadful table covered with sticky oilcloth and crowded with cooking pots and irons and half-darned stockings and pieces of stale bread and bits of cheese wrapped round with greasy newspaper! And the congestion in a tiny room where getting from one side to the other is a complicated voyage between pieces of furniture, with a line of damp washing getting you in the face every time you move and the children as thick underfoot as toadstools! There are scenes that stand out vividly in my memory. The almost bare living-room of a cottage in a little mining village, where the whole family was out of work and everyone seemed to be underfed; and the big family of grown-up sons and daughters sprawling aimlessly about, all strangely alike with red hair, splendid bones, and pinched faces ruined by malnutrition and idleness; and one tall son sitting by the fireplace, too listless even to notice the entry of a stranger, and slowly peeling a sticky sock from a bare foot. A dreadful room in Wigan where all the furniture seemed to be made of packing cases and barrel staves and was coming to pieces at that; and an old woman with a blackened neck and her hair coming down denouncing her landlord in a Lancashire-Irish accent; and her mother, aged well over ninety, sitting in the background on the barrel that served her as a commode and regarding us blankly with a yellow, cretinous face. I could fill up pages with memories of similar interiors.

Of course the squalor of these people's houses is sometimes their own fault. Even if you live in a back to back house and have four children and a total income of thirty-two and sixpence a week from the P.A.C., there is no *need* to have unemptied chamber-pots standing about in your living-room. But it is equally certain that their circumstances do not encourage self-respect. The determining factor is probably the number of children. The best-kept interiors I saw were always childless houses or houses where there were only one or two children; with, say, six children in a three-roomed house it is quite impossible to keep anything decent. One thing that is very noticeable is that the worst squalors are never downstairs. You might visit quite a number of houses, even among the poorest of the unemployed, and bring away a wrong impression. These people, you might reflect, cannot be so badly off if they still have a fair amount of furniture and crockery. But it is in the rooms upstairs that the gauntness of poverty really discloses itself. Whether this is because pride makes people cling to their living-room furniture to the last, or because bedding is more pawnable, I do not know, but certainly many of the bedrooms

I saw were fearful places. Among people who have been unemployed for several years continuously I should say it is the exception to have anything like a full set of bedclothes. Often there is nothing that can be properly called bedclothes at all—just a heap of old overcoats and miscellaneous rags on a rusty iron bedstead. In this way overcrowding is aggravated. One family of four persons that I knew, a father and mother and two children, possessed two beds but could only use one of them because they had not enough bedding for the other.

Anyone who wants to see the effects of the housing shortage at their very worse should visit the dreadful caravan-dwellings that exist in numbers in many of the northern towns. Ever since the war, in the complete impossibility of getting houses, parts of the population have overflowed into supposedly temporary quarters in fixed caravans. Wigan, for instance, with a population of about 85000, has round about 200 caravan-dwellings with a family in each—perhaps somewhere near 1000 people in all. How many of these caravan-colonies exist throughout the industrial areas it would be difficult to discover with any accuracy. The local authorities are reticent about them and the census report of 1931 seems to have decided to ignore them. But so far as I can discover by inquiry they are to be found in most of the larger towns in Lancashire and Yorkshire, and perhaps further north as well. The probability is that throughout the north of England there are some thousands, perhaps tens of thousands of *families* (not individuals) who have no home except a fixed caravan.

But the word 'caravan' is very misleading. It calls up a picture of a cosy gypsy-encampment (in fine weather, of course) with wood fires crackling and children picking blackberries and many-coloured washing fluttering on the lines. The caravan-colonies in Wigan and Sheffield are not like that. I had a look at several of them, I inspected those in Wigan with considerable care, and I have never seen comparable squalor except in the Far East. Indeed when I saw them I was immediately reminded of the filthy kennels in which I have seen Indian coolies living in Burma. But, as a matter of fact, nothing in the East could ever be quite as bad, for in the East you haven't our clammy, penetrating cold to contend with, and the sun is a disinfectant.

Along the banks of Wigan's miry canal are patches of waste ground on which the caravans have been dumped like rubbish shot out of a bucket. Some of them are actually gypsy caravans, but very old ones and in bad repair. The majority are old single-decker buses (the rather

smaller buses of ten years ago) which have been taken off their wheels
and propped up with struts of wood. Some are simply wagons with
semi-circular slats on top, over which canvas is stretched, so that the
people inside have nothing but canvas between them and the outer air.
Inside, these places are usually about five feet wide by six high (I could
not stand quite upright in any of them) and anything from six to fifteen
feet long. Some, I suppose, are inhabited by only one person, but I did
not see any that held less than two persons, and some of them contained large families. One, for instance, measuring fourteen feet long,
had seven people in it—seven people in about 450 cubic feet of space;
which is to say that each person had for his entire dwelling a space
a *good deal* smaller than one compartment of a public lavatory. The dirt
and congestion of these places is such that you cannot well imagine it
unless you have tested it with your own eyes and more particularly
your nose. Each contains a tiny cottage kitchener and such furniture as
can be crammed in—sometimes two beds, more usually one, into
which the whole family have to huddle as best they can. It is almost
impossible to sleep on the floor, because the damp soaks up from
below. I was shown mattresses which were still wringing wet at eleven
in the morning. In winter it is so cold that the kitcheners have to be
kept burning day and night, and the windows, needless to say, are
never opened. Water is got from a hydrant common to the whole colony, some of the caravan-dwellers having to walk 150 or 200 yards for
every bucket of water. There are no sanitary arrangements at all. Most
of the people construct a little hut to serve as a lavatory on the tiny
patch of ground surrounding their caravan, and once a week dig
a deep hole in which to bury the refuse. All the people I saw in these
places, especially the children, were unspeakably dirty, and I do not
doubt that they were lousy as well. They could not possibly be otherwise. The thought that haunted me as I went from caravan to caravan
was, What can happen in those cramped interiors when anybody dies?
But that, of course, is the kind of question you hardly care to ask.

Some of the people have been in their caravans for many years.
Theoretically the Corporation are doing away with the caravan-
colonies and getting the inhabitants out into houses; but as the houses
don't get built, the caravans remain standing. Most of the people
I talked to had given up the idea of ever getting a decent habitation
again. They were all out of work, and a job and a house seemed to
them about equally remote and impossible. Some hardly seemed to

care; others realized quite clearly in what misery they were living. One woman's face stays by me, a worn skull-like face on which was a look of intolerable misery and degradation. I gathered that in that dreadful pigsty, struggling to keep her large brood of children clean, she felt as I should feel if I were coated all over with dung. One must remember that these people are not gypsies; they are decent English people who have all, except the children born there, had homes of their own in their day; besides, their caravans are greatly inferior to those of gypsies and they have not the great advantage of being on the move. No doubt there are still middle-class people who think that the Lower Orders don't mind that kind of thing and who, if they happened to pass a caravan-colony in the train, would immediately assume that the people lived there from choice. I never argue nowadays with that kind of person. But it is worth noticing that the caravan-dwellers don't even save money by living there, for they are paying about the same rents as they would for houses. I could not hear of any rent lower than five shillings a week (five shillings for 200 cubic feet of space!) and there are even cases where the rent is as high as ten shillings. Somebody must be making a good thing out of those caravans! But clearly their continued existence is due to the housing shortage and not directly to poverty.

Talking once with a miner I asked him when the housing shortage first became acute in his district; he answered, 'When we were told about it', meaning that till recently people's standards were so low that they took almost any degree of overcrowding for granted. He added that when he was a child his family had slept eleven in a room and thought nothing of it, and that later, when he was grown-up, he and his wife had lived in one of the old-style back to back houses in which you not only had to walk a couple of hundred yards to the lavatory but often had to wait in a queue when you got there, the lavatory being shared by thirty-six people. And when his wife was sick with the illness that killed her, she still had to make that two hundred yards' journey to the lavatory. This, he said, was the kind of thing people would put up with 'till they were told about it'.

I do not know whether that is true. What is certain is that nobody *now* thinks it bearable to sleep eleven in a room, and that even people with comfortable incomes are vaguely troubled by the thought of 'the slums'. Hence the clatter about 'rehousing' and 'slum clearance' which we have had at intervals ever since the war. Bishops, politicians, philanthropists, and what not enjoy talking piously about 'slum clearance', because they can thus divert attention from more serious evils and pretend that if you abolish the slums you abolish poverty. But all this talk has led to surprisingly small results. So far as one can discover, the congestion is no better, perhaps slightly worse, than it was a dozen years ago. There is certainly great variation in the speed at which the different towns are attacking their housing problem. In some towns building seems to be almost at a standstill, in others it is proceeding rapidly and the private landlord is being driven out of business. Liverpool, for instance, has been very largely rebuilt, mainly by the efforts of the Corporation. Sheffield, too, is being torn down and rebuilt pretty fast, though perhaps, considering the unparalleled beastliness of its slums, not quite fast enough.[1]

Why rehousing has on the whole moved so slowly, and why some towns can borrow money for building purposes so much more easily than others, I do not know. Those questions would have to be answered by someone who knows more about the machinery of local government than I do. A Corporation house costs normally somewhere between three and four hundred pounds; it costs rather less when it is built by 'direct labour' than when built by contract. The rent of these houses would average something over twenty pounds a year not counting rates, so one would think that, even allowing for overhead expenses and interest on loans, it would pay any Corporation to build as many houses as could be tenanted. In many cases, of course, the houses would have to be inhabited by people on the P.A.C., so that the local bodies would merely be taking money out of one pocket and putting it into another—i.e. paying out money in the form of relief and taking it back in the form of rent. But they have got to pay the relief in any case, and at present a proportion of what they pay is being swallowed up by private landlords. The reasons given for the slow rate of building are lack of money and the difficulty of getting hold of sites—for Corporation houses are not erected piecemeal but in 'estates', sometimes of hundreds of houses at a time. One thing that always strikes me as mysterious is that so many of the northern towns see fit to build themselves immense and luxurious public buildings at the same time as they are in crying need of dwelling houses. The town of Barnsley, for instance,

---

[1] The number of Corporation houses in process of construction in Sheffield at the beginning of 1936 was 1398. To replace the slum areas entirely Sheffield is said to need 100000 houses.

recently spent close on £150000 on a new town hall, although admittedly needing at least 2000 new working-class houses, not to mention public baths. (The public baths in Barnsley contain *nineteen* men's slipper baths—this in a town of 70000 inhabitants, largely miners, not one of whom has a bath in his house!) For £150000 it could have built 350 Corporation houses and still had £10000 to spend on a town hall. However, as I say, I do not pretend to understand the mysteries of local government. I merely record the fact that houses are desperately needed and are being built, on the whole, with paralytic slowness.

Still, houses *are* being built, and the Corporation building estates, with their row upon row of little red houses, all much liker than two peas (where did that expression come from? Peas have great individuality) are a regular feature of the outskirts of the industrial towns. As to what they are like and how they compare with the slum houses, I can best give an idea by transcribing two more extracts from my diary. The tenants' opinions of their houses vary greatly, so I will give one favourable extract and one unfavourable. Both of these are from Wigan and both are the cheaper 'non-parlour type' houses:

1. House in Beech Hill Estate.
Downstairs. Large living-room with kitchener fireplace, cupboards, and fixed dresser, composition floor. Small hallway, largish kitchen. Up to date electric cooker hired from Corporation at much the same rate as a gas cooker.

Upstairs. Two largish bedrooms, one tiny one—suitable only for a boxroom or temporary bedroom. Bathroom, W.C., with hot and cold water.

Smallish garden. These vary throughout the estate, but mostly rather smaller than an allotment.

Four in family, parents and two children. Husband in good employ. Houses appear well built and are quite agreeable to look at. Various restrictions, e.g. it is forbidden to keep poultry or pigeons, take in lodgers, sub-let, or start any kind of business without leave from the Corporation. (This is easily granted in the case of taking in lodgers, but not in any of the others.) Tenant very well satisfied with house and proud of it. Houses in this estate all well kept. Corporation are good about repairs, but keep tenants up to the mark with regard to keeping the place tidy, etc.

Rent 11s. 3d. including rates. Bus fare into town 2d.

2. House in Welly Estate.
Downstairs. Living-room 14 ft by 10 ft, kitchen a good deal smaller, tiny larder under stairs, small but fairly good bathroom. Gas cooker, electric lighting. Outdoor W.C.

Upstairs. One bedroom 12 ft by 10 ft with tiny fireplace, another the same size without fireplace, another 7 ft by 6 ft. Best bedroom has small wardrobe let into wall.

Garden about 20 yards by 10.

Six in family, parents and four children, eldest son nineteen, eldest daughter twenty-two. None in work except eldest son. Tenants very discontented. Their complaints are: 'House is cold, draughty, and damp. Fireplace in living-room gives out no heat and makes room very dusty—attributed to its being set too low. Fireplace in best bedroom too small to be of any use. Walls upstairs cracking. Owing to uselessness of tiny bedroom, five are sleeping in one bedroom, one (the eldest son) in the other.'

Gardens in this estate all neglected.

Rent 10s. 3d., inclusive. Distance to town a little over a mile—there is no bus here.

I could multiply examples, but these two are enough, as the types of Corporation houses being built do not vary greatly from place to place. Two things are immediately obvious. The first is that at their very worst the Corporation houses are better than the slums they replace. The mere possession of a bathroom and a bit of garden would outweigh almost any disadvantage. The other is that they are much more expensive to live in. It is common enough for a man to be turned out of a condemned house where he is paying six or seven shillings a week and given a Corporation house where he has to pay ten. This only affects those who are in work or have recently been in work, because when a man is on the P.A.C. his rent is assessed at a quarter of his dole, and if it is more than this he gets an extra allowance; in any case, there are certain classes of Corporation houses to which people on the dole are not admitted. But there are other ways in which life in a Corporation estate is expensive, whether you are in work or out of it. To begin with, owing to the higher rents, the shops in the estate are much more expensive and there are not so many of them. Then again, in a comparatively large, detached house, away from the frowsy huddle of the slum, it is much colder and more fuel has to be burnt. And again there is the expense, especially for a man in work, of getting to and from town. This last is one of the more obvious problems of rehousing. Slum clearance means diffusion of the population. When you rebuild on a large scale, what you do in effect is to scoop out the centre of the town and redistribute it on the outskirts. This is all very well in a way; you have got the people out of fetid alleys into places where they have room to breathe; but from the point of view of the people themselves, what you have done is to pick them up and dump them down five miles from their work. The simplest solution is flats. If people are going to live in large towns at all they must learn to live on top of one another. But the northern working people do not take kindly to flats; even where flats exist they are contemptuously named 'tenements'. Almost everyone will tell you that he 'wants a house of his own', and apparently a house in the middle of an unbroken block of houses a hundred yards long seems to them more 'their own' than a flat situated in mid-air.

To revert to the second of the two Corporation houses I have just mentioned. The tenant complained that the house was cold, damp, and so forth. Perhaps the house was jerry-built, but equally probably he was exaggerating. He had come there from a filthy hovel in the middle of Wigan which I happened to have inspected previously; while there he had made every effort to get hold of a Corporation house, and he was no sooner in the Corporation house than he wanted to be back in the slum. This looks like mere captiousness but it covers a perfectly genuine grievance. In very many cases, perhaps in half the cases, I found that the people in Corporation houses don't really like them. They are glad to get out of the stink of the slum, they know that it is better for their children to have space to play about in, but they don't feel really at home. The exceptions are usually people in good employ who can afford to spend a little extra on fuel and furniture and journeys, and who in any case are of 'superior' type. The others, the typical slum-dwellers, miss the frowsy warmth of the slum. They complain that 'out in the country', i.e. on the edge of the town, they are 'starving' (freezing). Certainly most Corporation estates are pretty bleak in winter. Some I have been through, perched on treeless clayey hillsides and swept by icy winds, would be horrible places to live in. It is not that slum-dwellers want dirt and congestion for their own sakes, as the fat-bellied bourgeoisie love to believe. (See for instance the conversation about slum-clearance in Galsworthy's *Swan Song*, where the rentier's cherished belief that the slum-dweller makes the slum, and not vice versa, is put into the mouth of a philan-thropic Jew.) Give people a decent house and they will soon learn to keep it decent. Moreover, with a smart-looking house to live up to they improve in self-respect and cleanliness, and their children start life with better chances. Nevertheless, in a Corporation estate there is an uncomfortable, almost prison-like atmosphere, and the people who live there are perfectly well aware of it.

And it is here that one comes on the central difficulty of the housing problem. When you walk through the smoke-dim slums of Manchester you think that nothing is needed except to tear down these abominations and build decent houses in their place. But the trouble is that in destroying the slum you destroy other things as well. Houses are desperately needed and are not being built fast enough; but in so far as rehousing is being done, it is being done—perhaps it is unavoidable—in a monstrously inhuman manner. I don't mean merely that the houses are new and ugly. All houses have got to be new at some time, and as a matter of fact the type of Corporation house now being built is not at all offensive to look at. On the outskirts of Liverpool there are what amount to whole towns consisting entirely of Corporation houses, and they are quite pleasing to the eye; the blocks of workers' flats in the centre of the town modelled, I believe, on the workers' flats in Vienna, are definitely fine buildings. But there is something ruthless and soulless about the whole business. Take, for instance, the restrictions with which you are burdened in a Corporation house. You are not allowed to keep your house and garden as you want them—in some estates there is even a regulation that every garden must have the same kind of hedge. You are not allowed to keep poultry or pigeons. The Yorkshire miners are fond of keeping homer pigeons; they keep them in the back yard and take them out and race them on Sundays. But pigeons are messy birds and the Corporation suppresses them as a matter of course. The restrictions about shops are more serious. The number of shops in a Corporation estate is rigidly limited, and it is said that preference is given to the Co-op and the chain stores; this may not be strictly true, but certainly those are the shops that one usually sees there. This is bad enough for the general public, but from the point of view of the independent shopkeeper it is a disaster. Many a small shopkeeper is utterly ruined by some rehousing scheme which takes no notice of his existence. A whole section of the town is condemned *en bloc*; presently the houses are pulled down and the people are transferred to some housing estate miles away. In this way all the small shopkeepers of the quarter have their whole clientele taken away from them at a single swoop and receive not a penny of compensation. They cannot transfer their business to the estate, because even if they can afford the move and the much higher rents, they would probably be refused a licence. As for pubs, they are banished from the housing estates almost completely, and the few that remain are dismal sham-Tudor places fitted out by the big brewery companies and very expensive. For a middle-class population this would be a nuisance—it might mean walking a mile to get a glass of beer; for a working-class population, which uses the pub as a kind of club, it is a serious blow at communal life. It is a great achievement to get slum-dwellers into decent houses, but it is unfortunate that, owing to the peculiar temper of our time, it is also considered necessary to rob them of the last vestiges of their liberty. The people themselves feel this, and it is this feeling that they are rationalizing when they complain that their new houses—so much better, *as* houses, than those they have come out of—are cold and uncomfortable and 'unhomelike'.

I sometimes think that the price of liberty is not so much eternal vigilance as eternal dirt. There are some Corporation estates in which new tenants are systematically deloused before being allowed into their houses. All their possessions except what they stand up in are taken away from them, fumigated, and sent on to the new house. This procedure has its points, for it *is* a pity that people should take bugs into brand new houses (a bug will follow you about in your luggage if he gets half a chance), but it is the kind of thing that makes you wish that the word 'hygiene' could be dropped out of the dictionary. Bugs are bad, but a state of affairs in which men will allow themselves to be dipped like sheep is worse. Perhaps, however, when it is a case of slum clearance, one must take for granted a certain amount of restrictions and inhumanity. When all is said and done, the most important thing is that people shall live in decent houses and not in pigsties. I have seen too much of slums to go into Chestertonian raptures about them. A place where the children can breathe clean air, and women have a few conveniences to save them from drudgery, and a man has a bit of garden to dig in, *must* be better than the stinking back-streets of Leeds and Sheffield. On balance, the Corporation Estates are better than the slums; but only by a small margin.

When I was looking into the housing question I visited and inspected numbers of houses, perhaps a hundred or two hundred houses altogether, in various mining towns and villages. I cannot end this chapter without remarking on the extraordinary courtesy and good nature with which I was received everywhere. I did not go alone—I always had some local friend among the unemployed to show me round—but even so, it is an impertinence to go poking into strangers' houses and asking to see the cracks in the bedroom wall. Yet everyone was astonishingly patient and seemed to understand almost without explanation why I was questioning them and what I wanted to see. If any unauthorized person walked into *my* house and began asking me whether the roof leaked and whether I was much troubled by bugs and what I thought of my landlord, I should probably tell him to go to hell. This only happened to me once, and in that case the woman was slightly deaf and took me for a Means Test nark; but even she relented after a while and gave me the information I wanted.

I am told that it is bad form for a writer to quote his own reviews, but I want here to contradict a reviewer in the *Manchester Guardian* who says apropos of one of my books:

Set down in Wigan or Whitechapel Mr Orwell would still exercise an unerring power of closing his vision to all that is good in order to proceed with his wholehearted vilification of humanity.

Wrong. Mr Orwell was 'set down' in Wigan for quite a while and it did not inspire him with any wish to vilify humanity. He liked Wigan very much—the people, not the scenery. Indeed, he has only one fault to find with it, and that is in respect of the celebrated Wigan Pier, which he had set his heart on seeing. Alas! Wigan Pier had been demolished, and even the spot where it used to stand is no longer certain.

V

WHEN you see the unemployment figures quoted at two millions, it is fatally easy to take this as meaning that two million people are out of work and the rest of the population is comparatively comfortable. I admit that till recently I was in the habit of doing so myself. I used to calculate that if you put the registered unemployed at round about two millions and threw in the destitute and those who for one reason and another were not registered, you might take the number of underfed people in England (for *everyone* on the dole or thereabouts is underfed) as being, at the very most, five millions.

This is an enormous under-estimate, because, in the first place, the only people shown on unemployment figures are those actually drawing the dole—that is, in general, heads of families. An unemployed man's dependants do not figure on the list unless they too are drawing a separate allowance. A Labour Exchange officer told me that to get at the real number of people *living on* (not drawing) the dole, you have got to multiply the official figures by something over three. This alone brings the number of unemployed to round about six millions. But in addition there are great numbers of people who are in work but who, from a financial point of view, might equally well be unemployed, because they are not drawing anything that can be described as a living wage.[1] Allow for these and their dependants, throw in as before the old-age pensioners, the destitute, and other nondescripts, and you get an *underfed* population of well over ten millions. Sir John Orr puts it at twenty millions.

Take the figures for Wigan, which is typical enough of the industrial and mining districts. The number of insured workers is round about 36000 (26000 men and 10000 women). Of these, the number unemployed at the beginning of 1936 was about 10000. But this was in winter when the mines are working full time; in summer it would probably be 12000. Multiply by three, as above, and you get 30000 or 36000. The total population of Wigan is a little under 87000; so that

[1] For instance, a recent census of the Lancashire cotton mills revealed the fact that over 40000 *full-time* employees receive less than thirty shillings a week each. In Preston, to take only one town, the number receiving *over* thirty shillings a week was 640 and the number receiving *under* thirty shillings was 3113.

at any moment more than one person in three out of the whole population—not merely the registered workers—is either drawing or living on the dole. Those ten or twelve thousand unemployed contain a steady core of from four to five thousand miners who have been continuously unemployed for the past seven years. And Wigan is not especially badly off as industrial towns go. Even in Sheffield, which has been doing well for the last year or so because of wars and rumours of war, the proportion of unemployment is about the same—one in three of registered workers unemployed.

When a man is first unemployed, until his insurance stamps are exhausted, he draws 'full benefit', of which the rates are as follows:

	per week
Single man	17s.
Wife	9s.
Each child below 14	3s.

Thus in a typical family of parents and three children of whom one was over fourteen, the total income would be 32s. per week, plus anything that might be earned by the eldest child. When a man's stamps are exhausted, before being turned over to the P.A.C. (Public Assistance Committee), he receives twenty-six weeks' 'transitional benefit' from the U.A.B. (Unemployment Assistance Board), the rates being as follows:

	per week
Single man	15s.
Man and wife	24s.
Children, 14–18	6s.
Children, 11–14	4s. 6d.
Children, 8–11	4s.
Children, 5–8	3s. 6d.
Children, 3–5	3s.

Thus on the U.A.B. the income of the typical family of five persons would be 37s. 6d. a week if no child was in work. When a man is on the U.A.B. a quarter of his dole is regarded as rent, with a minimum of 7s. 6d. a week. If the rent he is paying is more than a quarter of his dole he receives an extra allowance, but if it is less than 7s. 6d., a corresponding amount is deducted. Payments on the P.A.C. theoretically come out of the local rates, but are backed by a central fund. The rates of benefit are:

	per week
Single man	12s. 6d.
Man and wife	23s.
Eldest child	4s.
Any other child	3s.

Being at the discretion of the local bodies these rates vary slightly, and a single man may or may not get an extra 2s. 6d. weekly, bringing his benefit up to 15s. As on the U.A.B., a quarter of a married man's dole is regarded as rent. Thus in the typical family considered above the total income would be 33s. a week, a quarter of this being regarded as rent. In addition, in most districts a coal allowance of 1s. 6d. a week (1s. 6d. is equivalent to about a hundredweight of coal) is granted for six weeks before and six weeks after Christmas.

It will be seen that the income of a family on the dole normally averages round about thirty shillings a week. One can write at least a quarter of this off as rent, which is to say that the average person, child or adult, has got to be fed, clothed, warmed, and otherwise cared-for for six or seven shillings a week. Enormous groups of people, probably at least a third of the whole population of the industrial areas, are living at this level. The Means Test is very strictly enforced, and you are liable to be refused relief at the slightest hint that you are getting money from another source. Dock-labourers, for instance, who are generally hired by the half-day, have to sign on at a Labour Exchange twice daily; if they fail to do so it is assumed that they have been working and their dole is reduced correspondingly. I have seen cases of evasion of the Means Test, but I should say that in the industrial towns, where there is still a certain amount of communal life and everyone has neighbours who know him, it is much harder than it would be in London. The usual method is for a young man who is actually living with his parents to get an accommodation address, so that supposedly he has a separate establishment and draws a separate allowance. But there is much spying and tale-bearing. One man I knew, for instance, was seen feeding his neighbour's chickens while the neighbour was away. It was reported to the authorities that he 'had a job feeding chickens' and he had great difficulty in refuting this. The favourite joke in Wigan was about a man who was refused relief on the ground that he 'had a job carting firewood'. He had been seen, it was said, carting firewood at night. He had to explain that he was not carting firewood but doing a moonlight flit. The 'firewood' was his furniture.

The most cruel and evil effect of the Means Test is the way in which it breaks up families. Old people, sometimes bedridden, are driven out of their homes by it. An old age pensioner, for instance, if a widower, would normally live with one or other of his children; his weekly ten shillings goes towards the household expenses, and probably he is not badly cared for. Under the Means Test, however, he counts as a 'lodger' and if he stays at home his children's dole will be docked. So, perhaps at seventy or seventy-five years of age, he has to turn out into lodgings, handing his pension over to the lodging-house keeper and existing on the verge of starvation. I have seen several cases of this myself. It is happening all over England at this moment, thanks to the Means Test.

Nevertheless, in spite of the frightful extent of unemployment, it is a fact that poverty—extreme poverty—is less in evidence in the industrial North than it is in London. Everything is poorer and shabbier, there are fewer motor-cars and fewer well-dressed people; but also there are fewer people who are obviously destitute. Even in a town the size of Liverpool or Manchester you are struck by the fewness of the beggars. London is a sort of whirlpool which draws derelict people towards it, and it is so vast that life there is solitary and anonymous. Until you break the law nobody will take any notice of you, and you can go to pieces as you could not possibly do in a place where you had neighbours who knew you. But in the industrial towns the old communal way of life has not yet broken up, tradition is still strong and almost everyone has a family—potentially, therefore, a home. In a town of 50000 or 100000 inhabitants there is no casual and as it were unaccounted-for population; nobody sleeping in the streets, for instance. Moreover, there is just this to be said for the unemployment regulations, that they do not discourage people from marrying. A man and wife on twenty-three shillings a week are not far from the starvation line, but they can make a home of sorts; they are vastly better off than a single man on fifteen shillings. The life of a single unemployed man is dreadful. He lives sometimes in a common lodging-house, more often in a 'furnished' room for which he usually pays six shillings a week, finding himself as best he can on the other nine (say six shillings a week for food and three for clothes, tobacco, and amusements). Of course he cannot feed or look after himself properly, and a man who pays six shillings a week for his room is not encouraged to be indoors more than is necessary. So he spends his days loafing in the public library or any other place where he can keep warm. That—keeping warm—is almost the sole preoccupation of a single unemployed man in winter. In Wigan a favourite refuge was the pictures, which are fantastically cheap there. You can always get a seat for fourpence, and at the matinée at some houses you can even get a seat for twopence. Even people on the verge of starvation will readily pay twopence to get out of the ghastly cold of a winter afternoon. In Sheffield I was taken to a public hall to listen to a lecture by a clergyman, and it was by a long way the silliest and worst-delivered lecture I have ever heard or ever expect to hear. I found it physically impossible to sit it out, indeed my feet carried me out, seemingly of their own accord, before it was half-way through. Yet the hall was thronged with unemployed men; they would have sat through far worse drivel for the sake of a warm place to shelter in.

At times I have seen unmarried men on the dole living in the extreme of misery. In one town I remember a whole colony of them who were squatting, more or less illicitly, in a derelict house which was practically falling down. They had collected a few scraps of furniture, presumably off refuse-tips, and I remember that their sole table was an old marble-topped wash-hand-stand. But this kind of thing is exceptional. A working-class bachelor is a rarity, and so long as a man is married unemployment makes comparatively little alteration in his way of life. His home is impoverished but it is still a home, and it is noticeable everywhere that the anomalous position created by unemployment—the man being out of work while the woman's work continues as before—has not altered the relative status of the sexes. In a working-class home it is the man who is the master and not, as in a middle-class home, the woman or the baby. Practically never, for instance, in a working-class home, will you see the man doing a stroke of the housework. Unemployment has not changed this convention, which on the face of it seems a little unfair. The man is idle from morning to night but the woman is as busy as ever—more so, indeed, because she has to manage with less money. Yet so far as my experience goes the women do not protest. I believe that they, as well as the men, feel that a man would lose his manhood if, merely because he was out of work, he developed into a 'Mary Ann'.*

But there is no doubt about the deadening, debilitating effect of unemployment upon everybody, married or single, and upon men more than upon women. The best intellects will not stand up against it. Once or twice it has happened to me to meet unemployed men of genuine literary ability; there are others whom I haven't met but whose work I occasionally see in the magazines. Now and again, at long intervals, these men will produce an article or a short story which is quite obviously better than most of the stuff that gets whooped up by the blurb-reviewers. Why, then, do they make so little use of their talents? They have all the leisure in the world; why don't they sit down and write books? Because to write books you need not only comfort and solitude—and solitude is never easy to attain in a working-class home—you also need peace of mind. You can't settle to anything, you can't command the spirit of *hope* in which anything has got to be created, with that dull evil cloud of unemployment hanging over you. Still, an unemployed man who feels at home with books can at any rate occupy himself by reading. But what about the man who cannot read without discomfort? Take a miner, for instance, who has worked in the pit since childhood and has been trained to be a miner and nothing else. How the devil is he to fill up the empty days? It is absurd to say that he ought to be looking for work. There is no work to look for, and everybody knows it. You can't go on looking for work every day for seven years. There are allotments, which occupy the time and help to feed a family, but in a big town there are only allotments for a small proportion of the people. Then there are the occupational centres which were started a few years ago to help the unemployed. On the whole this movement has been a failure, but some of the centres are still flourishing. I have visited one or two of them. There are shelters where the men can keep warm and there are periodical classes in carpentering, boot-making, leather-work, handloom-weaving, basket-work, sea-grass work, etc., etc.; the idea being that the men can make furniture and so forth, not for sale but for their own homes, getting tools free and materials cheaply. Most of the Socialists I have talked to denounce this movement as they denounce the project—it is always being talked about but it never comes to anything—to give the unemployed small-holdings. They say that the occupational centres are simply a device to keep the unemployed quiet and give them the illusion that something is being done for them. Undoubtedly that *is* the underlying motive. Keep a man busy mending boots and he is less likely to read the *Daily Worker*. Also there is a nasty Y.M.C.A. atmosphere about these places which you can feel as soon as you go in. The unemployed men who frequent them are mostly of the cap-touching type—the type who tells you oilily that he is 'Temperance' and votes Conservative. Yet even here you feel yourself torn both ways. For probably it is better that a man should waste his time even with such rubbish as sea-grass work than that for years upon end he should do absolutely *nothing*.

By far the best work for the unemployed is being done by the N.U.W.M.—National Unemployed Workers' Movement. This is a revolutionary organization intended to hold the unemployed together, stop them blacklegging during strikes, and give them legal advice against the Means Test. It is a movement that has been built out of nothing by the pennies and efforts of the unemployed themselves. I have seen a good deal of the N.U.W.M., and I greatly admire the men, ragged and underfed like the others, who keep the organization going. Still more I admire the tact and patience with which they do it; for it is not easy to coax even a penny-a-week subscription out of the pockets of people on the P.A.C. As I said earlier, the English working class do not show much capacity for leadership, but they have a wonderful talent for organization. The whole trade union movement testifies to this; so do the excellent working-men's clubs—really a sort of glorified coopera-tive pub, and splendidly organized—which are so common in Yorkshire. In many towns the N.U.W.M. have shelters and arrange speeches by Communist speakers. But even at these shelters the men who go there do nothing but sit round the stove and occasionally play a game of dominoes. If this movement could be combined with something along the lines of the occupational centres, it would be nearer what is needed. It is a deadly thing to see a skilled man running to seed, year after year, in utter, hopeless idleness. It ought not to be impossible to give him the chance of using his hands and making furniture and so forth for his own home, without turning him into a Y.M.C.A. cocoa-drunkard. We may as well face the fact that several million men in England will—unless another war breaks out—never have a real job this side the grave. One thing that probably could be done and certainly ought to be done as a matter of course is to give every unemployed man a patch of ground and free tools if he chose to apply for them. It is disgraceful that men who are expected to keep alive on the P.A.C. should not even have the chance to grow vegetables for their families.

To study unemployment and its effects you have got to go to the industrial areas. In the South unemployment exists, but it is scattered and queerly unobtrusive. There are plenty of rural districts where a man out of work is almost unheard-of, and you don't anywhere see the spectacle of whole blocks of cities living on the dole and the P.A.C. It is only when you lodge in streets where nobody has a job, where getting a job seems about as probable as owning an aeroplane and much *less* probable than winning fifty pounds in the Football Pool, that you begin to grasp the changes that are being worked in our civilization. For a change *is* taking place, there is no doubt about that. The attitude of the submerged working class is profoundly different from what it was seven or eight years ago.

I first became aware of the unemployment problem in 1928. At that time I had just come back from Burma, where unemployment was only a word, and I had gone to Burma when I was still a boy* and the post-war boom was not quite over. When I first saw unemployed men at close quarters, the thing that horrified and amazed me was to find that many of them were *ashamed* of being unemployed. I was very ignorant, but not so ignorant as to imagine that when the loss of foreign markets pushes two million men out of work, those two million are any more to blame than the people who draw blanks in the Calcutta Sweep. But at that time nobody cared to admit that unemployment was inevitable, because this meant admitting that it would probably continue. The middle classes were still talking about 'lazy idle loafers on the dole' and saying that 'these men could all find work if they wanted to', and naturally these opinions percolated to the working class themselves. I remember the shock of astonishment it gave me, when I first mingled with tramps and beggars, to find that a fair proportion, perhaps a quarter, of these beings whom I had been taught to regard as cynical parasites, were decent young miners and cotton-workers gazing at their destiny with the same sort of dumb amazement as an animal in a trap. They simply could not understand what was happening to them. They had been brought up to work, and behold! it seemed as if they were never going to have the chance of working again. In their circumstances it was inevitable, at first, that they should be haunted by a feeling of personal degradation. That was the attitude towards unemployment in those days: it was a disaster which happened to *you* as an individual and for which *you* were to blame.

When a quarter of a million miners are unemployed, it is part of the order of things that Alf Smith, a miner living in the back streets of Newcastle, should be out of work. Alf Smith is merely one of the quarter million, a statistical unit. But no human being finds it easy to regard himself as a statistical unit. So long as Bert Jones across the street is still at work, Alf Smith is bound to feel himself dishonoured and a failure. Hence that frightful feeling of impotence and despair which is almost the worst evil of unemployment—far worse than any hardship, worse than the demoralization of enforced idleness, and only less bad than the physical degeneracy of Alf Smith's children, born on the P.A.C. Everyone who saw Greenwood's play *Love on the Dole* must remember that dreadful moment when the poor, good, stupid working man beats on the table and cries out, 'O God, send me some work!' This was not dramatic exaggeration, it was a touch from life. That cry must have been uttered, in almost those words, in tens of thousands, perhaps hundreds of thousands of English homes, during the past fifteen years.

But, I think not again—or at least, not so often. That is the real point: people are ceasing to kick against the pricks. After all, even the middle classes—yes, even the bridge clubs in the country towns—are beginning to realize that there is such a thing as unemployment. The 'My dear, I don't *believe* in all this nonsense about unemployment. Why, only last week we wanted a man to weed the garden, and we simply couldn't get one. They don't *want* to work, that's all it is!' which you heard at every decent tea-table five years ago, is growing perceptibly less frequent. As for the working class themselves, they have gained immensely in economic knowledge. I believe that the *Daily Worker* has accomplished a great deal here: its influence is out of all proportion to its circulation. But in any case they have had their lesson well rubbed into them, not only because unemployment is so widespread but because it has lasted so long. When people live on the dole for years at a time they grow used to it, and drawing the dole, though it remains unpleasant, ceases to be shameful. Thus the old, independent, workhouse-fearing tradition is undermined, just as the ancient fear of debt is undermined by the hire-purchase system. In the back streets of Wigan and Barnsley I saw every kind of privation, but I probably saw much less *conscious* misery than I should have seen ten years ago. The people have at any rate grasped that unemployment is a thing they cannot help. It is not only Alf Smith who is out of work now; Bert Jones is out of work as well, and both of them have been 'out' for years. It makes a great deal of difference when things are the same for everybody.

So you have whole populations settling down, as it were, to a lifetime on the P.A.C. And what I think is admirable, perhaps even hopeful, is that they have managed to do it without going spiritually to pieces. A working man does not disintegrate under the strain of poverty as a middle-class person does. Take, for instance, the fact that the working class think nothing of getting married on the dole. It annoys the old ladies in Brighton, but it is a proof of their essential good sense; they realize that losing your job does not mean that you cease to be a human being. So that in one way things in the distressed areas are not as bad as they might be. Life is still fairly normal, more normal than one really has the right to expect. Families are impoverished, but the family-system has not broken up. The people are in effect living a reduced version of their former lives. Instead of raging against their destiny they have made things tolerable by lowering their standards.

But they don't necessarily lower their standards by cutting out luxuries and concentrating on necessities; more often it is the other way about—the more natural way, if you come to think of it. Hence the fact that in a decade of unparalleled depression, the consumption of all cheap luxuries has increased. The two things that have probably made the greatest difference of all are the movies and the mass-production of cheap smart clothes since the war. The youth who leaves school at fourteen and gets a blind-alley job is out of work at twenty, probably for life; but for two pounds ten on the hire-purchase he can buy himself a suit which, for a little while and at a little distance, looks as though it had been tailored in Savile Row. The girl can look like a fashion plate at an even lower price. You may have three halfpence in your pocket and not a prospect in the world, and only the corner of a leaky bedroom to go home to; but in your new clothes you can stand on the street corner, indulging in a private daydream of yourself as Clark Gable or Greta Garbo, which compensates you for a great deal. And even at home there is generally a cup of tea going—a 'nice cup of tea'—and Father, who has been out of work since 1929, is temporarily happy because he has a sure tip for the Cesarewitch.

Trade since the war has had to adjust itself to meet the demands of underpaid, underfed people, with the result that a luxury is nowadays almost always cheaper than a necessity. One pair of plain solid shoes costs as much as two ultra-smart pairs. For the price of one square meal you can get two pounds of cheap sweets. You can't get much meat for threepence, but you can get a lot of fish-and-chips. Milk costs threepence a pint and even 'mild' beer costs fourpence, but aspirins are seven a penny and you can wring forty cups of tea out of a quarter-pound packet. And above all there is gambling, the cheapest of all luxuries. Even people on the verge of starvation can buy a few days' hope ('Something to live for', as they call it) by having a penny on a sweepstake. Organized gambling has now risen almost to the status of a major industry. Consider, for instance, a phenomenon like the Football Pools, with a turnover of about six million pounds a year, almost all of it from the pockets of working-class people. I happened to be in Yorkshire when Hitler re-occupied the Rhineland. Hitler, Locarno, Fascism, and the threat of war aroused hardly a flicker of interest locally, but the decision of the Football Association to stop publishing their fixtures in advance (this was an attempt to quell the Football Pools) flung all Yorkshire into a storm of fury. And then there is the queer spectacle of modern electrical science showering miracles upon people with empty bellies. You may shiver all night for lack of bedclothes, but in the morning you can go to the public library and read the news that has been telegraphed for your benefit from San Francisco and Singapore. Twenty million people are underfed but literally everyone in England has access to a radio. What we have lost in food we have gained in electricity. Whole sections of the working class who have been plundered of all they really need are being compensated, in part, by cheap luxuries which mitigate the surface of life.

Do you consider all this desirable? No, I don't. But it may be that the psychological adjustment which the working class are visibly making is the best they could make in the circumstances. They have neither turned revolutionary nor lost their self-respect; merely they have kept their tempers and settled down to make the best of things on a fish-and-chip standard. The alternative would be God knows what continued agonies of despair; or it might be attempted insurrections which, in a strongly governed country like England, could only lead to futile massacres and a régime of savage repression.

Of course the post-war development of cheap luxuries has been a very fortunate thing for our rulers. It is quite likely that fish-and-chips, art-silk stockings, tinned salmon, cut-price chocolate (five two-ounce bars for sixpence), the movies, the radio, strong tea, and the Football Pools have between them averted revolution. Therefore we are sometimes told that the whole thing is an astute manoeuvre by the governing class—a sort of 'bread and circuses' business—to hold the unemployed down. What I have seen of our governing class does not convince me that they have that much intelligence. The thing has happened, but by an unconscious process—the quite natural inter-action between the manufacturer's need for a market and the need of half-starved people for cheap palliatives.

VI

WHEN I was a small boy at school a lecturer used to come once a term and deliver excellent lectures on famous battles of the past, such as Blenheim, Austerlitz, etc. He was fond of quoting Napoleon's maxim 'An army marches on its stomach', and at the end of his lecture he would suddenly turn to us and demand, 'What's the most important thing in the world?' We were expected to shout 'Food!' and if we did not do so he was disappointed.

Obviously he was right in a way. A human being is primarily a bag for putting food into; the other functions and faculties may be more godlike, but in point of time they come afterwards. A man dies and is buried, and all his words and actions are forgotten, but the food he has eaten lives after him in the sound or rotten bones of his children. I think it could be plausibly argued that changes of diet are more important than changes of dynasty or even of religion. The Great War, for instance, could never have happened if tinned food had not been invented. And the history of the past four hundred years in England would have been immensely different if it had not been for the introduction of root-crops and various other vegetables at the end of the Middle Ages, and a little later the introduction of non-alcoholic drinks (tea, coffee, cocoa) and also of distilled liquors to which the beer-drinking English were not accustomed. Yet it is curious how seldom the all-importance of food is recognized. You see statues everywhere to politicians, poets, bishops, but none to cooks or bacon-curers or market-gardeners. The Emperor Charles V is said to have erected a statue to the inventor of bloaters, but that is the only case I can think of at the moment.

So perhaps the really important thing about the unemployed, the really basic thing if you look to the future, is the diet they are living on. As I said earlier, the average unemployed family lives on an income of round about thirty shillings a week, of which at least a quarter goes in rent. It is worth considering in some detail how the remaining money is spent. I have here a budget which was made out for me by an unemployed miner and his wife. I asked them to make a list which represented as exactly as possible their expenditure in a typical week. This man's allowance was thirty-two shillings a week, and besides his wife he had two children, one aged two years and five months and the other ten months. Here is the list:

	s.	d.
Rent	9	0½
Clothing Club	3	0
Coal	2	0
Gas	1	3
Milk	0	10½
Union fees	0	3
Insurance (on the children)	0	2
Meat	2	6
Flour (2 stone)	3	4
Yeast	0	4
Potatoes	1	0
Dripping	0	10
Margarine	0	10
Bacon	1	2
Sugar	1	9
Tea	1	0
Jam	0	7½
Peas and cabbage	0	6
Carrots and onions	0	4
Quaker oats	0	4½
Soap, powders, blue, etc.	0	10
Total	£1 12	0

In addition to this, three packets of dried milk were supplied weekly for the baby by the Infants' Welfare Clinic.

One or two comments are needed here. To begin with the list leaves out a great deal—blacking, pepper, salt, vinegar, matches, kindling-wood, razor blades, replacements of utensils, and wear and tear of furniture and bedding, to name the first few that come to mind. Any money spent on these would mean reduction on some other item. A more serious charge is tobacco. This man happened to be a small smoker, but even so his tobacco would hardly cost less than a shilling a week, meaning a further reduction on food. The 'clothing clubs' into which unemployed people pay so much a week are run by big drapers in all the industrial towns. Without them it would be impossible for unemployed people to buy new clothes at all. I don't know whether or not they buy bedding through these clubs. This particular family, as I happen to know, possessed next to no bedding.

In the above list, if you allow a shilling for tobacco and deduct this and the other non-food items, you are left with sixteen and fivepence halfpenny. Call it sixteen shillings and leave the baby out of account—for the baby was getting its weekly packets of milk from the Welfare Clinic. This sixteen shillings has got to provide the entire nourishment, *including fuel*, of three persons, two of them adult. The first question is whether it is even theoretically possible for three persons to be properly nourished on sixteen shillings a week. When the dispute over the Means Test was in progress there was a disgusting public wrangle about the minimum weekly sum on which a human being could keep alive. So far as I remember, one school of dietitians worked it out at five and ninepence, while another school, more generous, put it at five and ninepence halfpenny. After this there were letters to the papers from a number of people who claimed to be feeding themselves on four shillings a week. Here is a weekly budget (it was printed in the *New Statesman* and also in the *News of the World*) which I picked out from among a number of others:

	s.	d.
3 wholemeal loaves	1	0
½ lb. margarine	0	2½
½ lb. dripping	0	3
1 lb. cheese	0	7
1 lb. onions	0	1½
1 lb. carrots	0	1½
1 lb. broken biscuits	0	4
2 lb. dates	0	6
1 tin evaporated milk	0	5
10 oranges	0	5
Total	3	11½

Please notice that this budget contains *nothing for fuel*. In fact, the writer explicitly stated that he could not afford to buy fuel and ate all his food raw. Whether the letter was genuine or a hoax does not matter at the moment. What I think will be admitted is that this list represents about as wise an expenditure as could be contrived; if you *had* to live on three and elevenpence halfpenny a week, you could hardly extract more food-value from it than that. So perhaps it is possible to feed yourself adequately on the P.A.C. allowance if you concentrate on essential foodstuffs; but not otherwise.

Now compare this list with the unemployed miner's budget that I gave earlier. The miner's family spend only tenpence a week on green vegetables and tenpence half-penny on milk (remember that one of them is a child less than three years old), and nothing on fruit; but they spend one and nine on sugar (about eight pounds of sugar, that is) and a shilling on tea. The half-crown spent on meat *might* represent a small joint and the materials for a stew; probably as often as not it would represent four or five tins of bully beef. The basis of their diet, therefore, is white bread and margarine, corned beef, sugared tea, and potatoes—an appalling diet. Would it not be better if they spent more money on wholesome things like oranges and wholemeal bread or if they even, like the writer of the letter to the *New Statesman*, saved on fuel and ate their carrots raw? Yes, it would, but the point is that no ordinary human being is ever going to do such a thing. The ordinary human being would sooner starve than live on brown bread and raw carrots. And the peculiar evil is this, that the less money you have, the less inclined you feel to spend it on wholesome food. A millionaire may enjoy breakfasting off orange juice and Ryvita biscuits; an unemployed man doesn't. Here the tendency of which I spoke at the end of the last chapter comes into play. When you are unemployed, which is to say when you are underfed, harassed, bored, and miserable, you don't *want* to eat dull wholesome food. You want something a little bit 'tasty'. There is always some cheaply pleasant thing to tempt you. Let's have three pennorth of chips! Run out and buy us a twopenny ice-cream! Put the kettle on and we'll all have a nice cup of tea! *That* is how your mind works when you are at the P.A.C. level. White bread-and-marg and sugared tea don't nourish you to any extent, but they are *nicer* (at least most people think so) than brown bread-and-dripping and cold water. Unemployment is an endless misery that has got to be constantly palliated, and especially with tea, the Englishman's opium. A cup of tea or even an aspirin is much better as a temporary stimulant than a crust of brown bread.

The results of all this are visible in a physical degeneracy which you can study directly, by using your eyes, or inferentially, by having a look at the vital statistics. The physical average in the industrial towns is terribly low, lower even than in London. In Sheffield you have the feeling of walking among a population of troglodytes. The miners are splendid men, but they are usually small, and the mere fact that their muscles are toughened by constant work does not mean that their children start life with a better physique. In any case the miners are physically the pick of the population. The most obvious sign of under-nourishment is the badness of everybody's teeth. In Lancashire you would have to look for a long time before you saw a working-class person with good natural teeth. Indeed, you see very few people with natural teeth at all, apart from the children; and even the children's teeth have a frail bluish appearance which means, I suppose, calcium deficiency. Several dentists have told me that in industrial districts a person over thirty with any of his or her own teeth is coming to be an abnormality. In Wigan various people gave me their opinion that it is best to 'get shut of' your teeth as early in life as possible. 'Teeth is just a misery,' one woman said to me. In one house where I stayed there were, apart from myself, five people, the oldest being forty-three and the youngest a boy of fifteen. Of these the boy was the only one who possessed a single tooth of his own, and his teeth were obviously not going to last long. As for the vital statistics, the fact that in any large industrial town the death rate and infant mortality of the poorest quarters are always about double those of the well-to-do residential quarters—a good deal more than double in some cases—hardly needs commenting on.

Of course one ought not to imagine that the prevailing bad physique is due solely to unemployment, for it is probable that the physical average has been declining all over England for a long time past, and not merely among the unemployed in the industrial areas. This cannot be proved statistically, but it is a conclusion that is forced upon you if you use your eyes, even in rural places and even in a prosperous town like London. On the day when King George V's body passed through London on its way to Westminster, I happened to be caught for an hour or two in the crowd in Trafalgar Square. It was impossible, looking about one then, not to be struck by the physical degeneracy of modern England. The people surrounding me were *not* working-class people for the most part; they were the shopkeeper—commercial-traveller type, with a sprinkling of the well-to-do. But what a set they looked! Puny limbs, sickly faces, under the weeping London sky! Hardly a well-built man or a decent-looking woman, and not a fresh complexion anywhere. As the King's coffin went by, the men took off their hats, and a friend who was in the crowd at the other side of the Strand said to me afterwards, 'The only touch of colour anywhere was the bald heads.' Even the Guards, it seemed to me—there was a squad of guardsmen marching beside the coffin—were not what they used to be. Where are the monstrous men with chests like barrels and moustaches like the wings of eagles who strode across my childhood's gaze twenty or thirty years ago? Buried, I suppose, in the Flanders mud. In their place there are these pale-faced boys who have been picked for their height and consequently look like hop-poles in overcoats—the truth being that in modern England a man over six feet high is usually skin and bone and not much else. If the English physique has declined, this is no doubt partly due to the fact that the Great War carefully selected the million best men in England and slaughtered them, largely before they had had time to breed. But the process must have begun earlier than that, and it must be due ultimately to unhealthy ways of living, i.e. to industrialism. I don't mean the habit of living in towns—probably the town is healthier than the country, in many ways—but the modern industrial technique which provides you with cheap substitutes for everything. We may find in the long run that tinned food is a deadlier weapon than the machine gun.

It is unfortunate that the English working class—the English nation generally, for that matter—are exceptionally ignorant about and wasteful of food. I have pointed out elsewhere how civilized is a French navvy's idea of a meal compared with an Englishman's, and I cannot believe that you would ever see such wastage in a French house as you habitually see in English ones. Of course, in the very poorest homes, where everybody is unemployed, you don't see much actual waste, but those who can afford to waste food often do so. I could give startling instances of this. Even the Northern habit of baking one's own bread is slightly wasteful in itself, because an over-worked woman cannot bake more than once or, at most, twice a week and it is impossible to tell beforehand how much bread will be wasted, so that a certain amount generally has to be thrown away. The usual thing is to bake six large loaves and twelve small ones at a time. All this is part of the old, generous English attitude to life, and it is an amiable quality, but a disastrous one at the present moment.

English working people everywhere, so far as I know, refuse brown bread; it is usually impossible to buy wholemeal bread in a working-class district. They sometimes give the reason that brown bread is 'dirty'. I suspect the real reason is that in the past brown bread has been confused with black bread, which is traditionally associated with Popery and wooden shoes. (They have plenty of Popery and wooden shoes in Lancashire. A pity they haven't the black bread as well!) But the English palate, especially the working-class palate, now rejects good food almost automatically. The number of people who *prefer* tinned peas and tinned fish to real peas and real fish must be increasing every year, and plenty of people who could afford real milk in their tea would much sooner have tinned milk—even that dreadful tinned milk which is made of sugar and corn-flour and has UNFIT FOR BABIES on the tin in huge letters. In some districts efforts are now being made to teach the unemployed more about food-values and more about the intelligent spending of money. When you hear of a thing like this you feel yourself torn both ways. I have heard a Communist speaker on the platform grow very angry about it. In London, he said, parties of Society dames now have the cheek to walk into East End houses and give shopping-lessons to the wives of the unemployed. He gave this as an instance of the mentality of the English governing class. First you condemn a family to live on thirty shillings a week, and then you have the damned impertinence to tell them how they are to spend their money. He was quite right—I agree heartily. Yet all the same it *is* a pity that, merely for the lack of a proper tradition, people should pour muck like tinned milk down their throats and not even know that it is inferior to the product of the cow.

I doubt, however, whether the unemployed would ultimately benefit if they learned to spend their money more economically. For it is only the fact that they are *not* economical that keeps their allowances so high. An Englishman on the P.A.C. gets fifteen shillings a week because fifteen shillings is the smallest sum on which he can conceivably keep alive. If he were, say, an Indian or Japanese coolie, who can live on rice and onions, he wouldn't get fifteen shillings a week—he would be lucky if he got fifteen shillings a month. Our unemployment allowances, miserable though they are, are framed to suit a population with very high standards and not much notion of economy. If the unemployed learned to be better managers they would be visibly better off, and I fancy it would not be long before the dole was docked correspondingly.

There is one great mitigation of unemployment in the North, and that is the cheapness of fuel. Anywhere in the coal areas the retail price of coal is about one and sixpence a hundredweight; in the South of England it is about half a crown. Moreover, miners in work can usually buy coal direct from the pit at eight or nine shillings a ton, and those who have a cellar in their homes sometimes store a ton and sell it (illicitly, I suppose) to those who are out of work. But apart from this there is immense and systematic thieving of coal by the unemployed. I call it thieving because technically it is that, though it does no harm to anybody. In the 'dirt' that is sent up from the pits there is a certain amount of broken coal, and unemployed people spend a lot of time in picking it out of the slag-heaps. All day long over those strange grey mountains you see people wandering to and fro with sacks and baskets across the sulphurous smoke (many slag-heaps are on fire under the surface), prising out the tiny nuggets of coal which are buried here and there. You meet men coming away, wheeling strange and wonderful home-made bicycles—bicycles made of rusty parts picked off refuse-tips, without saddles, without chains and almost always without tyres—across which are slung bags containing perhaps half a hundredweight of coal, fruit of half a day's searching. In times of strikes, when everybody is short of fuel, the miners turn out with pick and shovel and burrow into the slag-heaps, whence the hummocky appearance which most slag-heaps have. During long strikes, in places where there are outcrops of coal, they have sunk surface mines and carried them scores of yards into the earth.

In Wigan the competition among unemployed people for the waste coal has become so fierce that it has led to an extraordinary custom called 'scrambling for the coal', which is well worth seeing. Indeed I rather wonder that it has never been filmed. An unemployed miner took me to see it one afternoon. We got to the place, a mountain range of ancient slag-heaps with a railway running through the valley below. A couple of hundred ragged men, each with a sack and coal-hammer strapped under his coat-tails, were waiting on the 'broo'. When the dirt comes up from the pit it is loaded on to trucks and an engine runs these to the top of another slag-heap a quarter of a mile away and there leaves them. The process of 'scrambling for the coal' consists in getting on to the train while it is moving; any truck which you have succeeded in boarding while it is in motion counts as 'your' truck. Presently the train hove in sight. With a wild yell a hundred men dashed down the slope to catch her as she rounded the bend. Even at the bend the train was making twenty miles an hour. The men hurled themselves upon it, caught hold of the rings at the rear of the trucks and hoisted themselves up by way of the bumpers, five or ten of them on each truck. The driver took no notice, He drove up to the top of the slag-heap, uncoupled the trucks, and ran the engine back to the pit, presently returning with a fresh string of trucks. There was the same wild rush of ragged figures as before. In the end only about fifty men had failed to get on to either train.

We walked up to the top of the slag-heap. The men were shovelling the dirt out of the trucks, while down below their wives and children were kneeling, swiftly scrabbling with their hands in the damp dirt and picking out lumps of coal the size of an egg or smaller. You would see a woman pounce on a tiny fragment of stuff, wipe it on her apron, scrutinize it to make sure it was coal, and pop it jealously into her sack. Of course, when you are boarding a truck you don't know beforehand what is in it; it may be actual 'dirt' from the roads or it may merely be shale from the roofing. If it is a shale truck there will be no coal in it, but there occurs among the shale another inflammable rock called cannel, which looks very like ordinary shale but is slightly darker and is known by splitting in parallel lines, like slate. It makes tolerable fuel, not good enough to be commercially valuable, but good enough to be eagerly sought after by the unemployed. The miners on the shale trucks were picking out the cannel and splitting it up with their hammers. Down at the bottom of the 'broo' the people who had failed to get on to either train were gleaning the tiny chips of coal that came rolling down from above—fragments no bigger than a hazel-nut, these, but the people were glad enough to get them.

We stayed there till the train was empty. In a couple of hours the people had picked the dirt over to the last grain. They slung their sacks over shoulder or bicycle, and started on the two-mile trudge back to Wigan. Most of the families had gathered about half a hundredweight of coal or cannel, so that between them they must have stolen five or ten tons of fuel. This business of robbing the dirt trains takes place every day in Wigan, at any rate in winter, and at more collieries than one. It is of course extremely dangerous. No one was hurt the afternoon I was there, but a man had had both his legs cut off a few weeks earlier, and another man lost several fingers a week later. Technically it is stealing but, as everybody knows, if the coal were not stolen it would simply be wasted. Now and again, for form's sake, the colliery companies prosecute somebody for coal-picking, and in that

morning's issue of the local paper there was a paragraph saying that
two men had been fined ten shillings. But no notice is taken of the
prosecutions—in fact, one of the men named in the paper was there
that afternoon—and the coal-pickers subscribe among themselves to
pay the fines. The thing is taken for granted. Everyone knows that the
unemployed have got to get fuel somehow. So every afternoon several
hundred men risk their necks and several hundred women scrabble in
the mud for hours—and all for half a hundredweight of inferior fuel,
value ninepence.

That scene stays in my mind as one of my pictures of Lancashire:
the dumpy, shawled women, with their sacking aprons and their
heavy black clogs, kneeling in the cindery mud and the bitter wind,
searching eagerly for tiny chips of coal. They are glad enough to do it.
In winter they are desperate for fuel; it is more important almost than
food. Meanwhile all round, as far as the eye can see, are the slag-heaps
and hoisting gear of collieries, and not one of those collieries can sell
all the coal it is capable of producing. This ought to appeal to Major
Douglas.

VII

As you travel northward your eye, accustomed to the South or East, does not notice much difference until you are beyond Birmingham. In Coventry you might as well be in Finsbury Park, and the Bull Ring in Birmingham is not unlike Norwich Market, and between all the towns of the Midlands there stretches a villa-civilization indistinguishable from that of the South. It is only when you get a little further north, to the pottery towns and beyond, that you begin to encounter the real ugliness of industrialism—an ugliness so frightful and so arresting that you are obliged, as it were, to come to terms with it.

A slag-heap is at best a hideous thing, because it is so planless and functionless. It is something just dumped on the earth, like the emptying of a giant's dust-bin. On the outskirts of the mining towns there are frightful landscapes where your horizon is ringed completely round by jagged grey mountains, and underfoot is mud and ashes and overhead the steel cables where tubs of dirt travel slowly across miles of country. Often the slag-heaps are on fire, and at night you can see the red rivulets of fire winding this way and that, and also the slow-moving blue flames of sulphur, which always seem on the point of expiring and always spring out again. Even when a slag-heap sinks, as it does ultimately, only an evil brown grass grows on it, and it retains its hummocky surface. One in the slums of Wigan, used as a playground, looks like a choppy sea suddenly frozen; 'the flock mattress', it is called locally. Even centuries hence when the plough drives over the places where coal was once mined, the sites of ancient slag-heaps will still be distinguishable from an aeroplane.

I remember a winter afternoon in the dreadful environs of Wigan. All round was the lunar landscape of slag-heaps, and to the north, through the passes, as it were, between the mountains of slag, you could see the factory chimneys sending out their plumes of smoke. The canal path was a mixture of cinders and frozen mud, criss-crossed by the imprints of innumerable clogs, and all round, as far as the slag-heaps in the distance, stretched the 'flashes'—pools of stagnant water that had seeped into the hollows caused by the subsidence of ancient pits. It was horribly cold. The 'flashes' were covered with ice the colour of raw umber, the bargemen were muffled to the eyes in sacks, the lock gates wore beards of ice. It seemed a world from which vegetation had been banished; nothing existed except smoke, shale, ice, mud, ashes, and foul water. But even Wigan is beautiful compared with Sheffield. Sheffield, I suppose, could justly claim to be called the ugliest town in the Old World: its inhabitants, who want it to be pre-eminent in everything, very likely do make that claim for it. It has a population of half a million and it contains fewer decent buildings than the average East Anglian village of five hundred. And the stench! If at rare moments you stop smelling sulphur it is because you have begun smelling gas. Even the shallow river that runs through the town is usually bright yellow with some chemical or other. Once I halted in the street and counted the factory chimneys I could see; there were thirty-three of them, but there would have been far more if the air had not been obscured by smoke. One scene especially lingers in my mind. A frightful patch of waste ground (somehow, up there, a patch of waste ground attains a squalor that would be impossible even in London) trampled bare of grass and littered with newspapers and old saucepans. To the right an isolated row of gaunt four-roomed houses, dark red, blackened by smoke. To the left an interminable vista of factory chimneys, chimney beyond chimney, fading away into a dim blackish haze. Behind me a railway embankment made of the slag from furnaces. In front, across the patch of waste ground, a cubical building of red and yellow brick, with the sign 'Thomas Grocock, Haulage Contractor'.

At night, when you cannot see the hideous shapes of the houses and the blackness of everything, a town like Sheffield assumes a kind of sinister magnificence. Sometimes the drifts of smoke are rosy with sulphur, and serrated flames, like circular saws, squeeze themselves out from beneath the cowls of the foundry chimneys. Through the open doors of foundries you see fiery serpents of iron being hauled to and fro by redlit boys, and you hear the whizz and thump of steam hammers and the scream of the iron under the blow. The pottery towns are almost equally ugly in a pettier way. Right in among the rows of tiny blackened houses, part of the street as it were, are the 'pot banks'—conical brick chimneys like gigantic burgundy bottles buried in the soil and belching their smoke almost in your face. You come upon monstrous clay chasms hundreds of feet across and almost as deep, with little rusty tubs creeping on chain railways up one side, and on the other workmen clinging like samphire-gatherers and cutting into the face of the cliff with their picks. I passed that way in snowy weather, and even the snow was black. The best thing one can say for the pottery towns is that they are fairly small and stop abruptly. Less than ten miles away you can stand in undefiled country, on the almost naked hills, and the pottery towns are only a smudge in the distance.

When you contemplate such ugliness as this, there are two questions that strike you. First, is it inevitable? Secondly, does it matter?

I do not believe that there is anything inherently and unavoidably ugly about industrialism. A factor or even a gasworks is not obliged of its own nature to be ugly, any more than a palace or a dog-kennel or a cathedral. It all depends on the architectural tradition of the period. The industrial towns of the North are ugly because they happen to have been built at a time when modern methods of steel-construction and smoke-abatement were unknown, and when everyone was too busy making money to think about anything else. They go on being ugly largely because the Northerners have got used to that kind of thing and do not notice it. Many of the people in Sheffield or Manchester, if they smelled the air along the Cornish cliffs, would probably declare that it had no taste in it. But since the war, industry has tended to shift southward and in doing so has grown almost comely. The typical post-war factory is not a gaunt barrack or an awful chaos of blackness and belching chimneys; it is a glittering white structure of concrete, glass, and steel, surrounded by green lawns and beds of tulips. Look at the factories you pass as you travel out of London on the G.W.R.; they may not be aesthetic triumphs but certainly they are not ugly in the same way as the Sheffield gasworks. But in any case, though the ugliness of industrialism is the most obvious thing about it and the thing every newcomer exclaims against, I doubt whether it is centrally important. And perhaps it is not even desirable, industrialism being what it is, that it should learn to disguise itself as something else. As Mr Aldous Huxley has truly remarked, a dark Satanic mill ought to look like a dark Satanic mill and not like the temple of mysterious and splendid gods. Moreover, even in the worst of the industrial towns one sees a great deal that is not ugly in the narrow aesthetic sense. A belching chimney or a stinking slum is repulsive chiefly because it implies warped lives and ailing children. Look at it from a purely aesthetic standpoint and it may have a certain macabre appeal. I find that anything outrageously strange generally ends by fascinating me even when I abominate it. The landscapes of Burma, which, when I was among them, so appalled me as to assume the qualities of nightmare, afterwards stayed so hauntingly in my mind that I was obliged to write a novel about them to get rid of them. (In all novels about the East the scenery is the real subject-matter.) It would probably be quite easy to extract a sort of beauty, as Arnold Bennett did, from the blackness of the industrial towns; one can easily imagine Baudelaire, for instance, writing a poem about a slag-heap. But the beauty or ugliness of industrialism hardly matters. Its real evil lies far deeper and is quite uneradicable. It is important to remember this, because there is always a temptation to think that industrialism is harmless so long as it is clean and orderly.

But when you go to the industrial North you are conscious, quite apart from the unfamiliar scenery, of entering a strange country. This is partly because of certain real differences which do exist, but still more because of the North–South antithesis which has been rubbed into us for such a long time past. There exists in England a curious cult of Northernness, sort of Northern snobbishness. A Yorkshireman in the South will always take care to let you know that he regards you as an inferior. If you ask him why, he will explain that it is only in the North that life is 'real' life, that the industrial work done in the North is the only 'real' work, that the North is inhabited by 'real' people, the South merely by rentiers and their parasites. The Northerner has 'grit', he is grim, 'dour', plucky, warm-hearted, and democratic; the Southerner is snobbish, effeminate, and lazy—that at any rate is the theory. Hence the Southerner goes north, at any rate for the first time, with the vague inferiority-complex of a civilized man venturing among savages, while the Yorkshireman, like the Scotchman, comes to London in the spirit of a barbarian out for loot. And feelings of this kind, which are the result of tradition, are not affected by visible facts. Just as an Englishman five feet four inches high and twenty-nine inches round the chest feels that as an Englishman he is the physical superior of Carnera (Carnera being a Dago), so also with the Northerner and the Southerner. I remember a weedy little Yorkshireman, who would almost certainly have run away if a fox-terrier had snapped at him, telling me that in the South of England he felt 'like a wild invader'. But the cult is often adopted by people who are not by birth Northerners themselves. A year or two ago a friend of mine, brought up in the South but now living in the North, was driving me through Suffolk in a car. We passed through a rather beautiful village. He glanced disapprovingly at the cottages and said:

'Of course most of the villages in Yorkshire are hideous; but the Yorkshiremen are splendid chaps. Down here it's just the other way about—beautiful villages and rotten people. All the people in those cottages there are worthless, absolutely worthless.'

I could not help inquiring whether he happened to know anybody in that village. No, he did not know them; but because this was East Anglia they were obviously worthless. Another friend of mine, again a Southerner by birth, loses no opportunity of praising the North to the detriment of the South. Here is an extract from one of his letters to me:

I am in Clitheroe, Lancs....I think running water is much more attractive in moor and mountain country than in the fat and sluggish South. 'The smug and silver Trent,' Shakespeare says; and the South-er the smugger, I say.

Here you have an interesting example of the Northern cult. Not only are you and I and everyone else in the South of England written off as 'fat and sluggish', but even water when it gets north of a certain latitude, ceases to be H_2O and becomes something mystically superior. But the interest of this passage is that its writer is an extremely intelligent man of 'advanced' opinions who would have nothing but contempt for nationalism in its ordinary form. Put to him some such proposition as 'One Britisher is worth three foreigners', and he would repudiate it with horror. But when it is a question of North versus South, he is quite ready to generalize. *All* nationalistic distinctions— all claims to be better than somebody else because you have a different-shaped skull or speak a different dialect—are entirely spurious, but they are important so long as people believe in them. There is no doubt about the Englishman's inbred conviction that those who live to the south of him are his inferiors; even our foreign policy is governed by it to some extent. I think, therefore, that it is worth pointing out when and why it came into being.

When nationalism first became a religion, the English looked at the map, and, noticing that their island lay very high in the Northern Hemisphere, evolved the pleasing theory that the further north you live the more virtuous you become. The histories I was given when I was a little boy generally started off by explaining in the naïvest way that a cold climate made people energetic while a hot one made them lazy, and hence the defeat of the Spanish Armada. This nonsense about the superior energy of the English (actually the laziest people in Europe) has been current for at least a hundred years. 'Better is it for us', writes a Quarterly Reviewer of 1827, 'to be condemned to labour for our country's good than to luxuriate amid olives, vines, and vices.' 'Olives, vines, and vices' sums up the normal English attitude towards the Latin races. In the mythology of Carlyle, Creasey, etc., the Northerner ('Teutonic', later 'Nordic') is pictured as a hefty, vigorous chap with blond moustaches and pure morals, while the Southerner is sly, cowardly, and licentious. This theory was never pushed to its logical end, which would have meant assuming that the finest people in the world were the Eskimos, but it did involve admitting that the people who lived to the north of us were superior to ourselves. Hence, partly, the cult of Scotland and of Scotch things which has so deeply marked English life during the past fifty years. But it was the industrialization of the North that gave the North–South antithesis its peculiar slant. Until comparatively recently the northern part of England was the backward and feudal part, and such industry as existed was concentrated in London and the South-East. In the Civil War for instance, roughly speaking a war of money versus feudalism, the North and West were for the King and the South and East for the Parliament. But with the increasing use of coal industry passed to the North, and there grew up a new type of man, the self-made Northern business man—the Mr Rouncewell and Mr Bounderby of Dickens. The Northern business man, with his hateful 'get on or get out' philosophy, was the dominant figure of the nineteenth century, and as a sort of tyrannical corpse he rules us still. This is the type edified by Arnold Bennett—the type who starts off with half a crown and ends up with fifty thousand pounds, and whose chief pride is to be an even greater boor after he has made his money than before. On analysis his sole virtue turns out to be a talent for making money. We were bidden to admire him because though he might be narrow-minded, sordid, ignorant, grasping, and uncouth, he had 'grit', he 'got on'; in other words, he knew how to make money.

This kind of cant is nowadays a pure anachronism, for the Northern business man is no longer prosperous. But traditions are not killed by facts, and the tradition of Northern 'grit' lingers. It is still dimly felt that a Northerner will 'get on', i.e. make money, where a Southerner will fail. At the back of the mind of every Yorkshireman and every

Scotchman who comes to London is a sort of Dick Whittington picture of himself as the boy who starts off by selling newspapers and ends up as Lord Mayor. And that, really, is at the bottom of his bumptiousness. But where one can make a great mistake is in imagining that this feeling extends to the genuine working class. When I first went to Yorkshire, some years ago, I imagined that I was going to a country of boors. I was used to the London Yorkshireman with his interminable harangues and his pride in the supposed raciness of his dialect (' "A stitch in time saves nine", as we say in the West Riding'), and I expected to meet with a good deal of rudeness. But I met with nothing of the kind, and least of all among the miners. Indeed the Lancashire and Yorkshire miners treated me with a kindness and courtesy that were even embarrassing; for if there is one type of man to whom I do feel myself inferior, it is a coal-miner. Certainly no one showed any sign of despising me for coming from a different part of the country. This has its importance when one remembers that the English regional snobberies are nationalism in miniature; for it suggests that place-snobbery is not a working-class characteristic.

There is nevertheless a real difference between North and South, and there is at least a tinge of truth in that picture of Southern England as one enormous Brighton inhabited by lounge-lizards. For climatic reasons the parasitic dividend-drawing class tend to settle in the South. In a Lancashire cotton-town you could probably go for months on end without once hearing an 'educated' accent, whereas there can hardly be a town in the South of England where you could throw a brick without hitting the niece of a bishop. Consequently, with no petty gentry to set the pace, the bourgeoisification of the working class, though it is taking place in the North, is taking place more slowly. All the Northern accents, for instance, persist strongly, while the Southern ones are collapsing before the movies and the B.B.C. Hence your 'educated' accent stamps you rather as a foreigner than as a chunk of the petty gentry; and this is an immense advantage, for it makes it much easier to get into contact with the working class.

But is it ever possible to be really intimate with the working class? I shall have to discuss that later; I will only say here that I do not think it is possible. But undoubtedly it is easier in the North than it would be in the South to meet working-class people on approximately equal terms. It is fairly easy to live in a miner's house and be accepted as one of the family; with, say, a farm labourer in the Southern counties it probably would be impossible. I have seen just enough of the working class to avoid idealizing them, but I do know that you can learn a great deal in a working-class home, if only you can get there. The essential point is that your middle-class ideals and prejudices are tested by contact with others which are not necessarily better but are certainly different.

Take for instance the different attitude towards the family. A working-class family hangs together as a middle-class one does, but the relationship is far less tyrannical. A working man has not that deadly weight of family prestige hanging round his neck like a millstone. I have pointed out earlier that a middle-class person goes utterly to pieces under the influence of poverty; and this is generally due to the behaviour of his family—to the fact that he has scores of relations nagging and badgering him night and day for failing to 'get on'. The fact that the working class know how to combine and the middle class don't is probably due to their different conceptions of family loyalty. You cannot have an effective trade union of middle-class workers, because in times of strikes almost every middle-class wife would be egging her husband on to blackleg and get the other fellow's job. Another working-class characteristic, disconcerting at first, is their plain-spokenness towards anyone they regard as an equal. If you offer a working man something he doesn't want, he tells you that he doesn't want it; a middle-class person would accept it to avoid giving offence. And again, take the working-class attitude towards 'education'. How different it is from ours, and how immensely sounder! Working people often have a vague reverence for learning in others, but where 'education' touches their own lives they see through it and reject it by a healthy instinct. The time was when I used to lament over quite imaginary pictures of lads of fourteen dragged protesting from their lessons and set to work at dismal jobs. It seemed to me dreadful that the doom of a 'job' should descend upon anyone at fourteen. Of course I know now that there is not one working-class boy in a thousand who does not pine for the day when he will leave school. He wants to be doing real work, not wasting his time on ridiculous rubbish like history and geography. To the working class, the notion of staying at school till you are nearly grown-up seems merely contemptible and unmanly. The idea of a great big boy of eighteen, who ought to be bringing a pound a week home to his parents, going to school in a ridiculous uniform and even being caned for not doing his lessons! Just fancy a working-class boy of eighteen allowing himself to be caned! He is a man when the other is still a baby. Ernest Pontifex, in Samuel Butler's *Way of All Flesh*, after he had had a few glimpses of real life, looked back on his public school and university education and found it a 'sickly, debilitating debauch'. There is much in middle-class life that looks sickly and debilitating when you see it from a working-class angle.

In a working-class home—I am not thinking at the moment of the unemployed, but of comparatively prosperous homes—you breathe a warm, decent, deeply human atmosphere which it is not so easy to find elsewhere. I should say that a manual worker, if he is in steady work and drawing good wages—an 'if' which gets bigger and bigger— has a better chance of being happy than an 'educated' man. His home life seems to fall more naturally into a sane and comely shape. I have often been struck by the peculiar easy completeness, the per- fect symmetry as it were, of a working-class interior at its best. Especially on winter evenings after tea, when the fire glows in the open range and dances mirrored in the steel fender, when Father, in shirt-sleeves, sits in the rocking chair at one side of the fire reading the racing finals, and Mother sits on the other with her sewing, and the children are happy with a pennorth of mint humbugs, and the dog lolls roasting himself on the rag mat—it is a good place to be in, provided that you can be not only in it but sufficiently *of* it to be taken for granted.

This scene is still reduplicated in a majority of English homes, though not in so many as before the war. Its happiness depends mainly upon one question—whether Father is in work. But notice that the picture I have called up, of a working-class family sitting round the coal fire after kippers and strong tea, belongs only to our own moment of time and could not belong either to the future or the past. Skip forward two hundred years into the Utopian future, and the scene is totally different. Hardly one of the things I have imagined will still be there. In that age when there is no manual labour and everyone is 'educated', it is hardly likely that Father will still be a rough man with enlarged hands who likes to sit in shirt-sleeves and says 'Ah wur coomin' oop street'. And there won't be a coal fire in the grate, only some kind of invisible heater. The furniture will be made of rubber, glass, and steel. If there are still such things as evening papers there will certainly be no racing news in them, for gambling will be mean- ingless in a world where there is no poverty and the horse will have vanished from the face of the earth. Dogs, too, will have been suppressed on grounds of hygiene. And there won't be so many children, either, if the birth-controllers have their way. But move backwards into the Middle Ages and you are in a world almost equally foreign. A windowless hut, a wood fire which smokes in your face because there is no chimney, mouldy bread, 'Poor John', lice, scurvy, a yearly child-birth and a yearly child-death, and the priest terrifying you with tales of Hell.

Curiously enough it is *not* the triumphs of modern engineering, nor the radio, nor the cinematograph, nor the five thousand novels which are published yearly, nor the crowds at Ascot and the Eton and Harrow match, but the memory of working-class interiors—especially as I sometimes saw them in my childhood before the war, when England was still prosperous—that reminds me that our age has not been altogether a bad one to live in.

PART TWO

VIII

THE road from Mandalay to Wigan is a long one and the reasons for taking it are not immediately clear.

In the earlier chapters of this book I have given a rather fragmentary account of various things I saw in the coal areas of Lancashire and Yorkshire. I went there partly because I wanted to see what mass-unemployment is like at its worst, partly in order to see the most typical section of the English working class at close quarters. This was necessary to me as part of my approach to Socialism, for before you can be sure whether you are genuinely in favour of Socialism, you have got to decide whether things at present are tolerable or not tolerable, and you have got to take up a definite attitude on the terribly difficult issue of class. Here I shall have to digress and explain how my own attitude towards the class question was developed. Obviously this involves writing a certain amount of autobiography, and I would not do it if I did not think that I am sufficiently typical of my class, or rather sub-caste, to have a certain symptomatic importance.

I was born into what you might describe as the lower-upper-middle class. The upper-middle class, which had its heyday in the eighties and nineties, with Kipling as its poet laureate, was a sort of mound of wreckage left behind when the tide of Victorian prosperity receded. Or perhaps it would be better to change the metaphor and describe it not as a mound but as a layer—the layer of society lying between £2000 and £300 a year: my own family was not far from the bottom. You notice that I define it in terms of money, because that is always the quickest way of making yourself understood. Nevertheless, the essential point about the English class-system is that it is *not* entirely explicable in terms of money. Roughly speaking it is a money-stratification, but it is also interpenetrated by a sort of shadowy caste-system; rather like a jerry-built modern bungalow haunted by medieval ghosts. Hence the fact that the upper-middle class extends or extended to incomes as low as £300 a year—to incomes, that is, much lower than those of merely middle-class people with no social pretensions. Probably there are countries where you can predict a man's opinions from his income, but it is never quite safe to do so in England; you have always got to take his traditions into consideration as well. A naval officer and his grocer very likely have the same income, but they are not equivalent persons and they would only be on the same side in very large issues such as a war or a general strike—possibly not even then.

Of course it is obvious now that the upper-middle class is done for. In every country town in Southern England, not to mention the dreary wastes of Kensington and Earl's Court, those who knew it in the days of its glory are dying, vaguely embittered by a world which has not behaved as it ought. I never open one of Kipling's books or go into one of the huge dull shops which were once the favourite haunt of the upper-middle class, without thinking 'Change and decay in all around I see'. But before the war the upper-middle class, though already none too prosperous, still felt sure of itself. Before the war you were either a gentleman or not a gentleman, and if you were a gentleman you struggled to behave as such, whatever your income might be. Between those with £400 a year and those with £2000 or even £1000 a year there was a great gulf fixed, but it was a gulf which those with £400 a year did their best to ignore. Probably the distinguishing mark of the upper-middle class was that its traditions were not to any extent commercial, but mainly military, official, and professional. People in this class owned no land, but they felt that they were landowners in the sight of God and kept up a semi-aristocratic outlook by going into the professions and the fighting services rather than into trade. Small boys used to count the plum stones on their plates and foretell their destiny by chanting, 'Army, Navy, Church, Medicine, Law'; and even of these 'Medicine' was faintly inferior to the others and only put in for the sake of symmetry. To belong to this class when you were at the £400 a year level was a queer business, for it meant that your gentility was almost purely theoretical. You lived, so to speak, at two levels simultaneously. Theoretically you knew all about servants and how to tip them, although in practice you had one, at most, two resident servants. Theoretically you knew how to wear your clothes and how to order a dinner, although in practice you could never afford to go to a decent tailor or a decent restaurant. Theoretically you knew how to shoot and ride, although in practice you had no horses to ride and not an inch of ground to shoot over. It was this that explained the attraction of India (more recently Kenya, Nigeria, etc.) for the lower-upper-middle class. The people who went there as soldiers and officials did not go there to make money, for a soldier or an official does not want money; they went there because in India, with cheap horses, free shooting, and hordes of black servants, it was so easy to play at being a gentleman.

In the kind of shabby-genteel family that I am talking about there is far more *consciousness* of poverty than in any working-class family above the level of the dole. Rent and clothes and school-bills are an unending nightmare, and every luxury, even a glass of beer, is an unwarrantable extravagance. Practically the whole family income goes in keeping up appearances. It is obvious that people of this kind are in an anomalous position, and one might be tempted to write them off as mere exceptions and therefore unimportant. Actually, however, they are or were fairly numerous. Most clergymen and schoolmasters, for instance, nearly all Anglo-Indian officials, a sprinkling of soldiers and sailors, and a fair number of professional men and artists, fall into this category. But the real importance of this class is that they are the shock-absorbers of the bourgeoisie. The real bourgeoisie, those in the £2000 a year class and over, have their money as a thick layer of padding between themselves and the class they plunder; in so far as they are aware of the Lower Orders at all they are aware of them as employees, servants, and tradesmen. But it is quite different for the poor devils lower down who are struggling to live genteel lives on what are virtually working-class incomes. These last are forced into close and, in a sense, intimate contact with the working class, and I suspect it is from them that the traditional upper-class attitude towards 'common' people is derived.

And what is this attitude? An attitude of sniggering superiority punctuated by bursts of vicious hatred. Look at any number of *Punch* during the past thirty years. You will find it everywhere taken for granted that a working-class person, as such, is a figure of fun, except at odd moments when he shows signs of being too prosperous, whereupon he ceases to be a figure of fun and becomes a demon. It is no use wasting breath in denouncing this attitude. It is better to consider how it has arisen, and to do that one has got to realize what the working classes look like to those who live among them but have different habits and traditions.

A shabby genteel family is in much the same position as a family of 'poor whites' living in a street where everyone else is a Negro. In such circumstances you have got to cling to your gentility because it is the only thing you have; and meanwhile you are hated for your stuck-up-ness and for the accent and manners which stamp you as one of the boss class. I was very young, not much more than six, when I first became aware of class-distinctions. Before that age my chief heroes had generally been working-class people, because they always seemed to do such interesting things, such as being fishermen and black-smiths and bricklayers. I remember the farm hands on a farm in Cornwall who used to let me ride on the drill when they were sowing turnips and would sometimes catch the ewes and milk them to give me a drink; and the workmen building the new house next door, who let me play with the wet mortar and from whom I first learned the word 'b——'; and the plumber up the road with whose children I used to go out bird-nesting. But it was not long before I was forbid-den to play with the plumber's children; they were 'common' and I was told to keep away from them. This was snobbish, if you like, but it was also necessary, for middle-class people cannot afford to let their children grow up with vulgar accents. So, very early, the working class ceased to be a race of friendly and wonderful beings and became a race of enemies. We realized that they hated us, but we could never understand why, and naturally we set it down to pure, vicious malig-nity. To me in my early boyhood, to nearly all children of families like mine, 'common' people seemed almost sub-human. They had coarse faces, hideous accents, and gross manners, they hated everyone who was not like themselves, and if they got half a chance they would insult you in brutal ways. That was our view of them, and though it was false it was understandable. For one must remember that before the war there was much more *overt* class-hatred in England than there is now. In those days you were quite likely to be insulted simply for looking like a member of the upper classes; nowadays, on the other hand, you are more likely to be fawned upon. Anyone over thirty can remember the time when it was impossible for a well-dressed person to walk through a slum street without being hooted at. Whole quarters of big towns were considered unsafe because of 'hoo-ligans' (now almost an extinct type), and the London gutter-boy everywhere, with his loud voice and lack of intellectual scruples, could make life a misery for people who considered it beneath their dignity to answer back. A recurrent terror of my holidays, when I was a small boy, was the gangs of 'cads' who were liable to set upon you five or ten to one. In term time, on the other hand, it was we who were in the majority and the 'cads' who were oppressed; I remember a couple of savage mass-battles in the cold winter of 1916–17. And this tradition of open hostility between upper and lower class had apparently been the same for at least a century past. A typical joke in *Punch* in the sixties is a picture of a small, nervous-looking gentleman riding through a slum street and a crowd of street-boys closing in on him with shouts "Ere comes a swell! Let's frighten 'is 'oss!' Just fancy the street boys trying to frighten his horse now! They would be much likelier to hang round him in vague hopes of a tip. During the past dozen years the English working class have grown servile with a rather horrifying rapidity. It was bound to happen, for the frightful weapon of unemployment has cowed them. Before the war their economic position was comparatively strong, for though there was no dole to fall back upon, there was not much unemployment, and the power of the boss class was not so obvious as it is now. A man did not see ruin staring him in the face every time he cheeked a 'toff', and naturally he did cheek a 'toff' whenever it seemed safe to do so. G. J. Renier, in his book on Oscar Wilde, points out that the strange, obscene burst of popular fury which followed the Wilde trial was essentially social in character. The London mob had caught a member of the upper classes on the hop, and they took care to keep him hopping. All this was natural and even proper. If you treat people as the English working class have been treated during the past two centuries, you must expect them to resent it. On the other hand the children of shabby-genteel families could not be blamed if they grew up with a hatred of the working class, typified for them by prowling gangs of 'cads'.

But there was another and more serious difficulty. Here you come to the real secret of class-distinctions in the West—the real reason why a European of bourgeois upbringing, even when he calls himself a Communist, cannot without a hard effort think of a working man as his equal. It is summed up in four frightful words which people nowadays are chary of uttering, but which were bandied about quite freely in my childhood. The words were: *The lower classes smell*.

That was what we were taught—*the lower classes smell*. And here, obviously, you are at an impassable barrier. For no feeling of like or dislike is quite so fundamental as a *physical* feeling. Race-hatred, religious hatred, differences of education, of temperament, of intellect, even differences of moral code, can be got over; but physical repulsion cannot. You can have an affection for a murderer or a sodomite, but you cannot have an affection for a man whose breath stinks—habitually stinks, I mean. However well you may wish him, however much you may admire his mind and character, if his breath stinks he is horrible and in your heart of hearts you will hate him. It may not greatly matter if the average middle-class person is brought up to believe that the working classes are ignorant, lazy, drunken, boorish, and dishonest; it is when he is brought up to believe that they are dirty that the harm is done. And in my childhood we *were* brought up to believe that they were dirty. Very early in life you acquired the idea that there was something subtly repulsive about a working-class body; you would not get nearer to it than you could help. You watched a great sweaty navvy walking down the road with his pick over his shoulder; you looked at his discoloured shirt and his corduroy trousers stiff with the dirt of a decade; you thought of those nests and layers of greasy rags below, and, under all, the unwashed body, brown all over (that was how I used to imagine it), with its strong, bacon-like reek. You watched a tramp taking off his boots in a ditch—ugh! It did not seriously occur to you that the tramp might not enjoy having black feet. And even 'lower-class' people whom you knew to be quite clean—servants, for instance—were faintly unappetizing. The smell of their sweat, the very texture of their skins, were mysteriously different from yours.

Everyone who has grown up pronouncing his aitches and in a house with a bathroom and one servant is likely to have grown up with these feelings; hence the chasmic, impassable quality of class-distinctions in the West. It is queer how seldom this is admitted. At the moment I can think of only one book where it is set forth without humbug, and that is Mr Somerset Maugham's *On a Chinese Screen*. Mr Maugham describes a high Chinese official arriving at a wayside inn and blustering and calling everybody names in order to impress upon them that he is a supreme dignitary and they are only worms. Five minutes later, having asserted his dignity in the way he thinks proper, he is eating his dinner in perfect amity with the baggage coolies. As an official he feels that he has got to make his presence felt, but he has no feeling that the coolies are of different clay from himself. I have observed countless similar scenes in

Burma. Among Mongolians—among all Asiatics, for all I know—there is a sort of natural equality, an easy intimacy between man and man, which is simply unthinkable in the West. Mr Maugham adds:

In the West we are divided from our fellows by our sense of smell. The working man is our master, inclined to rule us with an iron hand, but it cannot be denied that he stinks: none can wonder at it, for a bath in the dawn when you have to hurry to your work before the factory bell rings is no pleasant thing, nor does heavy labour tend to sweetness; and you do not change your linen more than you can help when the week's washing must be done by a sharp-tongued wife. I do not blame the working man because he stinks, but stink he does. It makes social intercourse difficult to persons of sensitive nostril. The matutinal tub divides the classes more effectually than birth, wealth, or education.

Meanwhile, *do* the 'lower classes' smell? Of course, as a whole, they are dirtier than the upper classes. They are bound to be, considering the circumstances in which they live, for even at this late date less than half the houses in England have bathrooms. Besides, the habit of washing yourself all over every day is a very recent one in Europe, and the working classes are generally more conservative than the bourgeoisie. But the English are growing visibly cleaner, and we may hope that in a hundred years they will be almost as clean as the Japanese. It is a pity that those who idealize the working class so often think it necessary to praise every working-class characteristic and therefore to pretend that dirtiness is somehow meritorious in itself. Here, curiously enough, the Socialist and the sentimental democratic Catholic of the type of Chesterton sometimes join hands; both will tell you that dirtiness is healthy and 'natural' and cleanliness is a mere fad or at best a luxury.[1] They seem not to see that they are merely giving colour to the notion that working-class people are dirty from choice and not from necessity. Actually, people who have access to a bath will generally use it. But the essential thing is that middle-class people *believe* that the working class are dirty—you see from the passage quoted above that Mr Maugham himself believes it—and, what is worse, that they are somehow *inherently* dirty. As a child, one of the most dreadful things I could imagine was to drink out of a bottle after

[1] According to Chesterton, dirtiness is merely a kind of 'discomfort' and therefore ranks as self-mortification. Unfortunately, the discomfort of dirtiness is chiefly suffered by other people. It is not really very uncomfortable to be dirty—not nearly so uncomfortable as having a cold bath on a winter morning.

a navvy. Once when I was thirteen, I was in a train coming from a market town, and the third-class carriage was packed full of shepherds and pig-men who had been selling their beasts. Somebody produced a quart bottle of beer and passed it round; it travelled from mouth to mouth to mouth, everyone taking a swig. I cannot describe the horror I felt as that bottle worked its way towards me. If I drank from it after all those lower-class male mouths I felt certain I should vomit; on the other hand, if they offered it to me I dared not refuse for fear of offending them—you see here how the middle-class squeamishness works both ways. Nowadays, thank God, I have no feelings of that kind. A working man's body, as such, is no more repulsive to me than a millionaire's. I still don't like drinking out of a cup or bottle after another person—another man, I mean; with women I don't mind—but at least the question of class does not enter. It was rubbing shoulders with the tramps that cured me of it. Tramps are not really very dirty as English people go, but they have the name for being dirty, and when you have shared a bed with a tramp and drunk tea out of the same snuff-tin, you feel that you have seen the worst and the worst has no terrors for you.

I have dwelt on these subjects because they are vitally important. To get rid of class-distinctions you have got to start by understanding how one class appears when seen through the eyes of another. It is useless to say that the middle classes are 'snobbish' and leave it at that. You get no further if you do not realize that snobbishness is bound up with a species of idealism. It derives from the early training in which a middle-class child is taught almost simultaneously to wash his neck, to be ready to die for his country, and to despise the 'lower classes'.

Here I shall be accused of being behind the times, for I was a child before and during the war and it may be claimed that children nowadays are brought up with more enlightened notions. It is probably true that class-feeling is for the moment a very little less bitter than it was. The working class are submissive where they used to be openly hostile, and the post-war manufacture of cheap clothes and the general softening of manners have toned down the surface differences between class and class. But undoubtedly the essential feeling is still there. Every middle-class person has a dormant class-prejudice which needs only a small thing to arouse it; and if he is over forty he probably has a firm conviction that his own class has been sacrificed to the class below. Suggest to the average unthinking person of gentle birth who is struggling to keep up appearances on four or five hundred a year that he is a member of an exploiting parasite class, and he will think you are mad. In perfect sincerity he will point out to you a dozen ways in which he is worse-off than a working man. In his eyes the workers are not a submerged race of slaves, they are a sinister flood creeping upwards to engulf himself and his friends and his family and to sweep all culture and all decency out of existence. Hence that queer watchful anxiety lest the working class shall grow too prosperous. In a number of *Punch* soon after the war, when coal was still fetching high prices, there is a picture of four or five miners with grim, sinister faces riding in a cheap motor-car. A friend they are passing calls out and asks them where they have borrowed it. They answer, 'We've bought the thing!' This, you see, is 'good enough for *Punch*'; for miners to buy a motor-car, even one car between four or five of them, is a monstrosity, a sort of crime against nature. That was the attitude of a dozen years ago, and I see no evidence of any fundamental change. The notion that the working class have been absurdly pampered, hopelessly demoralized by doles, old age pensions, free education, etc., is still widely held; it has merely been a little shaken, perhaps, by the recent recognition that unemployment does exist. For quantities of middle-class people, probably for a large majority of those over fifty, the typical working man still rides to the Labour Exchange on a motor-bike and keeps coal in his bath-tub: 'And, if you'll believe it, my dear, they actually *get married* on the dole!'

The reason why class-hatred seems to be diminishing is that nowadays it tends not to get into print, partly owing to the mealy-mouthed habits of our time, partly because newspapers and even books now have to appeal to a working-class public. As a rule you can best study it in private conversations. But if you want some printed examples, it is worth having a look at the *obiter dicta* of the late Professor Saintsbury. Saintsbury was a very learned man and along certain lines a judicious literary critic, but when he talked of political or economic matters he only differed from the rest of his class by the fact that he was too thick-skinned and had been born too early to see any reason for pretending to common decency. According to Saintsbury, unemployment insurance was simply 'contributing to the support of lazy ne'er-do-weels', and the whole trade union movement was no more than a kind of organized mendicancy:

'Pauper' is almost actionable now, is it not, when used as a word? though to *be* paupers, in the sense of being wholly or partly supported at the expense of other people, is the ardent, and to a considerable extent achieved, aspiration of a large proportion of our population, and of an entire political party.

(*Second Scrap Book*)

It is to be noticed, however, that Saintsbury recognizes that unemployment is bound to exist, and, in fact, thinks that it ought to exist, so long as the unemployed are made to suffer as much as possible:

Is not 'casual' labour the very secret and safety-valve of a safe and sound labour-system generally?

... In a complicated industrial and commercial state constant employment at regular wages is impossible; while dole-supported unemployment, at anything like the wages of employment, is demoralizing to begin with and ruinous at its more or less quickly arriving end.

(*Last Scrap Book*)

What exactly is to happen to the 'casual labourers' when no casual labour happens to be available is not made clear. Presumably (Saintsbury speaks approvingly of 'good Poor Laws') they are to go into the work-house or sleep in the streets. As to the notion that every human being ought as a matter of course to have the chance of earning at least a tolerable livelihood, Saintsbury dismisses it with contempt:

Even the 'right to live' ... extends no further than the right to protection against murder. Charity certainly will, morality possibly may, and public utility perhaps ought to add to this protection supererogatory provision for continuance of life; but it is questionable whether strict justice demands it.

As for the insane doctrine that being born in a country gives some right to the possession of the soil of that country, it hardly requires notice.

(*Last Scrap Book*)

It is worth reflecting for a moment upon the beautiful implications of this last passage. The interest of passages like these (and they are scattered all through Saintsbury's work) lies in their having been printed at all. Most people are a little shy of putting that kind of thing on paper. But what Saintsbury is saying here is what any little worm with a fairly safe five hundred a year *thinks*, and therefore in a way one must admire him for saying it. It takes a lot of guts to be *openly* such a skunk as that.

This is the outlook of a confessed reactionary. But how about the middle-class person whose views are not reactionary but 'advanced'? Beneath his revolutionary mask, is he really so different from the other?

A middle-class person embraces Socialism and perhaps even joins the Communist Party. How much real difference does it make? Obviously, living within the framework of capitalist society, he has got to go on earning his living, and one cannot blame him if he clings to his bourgeois economic status. But is there any change in his tastes, his habits, his manners, his imaginative background—his 'ideology', in Communist jargon? Is there *any* change in him except that he now votes Labour, or, when possible, Communist at the elections? It is noticeable that he still habitually associates with his own class; he is vastly more at home with a member of his own class, who thinks him a dangerous Bolshie, than with a member of the working class who supposedly agrees with him; his tastes in food, wine, clothes, books, pictures, music, ballet, are still recognizably bourgeois tastes; most significant of all, he invariably marries into his own class. Look at any bourgeois Socialist. Look at Comrade X, member of the C.P.G.B.* and author of *Marxism for Infants*. Comrade X, it so happens, is an old Etonian. He would be ready to die on the barricades, in theory anyway, but you notice that he still leaves his bottom waistcoat button undone. He idealizes the proletariat, but it is remarkable how little his habits resemble theirs. Perhaps once, out of sheer bravado, he has smoked a cigar with the band on, but it would be almost physically impossible for him to put pieces of cheese into his mouth on the point of his knife, or to sit indoors with his cap on, or even to drink his tea out of the saucer. I have known numbers of bourgeois Socialists, I have listened by the hour to their tirades against their own class, and yet never, not even once, have I met one who had picked up proletarian table-manners. Yet, after all, why not? Why should a man who thinks all virtue resides in the proletariat still take such pains to drink his soup silently? It can only be because in his heart he feels that proletarian manners are disgusting. So you see he is still responding to the training of his childhood, when he was taught to hate, fear, and despise the working class.

IX

WHEN I was fourteen or fifteen I was an odious little snob, but no worse than other boys of my own age and class. I suppose there is no place in the world where snobbery is quite so ever-present or where it is cultivated in such refined and subtle forms as in an English public school. Here at least one cannot say that English 'education' fails to do its job. You forget your Latin and Greek within a few months of leaving school—I studied Greek for eight or ten years, and now, at thirty-three, I cannot even repeat the Greek alphabet—but your snobbishness, unless you persistently root it out like the bindweed it is, sticks by you till your grave.

At school I was in a difficult position, for I was among boys who, for the most part, were much richer than myself, and I only went to an expensive public school because I happened to win a scholarship. This is the common experience of boys of the lower-upper-middle class, the sons of clergymen, Anglo-Indian officials, etc., and the effects it had on me were probably the usual ones. On the one hand it made me cling tighter than ever to my gentility; on the other hand it filled me with resentment against the boys whose parents were richer than mine and who took care to let me know it. I despised anyone who was not describable as a 'gentleman', but also I hated the hoggishly rich, especially those who had grown rich too recently. The correct and elegant thing, I felt, was to be of gentle birth but to have no money. This is part of the *credo* of the lower-upper-middle class. It has a romantic, Jacobite-in-exile feeling about it which is very comforting.

But those years, during and just after the war, were a queer time to be at school, for England was nearer revolution than she has been since or had been for a century earlier. Throughout almost the whole nation there was running a wave of revolutionary feeling which has since been reversed and forgotten, but which has left various deposits of sediment behind. Essentially, though of course one could not then see it in perspective, it was a revolt of youth against age, resulting directly from the war. In the war the young had been sacrificed and the old had behaved in a way which, even at this distance of time, is horrible to contemplate; they had been sternly patriotic in safe places while their sons went down like swathes of hay before the German machine guns. Moreover, the war had been conducted mainly by old men and had been conducted with supreme incompetence. By 1918 everyone under forty was in a bad temper with his elders, and the mood of anti-militarism which followed naturally upon the fighting was extended into a general revolt against orthodoxy and authority. At that time there was, among the young, a curious cult of hatred of 'old men'. The dominance of 'old men' was held to be responsible for every evil known to humanity, and every accepted institution from Scott's novels to the House of Lords was derided merely because 'old men' were in favour of it. For several years it was all the fashion to be a 'Bolshie', as people then called it. England was full of half-baked antinomian opinions. Pacifism, internationalism, humanitarianism of all kinds, feminism, free love, divorce-reform, atheism, birth-control— things like these were getting a better hearing than they would get in normal times. And of course the revolutionary mood extended to those who had been too young to fight, even to public schoolboys. At that time we all thought of ourselves as enlightened creatures of a new age, casting off the orthodoxy that had been forced upon us by those detested 'old men'. We retained, basically, the snobbish outlook of our class, we took it for granted that we could continue to draw our dividends or tumble into soft jobs, but also it seemed natural to us to be 'agin the Government'. We derided the O.T.C., the Christian religion, and perhaps even compulsory games and the Royal Family, and we did not realize that we were merely taking part in a world-wide gesture of distaste for war. Two incidents stick in my mind as examples of the queer revolutionary feeling of that time. One day the master who taught us English set us a kind of general knowledge paper of which one of the questions was, 'Whom do you consider the ten greatest men now living?' Of sixteen boys in the class (our average age was about seventeen) fifteen included Lenin in their list. This was at a snobbish expensive public school, and the date was 1920, when the horrors of the Russian Revolution was still fresh in everyone's mind. Also there were the so-called peace celebrations in 1919. Our elders had decided for us that we should celebrate peace in the traditional manner by whooping over the fallen foe. We were to march into the school-yard, carrying torches, and sing jingo songs of the type of 'Rule Britannia'. The boys—to their honour, I think—guyed the whole proceeding and sang blasphemous and seditious words to the tunes provided. I doubt whether things would happen in quite that manner now. Certainly the public schoolboys I meet nowadays, even the intelligent ones, are much more right-wing in their opinions than I and my contemporaries were fifteen years ago.

Hence, at the age of seventeen or eighteen, I was both a snob and a revolutionary. I was against all authority. I had read and re-read the entire published works of Shaw, Wells, and Galsworthy (at that time still regarded as dangerously 'advanced' writers), and I loosely described myself as a Socialist. But I had not much grasp of what Socialism meant, and no notion that the working class were human beings. At a distance, and through the medium of books—Jack London's *The People of the Abyss*, for instance—I could agonize over their sufferings, but I still hated them and despised them when I came anywhere near them. I was still revolted by their accents and infuriated by their habitual rudeness. One must remember that just then, immediately after the war, the English working class were in a fighting mood. That was the period of the great coal strikes, when a miner was thought of as a fiend incarnate and old ladies looked under their beds every night lest Robert Smillie should be concealed there. All through the war and for a little time afterwards there had been high wages and abundant employment; things were now returning to something worse than normal, and naturally the working class resisted. The men who had fought had been lured into the army by gaudy promises, and now they were coming home to a world where there were no jobs and not even any houses. Moreover, they had been at war and were coming home with the soldier's attitude to life, which is fundamentally, in spite of discipline, a lawless attitude. There was a turbulent feeling in the air. To that time belongs the song with the memorable refrain:

> There's nothing sure but
> The rich get richer and the poor get children;
> In the mean time,
> In between time,
> Ain't we got fun?

People had not yet settled down to a lifetime of unemployment mitigated by endless cups of tea. They still vaguely expected the Utopia for which they had fought, and even more than before they were openly hostile to the aitch-pronouncing class. So to the shock-absorbers of the bourgeoisie, such as myself, 'common people' still appeared brutal and repulsive. Looking back upon that period, I seem to have spent half the time in denouncing the capitalist system and the other half in raging over the insolence of bus-conductors.

When I was not yet twenty I went to Burma, in the Indian Imperial Police. In an 'outpost of Empire' like Burma the class-question appeared at first sight to have been shelved. There was no obvious class-friction here, because the all-important thing was not whether you had been to one of the right schools but whether your skin was technically white. As a matter of fact most of the white men in Burma were not of the type who in England would be called 'gentlemen', but except for the common soldiers and a few nondescripts they lived lives appropriate to 'gentlemen'—had servants, that is, and called their evening meal 'dinner'—and officially they were regarded as being all of the same class. They were 'white men', in contradistinction to the other and inferior class, the 'natives'. But one did not feel towards the 'natives' as one felt towards the 'lower classes' at home. The essential point was that the 'natives', at any rate the Burmese, were not felt to be physically repulsive. One looked down on them as 'natives', but one was quite ready to be physically intimate with them; and this, I noticed, was the case even with white men who had the most vicious colour prejudice. When you have a lot of servants you soon get into lazy habits, and I habitually allowed myself, for instance, to be dressed and undressed by my Burmese boy. This was because he was a Burman and undisgusting; I could not have endured to let an English manservant handle me in that intimate manner. I felt towards a Burman almost as I felt towards a woman. Like most other races, the Burmese have a distinctive smell—I cannot describe it: it is a smell that makes one's teeth tingle—but this smell never disgusted me. (Incidentally, Orientals say that *we* smell. The Chinese, I believe, say that a white man smells like a corpse. The Burmese say the same—though no Burman was ever rude enough to say so to me.) And in a way my attitude was defensible, for if one faces the fact one must admit that most Mongolians have much nicer bodies than most white men. Compare the firm-knit silken skin of the Burman, which does not wrinkle at all till he is past forty, and then merely withers up like a piece of dry leather, with the coarse-grained, flabby, sagging skin of the white man. The white man has lank ugly hair growing down his legs and the backs of his arms and in an ugly patch on his chest. The Burman has only a tuft or two of stiff black hair at the appropriate places; for the rest he is quite hairless and is usually beardless as well. The white man almost always goes bald, the Burman seldom or never. The Burman's teeth are perfect, though generally discoloured by betel juice, the white man's teeth invariably decay. The white man is generally ill-shaped, and when he grows fat he bulges in improbable places; the Mongol has beautiful bones and in old age he is almost as shapely as in youth. Admittedly the white races throw up a few individuals who for a few years are supremely beautiful; but on the whole, say what you will, they are far less comely than Orientals. But it was not of this that I was thinking when I found the English 'lower classes' so much more repellant than Burmese 'natives'. I was still thinking in terms of my early-acquired class-prejudice. When I was not much past twenty I was attached for a short time to a British regiment. Of course I admired and liked the private soldiers as any youth of twenty would admire and like hefty, cheery youths five years older than himself with the medals of the Great War on their chests. And yet, after all, they faintly repelled me; they were 'common people' and I did not care to be too close to them. In the hot mornings when the company marched down the road, myself in the rear with one of the junior subalterns, the steam of those hundred sweating bodies in front made my stomach turn. And this, you observe, was pure prejudice. For a soldier is probably as inoffensive, physically, as it is possible for a male white person to be. He is generally young, he is nearly always healthy from fresh air and exercise, and a rigorous discipline compels him to be clean. But I could not see it like that. All I knew was that it was *lower-class* sweat that I was smelling, and the thought of it made me sick.

When later on I got rid of my class-prejudice, or part of it, it was in a roundabout way and by a process that took several years. The thing that changed my attitude to the class-issue was something only indirectly connected with it—something almost irrelevant.

I was in the Indian Police five years, and by the end of that time I hated the imperialism I was serving with a bitterness which I probably cannot make clear. In the free air of England that kind of thing is not fully intelligible. In order to hate imperialism you have got to be part of it. Seen from the outside the British rule in India appears—indeed, it *is*—benevolent and even necessary; and so no doubt are the French rule in Morocco and the Dutch rule in Borneo, for people usually govern foreigners better than they govern themselves.

But it is not possible to be a part of such a system without recognizing it as an unjustifiable tyranny. Even the thickest-skinned Anglo-Indian is aware of this. Every 'native' face he sees in the street brings home to him his monstrous intrusion. And the majority of Anglo-Indians, intermittently at least, are not nearly so complacent about their position as people in England believe. From the most unexpected people, from gin-pickled old scoundrels high up in the Government service, I have heard some such remark as: 'Of course we've no right in this blasted country at all. Only now we're here for God's sake let's stay here.' The truth is that no modern man, in his heart of hearts, believes that it is right to invade a foreign country and hold the population down by force. Foreign oppression is a much more obvious, understandable evil than economic oppression. Thus in England we tamely admit to being robbed in order to keep half a million worthless idlers in luxury, but we would fight to the last man sooner than be ruled by Chinamen; similarly, people who live on unearned dividends without a single qualm of conscience, see clearly enough that it is wrong to go and lord it in a foreign country where you are not wanted. The result is that every Anglo-Indian is haunted by a sense of guilt which he usually conceals as best he can, because there is no freedom of speech, and merely to be overheard making a seditious remark may damage his career. All over India there are Englishmen who secretly loathe the system of which they are part; and just occasionally, when they are quite certain of being in the right company, their hidden bitterness overflows. I remember a night I spent on the train with a man in the Educational Service, a stranger to myself whose name I never discovered. It was too hot to sleep and we spent the night in talking. Half an hour's cautious questioning decided each of us that the other was 'safe'; and then for hours, while the train jolted slowly through the pitch-black night, sitting up in our bunks with bottles of beer handy, we damned the British Empire—damned it from the inside, intelligently and intimately. It did us both good. But we had been speaking forbidden things, and in the haggard morning light when the train crawled into Mandalay, we parted as guiltily as any adulterous couple.

So far as my observation goes nearly all Anglo-Indian officials have moments when their conscience troubles them. The exceptions are men who are doing something which is demonstrably useful and would still have to be done whether the British were in India or not:

forest officers, for instance, and doctors and engineers. But I was in
the police, which is to say that I was part of the actual machinery of
despotism. Moreover, in the police you see the dirty work of Empire
at close quarters, and there is an appreciable difference between doing
dirty work and merely profiting by it. Most people approve of capital
punishment, but most people wouldn't do the hangman's job. Even
the other Europeans in Burma slightly looked down on the police
because of the brutal work they had to do. I remember once when
I was inspecting a police station, an American missionary whom
I knew fairly well came in for some purpose or other. Like most
Nonconformist missionaries he was a complete ass but quite a good
fellow. One of my native sub-inspectors was bullying a suspect
(I described this scene in *Burmese Days*). The American watched it,
and then turning to me said thoughtfully, 'I wouldn't care to have your
job.' It made me horribly ashamed. So *that* was the kind of job I had!
Even an ass of an American missionary, a teetotal cock-virgin from
the Middle West, had the right to look down on me and pity me! But
I should have felt the same shame even if there had been no one to
bring it home to me. I had begun to have an indescribable loathing of
the whole machinery of so-called justice. Say what you will, our criminal law (far more humane, by the way, in India than in England) is
a horrible thing. It needs very insensitive people to administer it. The
wretched prisoners squatting in the reeking cages of the lock-ups, the
grey cowed faces of the long-term convicts, the scarred buttocks of
the men who had been flogged with bamboos, the women and children howling when their menfolk were led away under arrest—things
like these are beyond bearing when you are in any way directly responsible for them. I watched a man hanged once; it seemed to me worse
than a thousand murders. I never went into a jail without feeling
(most visitors to jails feel the same) that my place was on the other
side of the bars. I thought then—I think now, for that matter—that
the worst criminal who ever walked is morally superior to a hanging
judge. But of course I had to keep these notions to myself, because of
the almost utter silence that is imposed on every Englishman in the
East. In the end I worked out an anarchistic theory that all government is evil, that the punishment always does more harm than the
crime and that people can be trusted to behave decently if only you
will let them alone. This of course was sentimental nonsense. I see
now as I did not see then, that it is always necessary to protect peaceful

people from violence. In any state of society where crime can be profitable you have got to have a harsh criminal law and administer it ruthlessly; the alternative is Al Capone. But the feeling that punishment is evil arises inescapably in those who have to administer it. I should expect to find that even in England many policemen, judges, prison warders, and the like are haunted by a secret horror of what they do. But in Burma it was a double oppression that we were committing. Not only were we hanging people and putting them in jail and so forth; we were doing it in the capacity of unwanted foreign invaders. The Burmese themselves never really recognized our jurisdiction. The thief whom we put in prison did not think of himself as a criminal justly punished, he thought of himself as the victim of a foreign conqueror. The thing that was done to him was merely a wanton meaningless cruelty. His face, behind the stout teak bars of the lock-up and the iron bars of the jail, said so clearly. And unfortunately I had not trained myself to be indifferent to the expression of the human face.

When I came home on leave in 1927 I was already half determined to throw up my job, and one sniff of English air decided me. I was not going back to be a part of that evil despotism. But I wanted much more than merely to escape from my job. For five years I had been part of an oppressive system, and it had left me with a bad conscience. Innumerable remembered faces—faces of prisoners in the dock, of men waiting in the condemned cells, of subordinates I had bullied and aged peasants I had snubbed, of servants and coolies I had hit with my fist in moments of rage (nearly everyone does these things in the East, at any rate occasionally: Orientals can be very provoking)— haunted me intolerably. I was conscious of an immense weight of guilt that I had got to expiate. I suppose that sounds exaggerated; but if you do for five years a job that you thoroughly disapprove of, you will probably feel the same. I had reduced everything to the simple theory that the oppressed are always right and the oppressors are always wrong: a mistaken theory, but the natural result of being one of the oppressors yourself. I felt that I had got to escape not merely from imperialism but from every form of man's dominion over man. I wanted to submerge myself, to get right down among the oppressed, to be one of them and on their side against their tyrants. And, chiefly because I had had to think everything out in solitude, I had carried my hatred of oppression to extraordinary lengths. At that time failure seemed to me to be the only virtue. Every suspicion of self-advancement, even to 'succeed' in life to the extent of making a few hundreds a year, seemed to me spiritually ugly, a species of bullying.

It was in this way that my thoughts turned towards the English working class. It was the first time that I had ever been really aware of the working class, and to begin with it was only because they supplied an analogy. They were the symbolic victims of injustice, playing the same part in England as the Burmese played in Burma. In Burma the issue had been quite simple. The whites were up and the blacks were down, and therefore as a matter of course one's sympathy was with the blacks. I now realized that there was no need to go as far as Burma to find tyranny and exploitation. Here in England, down under one's feet, were the submerged working class, suffering miseries which in their different way were as bad as any an Oriental ever knows. The word 'unemployment' was on everyone's lips. That was more or less new to me, after Burma, but the drivel which the middle classes were still talking ('These unemployed are all unemployables', etc., etc.) failed to deceive me. I often wonder whether that kind of stuff deceives even the fools who utter it. On the other hand I had at that time no interest in Socialism or any other economic theory. It seemed to me then—it sometimes seems to me now, for that matter—that economic injustice will stop the moment we want it to stop, and no sooner, and if we genuinely want it to stop the method adopted hardly matters.

But I knew nothing about working-class conditions. I had read the unemployment figures but I had no notion of what they implied; above all, I did not know the essential fact that 'respectable' poverty is always the worst. The frightful doom of a decent working man suddenly thrown on the streets after a lifetime of steady work, his agonized struggles against economic laws which he does not understand, the disintegration of families, the corroding sense of shame—all this was outside the range of my experience. When I thought of poverty I thought of it in terms of brute starvation. Therefore my mind turned immediately towards the extreme cases, the social outcasts: tramps, beggars, criminals, prostitutes. These were 'the lowest of the low', and these were the people with whom I wanted to get in contact. What I profoundly wanted, at that time, was to find some way of getting out of the respectable world altogether. I meditated upon it a great deal, I even planned parts of it in detail; how one could sell everything, give everything away, change one's name and start out with no money and nothing but the clothes one stood up in. But in real life nobody ever does that kind of thing; apart from the relatives and friends who have to be considered, it is doubtful whether an educated man *could* do it if there were any other course open to him. But at least I could go among these people, see what their lives were like and feel myself temporarily part of their world. Once I had been among them and accepted by them, I should have touched bottom, and—this is what I felt: I was aware even then that it was irrational—part of my guilt would drop from me.

I thought it over and decided what I would do. I would go suitably disguised to Limehouse and Whitechapel and such places and sleep in common lodging-houses and pal up with dock labourers, street hawkers, derelict people, beggars, and, if possible, criminals. And I would find out about tramps and how you got in touch with them and what was the proper procedure for entering the casual ward; and then, when I felt that I knew the ropes well enough, I would go on the road myself.

At the start it was not easy. It meant masquerading and I have no talent for acting. I cannot, for instance, disguise my accent, at any rate not for more than a very few minutes. I imagined—notice the frightful class-consciousness of the Englishman—that I should be spotted as a 'gentleman' the moment I opened my mouth; so I had a hard luck story ready in case I should be questioned. I got hold of the right kind of clothes and dirtied them in appropriate places. I am a difficult person to disguise, being abnormally tall, but I did at least know what a tramp looks like. (How few people do know this, by the way! Look at any picture of a tramp in *Punch*. They are always twenty years out of date.) One evening, having made ready at a friend's house, I set out and wandered eastward till I landed up at a common lodging-house in Limehouse Causeway. It was a dark, dirty-looking place. I knew it was a common lodging-house by the sign 'Good Beds for Single Men' in the window. Heavens, how I had to screw up my courage before I went in! It seems ridiculous now. But you see I was still half afraid of the working class. I wanted to get in touch with them, I even wanted to become one of them, but I still thought of them as alien and dangerous; going into the dark doorway of that common lodging-house seemed to me like going down into some dreadful subterranean place—a sewer full of rats, for instance. I went in fully expecting a fight. The people would spot that I was not one of themselves and immediately infer that I had come to spy on them; and then they would set upon me and throw me out—that was what I expected. I felt that I had got to do it, but I did not enjoy the prospect.

Inside the door a man in shirt-sleeves appeared from somewhere or other. This was the 'deputy', and I told him that I wanted a bed for the night. My accent did not make him stare, I noticed; he merely demanded ninepence and then showed me the way to a frowsy firelit kitchen underground. There were stevedores and navvies and a few sailors sitting about and playing draughts and drinking tea. They barely glanced at me as I entered. But this was Saturday night and a hefty young stevedore was drunk and was reeling about the room. He turned, saw me, and lurched towards me with broad red face thrust out and a dangerous-looking fishy gleam in his eyes. I stiffened myself. So the fight was coming already! The next moment the stevedore collapsed on my chest and flung his arms round my neck. "Ave a cup of tea, chum!' he cried tearfully; ''ave a cup of tea!'

I had a cup of tea. It was a kind of baptism. After that my fears vanished. Nobody questioned me, nobody showed offensive curiosity; everybody was polite and gentle and took me utterly for granted. I stayed two or three days in that common lodging-house, and a few weeks later, having picked up a certain amount of information about the habits of destitute people, I went on the road for the first time.

I have described all this in *Down and Out in Paris and London* (nearly all the incidents described there actually happened, though they have been rearranged) and I do not want to repeat it. Later I went on the road for much longer periods, sometimes from choice, sometimes from necessity. I have lived in common lodging-houses for months together. But it is that first expedition that sticks most vividly in my mind, because of the strangeness of it—the strangeness of being at last down there among 'the lowest of the low', and on terms of utter equality with working-class people. A tramp, it is true, is not a typical working-class person; still, when you are among tramps you are at any rate merged in one section—one sub-caste—of the working class, a thing which so far as I know can happen to you in no other way. For several days I wandered through the northern outskirts of London with an Irish tramp. I was his mate, temporarily. We shared the same cell at night, and he told me the history of his life and I told him a fictitious history of mine, and we took it in turns to beg at likely-looking houses and divided up the proceeds. I was very happy. Here I was, among 'the lowest of the low', at the bedrock of the Western world! The class-bar was down, or seemed to be down. And down there in the squalid and, as a matter of fact, horribly boring sub-world of the tramp I had a feeling of release, of adventure, which seems absurd when I look back, but which was sufficiently vivid at the time.

X

BUT unfortunately you do not solve the class problem by making friends with tramps. At most you get rid of some of your own class-prejudice by doing so.

Tramps, beggars, criminals, and social outcasts generally are very exceptional beings and no more typical of the working class as a whole than, say, the literary intelligentsia are typical of the bourgeoisie. It is quite easy to be on terms of intimacy with a foreign 'intellectual', but it is not at all easy to be on terms of intimacy with an ordinary respectable foreigner of the middle class. How many Englishmen have seen the inside of an ordinary French bourgeois family, for instance? Probably it would be quite impossible to do so, short of marrying into it. And it is rather similar with the English working class. Nothing is easier than to be bosom pals with a pickpocket, if you know where to look for him; but it is very difficult to be bosom pals with a bricklayer.

But why is it so easy to be on equal terms with social outcasts? People have often said to me, 'Surely when you are with the tramps they don't really accept you as one of themselves? Surely they notice that you are different—notice the difference of accent?' etc., etc. As a matter of fact, a fair proportion of tramps, well over a quarter I should say, notice nothing of the kind. To begin with, many people have no ear for accent and judge you entirely by your clothes. I was often struck by this fact when I was begging at back doors. Some people were obviously surprised by my 'educated' accent, others completely failed to notice it; I was dirty and ragged and that was all they saw. Again, tramps come from all parts of the British Isles and the variation in English accents is enormous. A tramp is used to hearing all kinds of accents among his mates, some of them so strange to him that he can hardly understand them, and a man from, say, Cardiff or Durham or Dublin does not necessarily know which of the south English accents is an 'educated' one. In any case men with 'educated' accents, though rare among tramps, are not unknown. But even when tramps are aware that you are of different origin from themselves, it does not necessarily alter their attitude. From their point of view all that matters is that you, like themselves, are 'on the bum'. And in that world it is not done to ask too many questions. You can tell people the history of your life if you choose, and most tramps do so on the smallest provocation, but you are under no compulsion to tell it and whatever story you tell will be accepted without question. Even a bishop could be at home among tramps if he wore the right clothes; and even if they knew he was a bishop it might not make any difference, provided that they also knew or believed that he was genuinely destitute. Once you are in that world and seemingly *of* it, it hardly matters what you have been in the past. It is a sort of world-within-a-world where everyone is equal, a small squalid democracy—perhaps the nearest thing to a democracy that exists in England.

But when you come to the normal working class the position is totally different. To begin with, there is no short cut into their midst. You can become a tramp simply by putting on the right clothes and going to the nearest casual ward, but you can't become a navvy or a coal-miner. You couldn't get a job as a navvy or a coal-miner even if you were equal to the work. Via Socialist politics you can get in touch with the working-class intelligentsia, but they are hardly more typical than tramps or burglars. For the rest you can only mingle with the working class by staying in their houses as a lodger, which always has a dangerous resemblance to 'slumming'. For some months I lived entirely in coal-miners' houses. I ate my meals with the family, I washed at the kitchen sink, I shared bedrooms with miners, drank beer with them, played darts with them, talked to them by the hour together. But though I was among them, and I hope and trust they did not find me a nuisance, I was not one of them, and they knew it even better than I did. However much you like them, however interesting you find their conversation, there is always that accursed itch of class-difference, like the pea under the princess's mattress. It is not a question of dislike or distaste, only of *difference*, but it is enough to make real intimacy impossible. Even with miners who described themselves as Communists I found that it needed tactful manoeuvrings to prevent them from calling me 'sir'; and all of them, except in moments of great animation, softened their northern accents for my benefit. I liked them and hoped they liked me; but I went among them as a foreigner, and both of us were aware of it. Whichever way you turn this curse of class-difference confronts you like a wall of stone. Or rather it is not so much like a stone wall as the plate-glass pane of an aquarium; it is so easy to pretend that it isn't there, and so impossible to get through it.

Unfortunately it is nowadays the fashion to pretend that the glass is penetrable. Of course everyone knows that class-prejudice exists, but at the same time everyone claims that *he*, in some mysterious way, is exempt from it. Snobbishness is one of those vices which we can discern in everyone else but never in ourselves. Not only the *croyant et pratiquant* Socialist, but every 'intellectual' takes it as a matter of course that *he* at least is outside the class-racket; *he*, unlike his neighbours, can see through the absurdity of wealth, ranks, titles, etc., etc. 'I'm not a snob' is nowadays a kind of universal *credo*. Who is there who has not jeered at the House of Lords, the military caste, the Royal Family, the public schools, the huntin' and shootin' people, the old ladies in Cheltenham boarding-houses, the horrors of 'county' society, and the social hierarchy generally? To do so has become an automatic gesture. You notice this particularly in novels. Every novelist of serious pretensions adopts an ironic attitude towards his upper-class characters. Indeed when a novelist has to put a definitely upper-class person—a duke or a baronet or whatnot—into one of his stories he guys him more or less instinctively. There is an important subsidiary cause of this in the poverty of the modern upper-class dialect. The speech of 'educated' people is now so lifeless and characterless that a novelist can do nothing with it. By far the easiest way of making it amusing is to burlesque it, which means pretending that every upper-class person is an ineffectual ass. The trick is imitated from novelist to novelist, and in the end becomes almost a reflex action.

And yet all the while, at the bottom of his heart, everyone knows that this is humbug. We all rail against class-distinctions, but very few people seriously want to abolish them. Here you come upon the important fact that every revolutionary opinion draws part of its strength from a secret conviction that nothing can be changed.

If you want a good illustration of this, it is worth studying the novels and plays of John Galsworthy,* keeping one eye on their chronology. Galsworthy is a very fine specimen of the thin-skinned, tear-in-the-eye, pre-war humanitarian. He starts out with a morbid pity-complex which extends even to thinking that every married woman is an angel chained to a satyr. He is in a perpetual quiver of indignation over the sufferings of overworked clerks, of under-paid farm hands, of fallen women, of criminals, of prostitutes, of animals. The world, as he sees it in his earlier books (*The Man of Property*,

Justice, etc.), is divided into oppressors and oppressed, with the oppressors sitting on top like some monstrous stone idol which all the dynamite in the world cannot overthrow. But is it so certain that he really wants it overthrown? On the contrary, in his fight against an immovable tyranny he is upheld by the consciousness that it *is* immovable. When things happen unexpectedly and the world-order which he has known begins to crumble, he feels somewhat differently about it. So, having set out to be the champion of the underdog against tyranny and injustice, he ends by advocating (*vide The Silver Spoon*) that the English working class, to cure their economic ills, shall be deported to the colonies like batches of cattle. If he had lived ten years longer he would quite probably have arrived at some genteel version of Fascism. This is the inevitable fate of the sentimentalist. All his opinions change into their opposites at the first brush of reality.

The same streak of soggy half-baked insincerity runs through all 'advanced' opinion. Take the question of imperialism, for instance. Every left-wing 'intellectual' is, as a matter of course, an anti-imperialist. He claims to be outside the empire-racket as automatically and self-righteously as he claims to be outside the class-racket. Even the right-wing 'intellectual', who is not definitely in revolt against British imperialism, pretends to regard it with a sort of amused detachment. It is so easy to be witty about the British Empire. The White Man's Burden and 'Rule, Britannia' and Kipling's novels and Anglo-Indian bores—who could even mention such things without a snigger? And is there any cultured person who has not at least once in his life made a joke about that old Indian havildar who said that if the British left India there would not be a rupee or a virgin left between Peshawar and Delhi (or wherever it was)? That is the attitude of the typical left-winger towards imperialism, and a thoroughly flabby, boneless attitude it is. For in the last resort, the only important question is, Do you want the British Empire to hold together or do you want it to disintegrate? And at the bottom of his heart no Englishman, least of all the kind of person who is witty about Anglo–Indian colonels, does want it to disintegrate. For, apart from any other consideration, the high standard of life we enjoy in England depends upon our keeping a tight hold on the Empire, particularly the tropical portions of it such as India and Africa. Under the capitalist system, in order that England may live in comparative comfort, a hundred million Indians must live on the verge of starvation—an evil state of affairs, but you acquiesce in it every time you step into a taxi or eat a plate of straw-berries and cream. The alternative is to throw the Empire overboard and reduce England to a cold and unimportant little island where we should all have to work very hard and live mainly on herrings and potatoes. That is the very last thing that any left-winger wants. Yet the left-winger continues to feel that he has no moral responsibility for imperialism. He is perfectly ready to accept the products of Empire and to save his soul by sneering at the people who hold the Empire together.

It is at this point that one begins to grasp the unreality of most people's attitude towards the class question. So long as it is merely a question of ameliorating the worker's lot, every decent person is agreed. Take a coal-miner, for example. Everyone, barring fools and scoundrels, would *like* to see the miner better off. If, for instance, the miner could ride to the coal face in a comfortable trolley instead of crawling on his hands and knees, if he could work a three-hour shift instead of seven and a half hours, if he could live in a decent house with five bedrooms and a bathroom and have ten pounds a week wages—splendid! Moreover, anyone who uses his brain knows per-fectly well that this is within the range of possibility. The world, potentially at least, is immensely rich; develop it as it might be devel-oped, and we could all live like princes, supposing that we wanted to. And to a very superficial glance the social side of the question looks equally simple. In a sense it is true that almost everyone would like to see class-distinctions abolished. Obviously this perpetual uneasiness between man and man, from which we suffer in modern England, is a curse and a nuisance. Hence the temptation to believe that it can be shouted out of existence with a few scoutmasterish bellows of good-will. Stop calling me 'sir', you chaps! Surely we're all men? Let's pal up and get our shoulders to the wheel and remember that we're all equal, and what the devil does it matter if I know what kind of ties to wear and you don't, and I drink my soup comparatively quietly and you drink yours with the noise of water going down a waste-pipe—and so on and so on and so on; all of it the most pernicious rubbish, but quite alluring when it is suitably expressed.

But unfortunately you get no further by merely wishing class-distinctions away. More exactly, it *is* necessary to wish them away, but your wish has no efficacy unless you grasp what it involves. The fact that has got to be faced is that to abolish class-distinctions means abolishing a part of yourself. Here am I, a typical member of the middle class. It is easy for me to say that I want to get rid of class-distinctions, but nearly everything I think and do is a result of class-distinctions. All my notions—notions of good and evil, of pleasant and unpleasant, of funny and serious, of ugly and beautiful—are essentially *middle-class* notions; my taste in books and food and clothes, my sense of honour, my table manners, my turns of speech, my accent, even the characteristic movements of my body, are the products of a special kind of upbringing and a special niche about half-way up the social hierarchy. When I grasp this I grasp that it is no use clapping a proletarian on the back and telling him that he is as good a man as I am; if I want real contact with him, I have got to make an effort for which very likely I am unprepared. For to get outside the class-racket I have got to suppress not merely my private snobbishness, but most of my other tastes and prejudices as well. I have got to alter myself so completely that at the end I should hardly be recognizable as the same person. What is involved is not merely the amelioration of working-class conditions, nor an avoidance of the more stupid forms of snobbery, but a complete abandonment of the upper-class and middle-class attitude to life. And whether I say Yes or No probably depends upon the extent to which I grasp what is demanded of me.

Many people, however, imagine that they can abolish class-distinctions without making any uncomfortable change in their own habits and 'ideology'. Hence the eager class-breaking activities which one can see in progress on all sides. Everywhere there are people of goodwill who quite honestly believe that they are working for the overthrow of class-distinctions. The middle-class Socialist enthuses over the proletariat and runs 'summer schools' where the proletarian and the repentant bourgeois are supposed to fall upon one another's necks and be brothers for ever; and the bourgeois visitors come away saying how wonderful and inspiring it has all been (the proletarian ones come away saying something different). And then there is the outer-suburban creeping Jesus, a hangover from the William Morris period, but still surprisingly common, who goes about saying 'Why must we level *down*? Why not level *up*?' and proposes to level the working class 'up' (up to his own standard) by means of hygiene, fruit-juice, birth-control, poetry, etc. Even the Duke of York (now King George VI) runs a yearly camp where public-school boys and boys from the slums are supposed to mix on exactly equal terms, and *do* mix for the time being, rather like the animals in one of those 'Happy Family' cages where a dog, a cat, two ferrets, a rabbit, and three canaries preserve an armed truce while the showman's eye is on them.

All such deliberate, conscious efforts at class-breaking are, I am convinced, a very serious mistake. Sometimes they are merely futile, but where they do show a definite result it is usually to *intensify* class-prejudice. This, if you come to think of it, is only what might be expected. You have forced the pace and set up an uneasy, unnatural equality between class and class; the resultant friction brings to the surface all kinds of feelings that might otherwise have remained buried, perhaps for ever. As I said apropos of Galsworthy, the opinions of the sentimentalist change into their opposites at the first touch of reality. Scratch the average pacifist and you find a jingo. The middle-class I.L.P.'er* and the bearded fruit-juice drinker are all for a classless society so long as they see the proletariat through the wrong end of the telescope; force them into any *real* contact with a proletarian—let them get into a fight with a drunken fish-porter on Saturday night, for instance—and they are capable of swinging back to the most ordinary middle-class snobbishness. Most middle-class Socialists, however, are very unlikely to get into fights with drunken fish-porters; when they do make a genuine contact with the working class, it is usually with the working-class intelligentsia. But the working-class intelligentsia is sharply divisible into two different types. There is the type who remains working-class—who goes on working as a mechanic or a dock-labourer or whatever it may be and does not bother to change his working-class accent and habits, but who 'improves his mind' in his spare time and works for the I.L.P. or the Communist Party; and there is the type who does alter his way of life, at least externally, and who by means of State scholarships succeeds in climbing into the middle class. The first is one of the finest types of man we have. I can think of some I have met whom not even the most hidebound Tory could help liking and admiring. The other type, with exceptions—D. H. Lawrence, for example—is less admirable.

To begin with, it is a pity, though it is a natural result of the scholarship system, that the proletariat should tend to interpenetrate the middle class via the literary intelligentsia. For it is not easy to crash your way into the literary intelligentsia if you happen to be a decent human being. The modern English literary world, at any rate the high-brow section of it, is a sort of poisonous jungle where only weeds can flourish. It is just possible to be a literary gent and to keep your decency if you are a definitely *popular* writer—a writer of detective stories, for instance; but to be a highbrow, with a footing in the snootier magazines, means delivering yourself over to horrible campaigns of wire-pulling and backstairs-crawling. In the highbrow world you 'get on', if you 'get on' at all, not so much by your literary ability as by being the life and soul of cocktail parties and kissing the bums of verminous little lions. This, then, is the world that most readily opens its doors to the proletarian who is climbing out of his own class. The 'clever' boy of a working-class family, the sort of boy who wins scholarships and is obviously not fitted for a life of manual labour, may find other ways of rising into the class above—a slightly different type, for instance, rises via Labour Party politics—but the literary way is by far the most usual. Literary London now teems with young men who are of proletarian origin and have been educated by means of scholarships. Many of them are very disagreeable people, quite unrepresentative of their class, and it is most unfortunate that when a person of bourgeois origin does succeed in meeting a proletarian face to face on equal terms, this is the type he most commonly meets. For the result is to drive the bourgeois, who has idealized the proletariat so long as he knew nothing about them, back into frenzies of snobbishness. The process is sometimes very comic to watch, if you happen to be watching it from the outside. The poor well-meaning bourgeois, eager to embrace his proletarian brother, leaps forward with open arms; and only a little while later he is in retreat, minus a borrowed five pounds and exclaiming dolefully, 'But, dash it, the fellow's not a gentleman!'

The thing that disconcerts the bourgeois in a contact of this kind is to find certain of his own professions being taken seriously. I have pointed out that the left-wing opinions of the average 'intellectual' are mainly spurious. From pure imitativeness he jeers at things which in fact he believes in. As one example out of many, take the public-school code of honour, with its 'team spirit' and 'Don't hit a man when he's down', and all the rest of that familiar bunkum. Who has not laughed at it? Who, calling himself an 'intellectual', would dare *not* to laugh at it? But it is a bit different when you meet somebody who laughs at it *from the outside*; just as we spend our lives in abusing

England but grow very angry when we hear a foreigner saying exactly the same things. No one has been more amusing about the public schools than 'Beachcomber' of the *Express*. He laughs, quite rightly, at the ridiculous code which makes cheating at cards the worst of all sins. But would 'Beachcomber' like it if one of his own friends was caught cheating at cards? I doubt it. It is only when you meet someone of a different culture from yourself that you begin to realize what your own beliefs really are. If you are a bourgeois 'intellectual' you too readily imagine that you have somehow become unbourgeois because you find it easy to laugh at patriotism and the C. of E. and the Old School Tie and Colonel Blimp and all the rest of it. But from the point of view of the proletarian 'intellectual', who at least by origin is genuinely outside the bourgeois culture, your resemblances to Colonel Blimp may be more important than your differences. Very likely he looks upon you and Colonel Blimp as practically equivalent persons; and in a way he is right, though neither you nor Colonel Blimp would admit it. So that the meeting of proletarian and bourgeois, when they do succeed in meeting, is not always the embrace of long-lost brothers; too often it is the clash of alien cultures which can only meet in war.

I have been looking at this from the point of view of the bourgeois who finds his secret beliefs challenged and is driven back to a frightened conservatism. But one has also got to consider the antagonism that is aroused in the proletarian 'intellectual'. By his own efforts and sometimes with frightful agonies he has struggled out of his own class into another where he expects to find a wider freedom and a greater intellectual refinement; and all he finds, very often, is a sort of hollowness, a deadness, a lack of any warm human feeling—of any real life whatever. Sometimes the bourgeoisie seem to him just dummies with money and water in their veins instead of blood. This at any rate is what he *says*, and almost any young highbrow of proletarian origin will spin you this line of talk. Hence the 'proletarian' cant from which we now suffer. Everyone knows, or ought to know by this time, how it runs: the bourgeoisie are 'dead' (a favourite word of abuse nowadays and very effective because meaningless), bourgeois culture is bankrupt, bourgeois 'values' are despicable, and so on and so forth; if you want examples, see any number of the *Left Review** or any of the younger Communist writers such as Alec Brown, Philip Henderson, etc. The sincerity of much of this is suspect, but D. H. Lawrence, who was sincere, whatever else he may not have been, expresses the same thought over and over again. It is curious how he harps upon that idea that the English bourgeoisie are all *dead*, or at least gelded. Mellors, the gamekeeper in *Lady Chatterley's Lover* (really Lawrence himself), has had the opportunity to get out of his own class and does not particularly want to return to it, because English working people have various 'disagreeable habits'; on the other hand the bourgeoisie, with whom he has also mixed to some extent, seem to him half dead, a race of eunuchs. Lady Chatterley's husband, symbolically, is impotent in the actual physical sense. And then there is the poem about the young man (once again Lawrence himself) who 'got up to the top of the tree' but came down saying:

> Oh you've got to be like a monkey
> if you climb up the tree!
> You've no more use for the solid earth
> and the lad you used to be.
> You sit in the boughs and gibber
> with superiority.
> They all gibber and gibber and chatter,
> and never a word they say
> comes really out of their guts, lad,
> they make it up half-way....
> I tell you something's been done to 'em,
> to the pullets up above;
> there's not a cock bird among 'em, etc., etc.

You could hardly have it in plainer terms than that. Possibly by the people at 'the top of the tree' Lawrence only means the real bourgeoisie, those in the £2000 a year class and over, but I doubt it. More probably he means everyone who is more or less within the bourgeois culture—everyone who was brought up with a mincing accent and in a house where there were one or two servants. And at this point you realize the danger of the 'proletarian' cant—realize, I mean, the terrible antagonism that it is capable of arousing. For when you come to such an accusation as this, you are up against a blank wall. Lawrence tells me that because I have been to a public school I am a eunuch. Well, what about it? I can produce medical evidence to the contrary, but what good will that do? Lawrence's condemnation remains. If you tell me I am a scoundrel I may mend my ways, but if you tell me I am a eunuch you are tempting me to hit back in any way that seems feasible. If you want to make an enemy of a man, tell him that his ills are incurable.

This then is the net result of most meetings between proletarian and bourgeois: they lay bare a real antagonism which is intensified by the 'proletarian' cant, itself the product of forced contacts between class and class. The only sensible procedure is to go slow and not force the pace. If you secretly think of yourself as a gentleman and as such the superior of the greengrocer's errand boy, it is far better to say so than to tell lies about it. Ultimately you have got to drop your snobbishness, but it is fatal to pretend to drop it before you are really ready to do so.

Meanwhile one can observe on every side that dreary phenomenon, the middle-class person who is an ardent Socialist at twenty-five and a sniffish Conservative at thirty-five. In a way his recoil is natural enough—at any rate, one can see how his thoughts run. Perhaps a classless society *doesn't* mean a beatific state of affairs in which we shall all go on behaving exactly as before except that there will be no class-hatred and no snobbishness; perhaps it means a bleak world in which all our ideals, our codes, our tastes—our 'ideology', in fact—will have no meaning. Perhaps this class-breaking business isn't so simple as it looked! On the contrary, it is a wild ride into the darkness, and it may be that at the end of it the smile will be on the face of the tiger. With loving though slightly patronizing smiles we set out to greet our proletarian brothers, and behold! our proletarian brothers—in so far as we understand them—are not asking for our greetings, they are asking us to commit suicide. When the bourgeois sees it in *that* form he takes to flight, and if his flight is rapid enough it may carry him to Fascism.

XI

MEANWHILE what about Socialism?

It hardly needs pointing out that at this moment we are in a very serious mess, so serious that even the dullest-witted people find it difficult to remain unaware of it. We are living in a world in which nobody is free, in which hardly anybody is secure, in which it is almost impossible to be honest and to remain alive. For enormous blocks of the working class the conditions of life are such as I have described in the opening chapters of this book, and there is no chance of those conditions showing any fundamental improvement. The very best the English working class can hope for is an occasional temporary decrease in unemployment when this or that industry is artificially stimulated by, for instance, rearmament. Even the middle classes, for the first time in their history, are feeling the pinch. They have not known actual hunger yet, but more and more of them find themselves floundering in a sort of deadly net of frustration in which it is harder and harder to persuade yourself that you are either happy, active, or useful. Even the lucky ones at the top, the real bourgeoisie, are haunted periodically by a consciousness of the miseries below, and still more by fears of the menacing future. And this is merely a preliminary stage, in a country still rich with the loot of a hundred years. Presently there may be coming God knows what horrors—horrors of which, in this sheltered island, we have not even a traditional knowledge.

And all the while everyone who uses his brain knows that Socialism, as a world-system and wholeheartedly applied, is a way out. It would at least ensure our getting enough to eat even if it deprived us of everything else. Indeed, from one point of view, Socialism is such elementary common sense that I am sometimes amazed that it has not established itself already. The world is a raft sailing through space with, potentially, plenty of provisions for everybody; the idea that we must all cooperate and see to it that everyone does his fair share of the work and gets his fair share of the provisions seems so blatantly obvious that one would say that no one could possibly fail to accept it unless he had some corrupt motive for clinging to the present system. Yet the fact that we have got to face is that Socialism is *not* establishing itself. Instead of going forward, the cause of Socialism is visibly going back. At this moment Socialists almost everywhere are in retreat before the onslaught of Fascism, and events are moving at terrible speed. As I write this the Spanish Fascist forces are bombarding Madrid, and it is quite likely that before the book is printed we shall have another Fascist country to add to the list, not to mention a Fascist control of the Mediterranean which may have the effect of delivering British foreign policy into the hands of Mussolini. I do not, however, want here to discuss the wider political issues. What I am concerned with is the fact that Socialism is losing ground exactly where it ought to be gaining it. With so much in its favour—for every empty belly is an argument for Socialism—the *idea* of Socialism is less widely accepted than it was ten years ago. The average thinking person nowadays is not merely not a Socialist, he is actively hostile to Socialism. This must be due chiefly to mistaken methods of propaganda. It means that Socialism, in the form of which it is now presented to us, has about it something inherently distasteful—something that drives away the very people who ought to be flocking to its support.

A few years ago this might have seemed unimportant. It seems only yesterday that Socialists, especially orthodox Marxists, were telling me with superior smiles that Socialism was going to arrive of its own accord by some mysterious process called 'historic necessity'. Possibly that belief still lingers, but it has been shaken, to say the least of it. Hence the sudden attempts of Communists in various countries to ally themselves with democratic forces which they have been sabotaging for years past. At a moment like this it is desperately necessary to discover just *why* Socialism has failed in its appeal. And it is no use writing off the current distaste for Socialism as the product of stupidity or corrupt motives. If you want to remove that distaste you have got to understand it, which means getting inside the mind of the ordinary objector to Socialism, or at least regarding his viewpoint sympathetically. No case is really answered until it has had a fair hearing. Therefore, rather paradoxically, in order to defend Socialism it is necessary to start by attacking it.

In the last three chapters I tried to analyse the difficulties that are raised by our anachronistic class-system; I shall have to touch on that subject again, because I believe that the present intensely stupid handling of the class-issue may stampede quantities of potential Socialists into Fascism. In the chapter following this one I want to discuss certain underlying assumptions that alienate sensitive minds from

Socialism. But in the present chapter I am merely dealing with the obvious, preliminary objections—the kind of thing that the person who is not a Socialist (I don't mean the 'Where's the money to come from?' type) always starts by saying when you tax him on the subject. Some of these objections may appear frivolous or self-contradictory, but that is beside the point; I am merely discussing symptoms. Anything is relevant which helps to make clear why Socialism is not accepted. And please notice that I am arguing *for* Socialism, not *against* it. But for the moment I am *advocatus diaboli*. I am making out a case for the sort of person who is in sympathy with the fundamental aims of Socialism, who has the brains to see that Socialism would 'work', but who in practice always takes to flight when Socialism is mentioned.

Question a person of this type, and you will often get the semi-frivolous answer: 'I don't object to Socialism, but I do object to Socialists.' Logically it is a poor argument, but it carries weight with many people. As with the Christian religion, the worst advertisement for Socialism is its adherents.

The first thing that must strike any outside observer is that Socialism in its developed form is a theory confined entirely to the middle classes. The typical Socialist is not, as tremulous old ladies imagine, a ferocious-looking working man with greasy overalls and a raucous voice. He is either a youthful snob-Bolshevik who in five years' time will quite probably have made a wealthy marriage and been converted to Roman Catholicism; or, still more typically, a prim little man with a white-collar job, usually a secret teetotaller and often with vegetarian leanings, with a history of Nonconformity behind him, and, above all, with a social position which he has no intention of forfeiting. This last type is surprisingly common in Socialist parties of every shade; it has perhaps been taken over *en bloc* from the old Liberal Party. In addition to this there is the horrible—the really disquieting—prevalence of cranks wherever Socialists are gathered together. One sometimes gets the impression that the mere words 'Socialism' and 'Communism' draw towards them with magnetic force every fruit-juice drinker, nudist, sandal-wearer, sex-maniac, Quaker, 'Nature Cure' quack, pacifist, and feminist in England. One day this summer I was riding through Letchworth when the bus stopped and two dreadful-looking old men got on to it. They were both about sixty, both very short, pink, and chubby, and both hatless. One of them was obscenely bald, the other had long grey hair bobbed in the Lloyd George style. They were dressed in pistachio-coloured shirts and khaki shorts into which their huge bottoms were crammed so tightly that you could study every dimple. Their appearance created a mild stir of horror on top of the bus. The man next to me, a commercial traveller I should say, glanced at me, at them, and back again at me, and murmured 'Socialists', as who should say, 'Red Indians'. He was probably right—the I.L.P. were holding their summer school at Letchworth. But the point is that to him, as an ordinary man, a crank meant a Socialist and a Socialist meant a crank. Any Socialist, he probably felt, could be counted on to have *something* eccentric about him. And some such notion seems to exist even among Socialists themselves. For instance, I have here a prospectus from another summer school which states its terms per week and then asks me to say 'whether my diet is ordinary or vegetarian'. They take it for granted, you see, that it is necessary to ask this question. This kind of thing is by itself sufficient to alienate plenty of decent people. And their instinct is perfectly sound, for the food-crank is by definition a person willing to cut himself off from human society in hopes of adding five years on to the life of his carcase; that is, a person out of touch with common humanity.

To this you have got to add the ugly fact that most middle-class Socialists, while theoretically pining for a classless society, cling like glue to their miserable fragments of social prestige. I remember my sensations of horror on first attending an I.L.P. branch meeting in London. (It might have been rather different in the North, where the bourgeoisie are less thickly scattered.) Are *these* mingy little beasts, I thought, the champions of the working class? For every person there, male and female, bore the worst stigmata of sniffish middle-class superiority. If a real working man, a miner dirty from the pit, for instance, had suddenly walked into their midst, they would have been embarrassed, angry, and disgusted; some, I should think, would have fled holding their noses. You can see the same tendency in Socialist literature, which, even when it is not openly written *de haut en bas*, is always completely removed from the working class in idiom and manner of thought. The Coles, Webbs, Stracheys, etc., are not *exactly* proletarian writers. It is doubtful whether anything describable as proletarian literature now exists—even the *Daily Worker** is written in standard South English—but a good music-hall comedian comes nearer to producing it than any Socialist writer I can think of.

As for the technical jargon of the Communists, it is as far removed from the common speech as the language of a mathematical textbook. I remember hearing a professional Communist speaker address a working-class audience. His speech was the usual bookish stuff, full of long sentences and parentheses and 'Notwithstanding' and 'Be that as it may', besides the usual jargon of 'ideology' and 'class-consciousness' and 'proletarian solidarity' and all the rest of it. After him a Lancashire working man got up and spoke to the crowd in their own broad lingo. There was not much doubt which of the two was nearer to his audience, but I do not suppose for a moment that the Lancashire working man was an orthodox Communist.

For it must be remembered that a working man, so long as he remains a genuine working man, is seldom or never a Socialist in the complete, logically consistent sense. Very likely he votes Labour, or even Communist if he gets the chance, but his conception of Socialism is quite different from that of the book-trained Socialist higher up. To the ordinary working man, the sort you would meet in any pub on Saturday night, Socialism does not mean much more than better wages and shorter hours and nobody bossing you about. To the more revolutionary type, the type who is a hunger-marcher and is black-listed by employers, the word is a sort of rallying-cry against the forces of oppression, a vague threat of future violence. But, so far as my experience goes, no genuine working man grasps the deeper implications of Socialism. Often, in my opinion, he is a truer Socialist than the orthodox Marxist, because he does remember, what the other so often forgets, that Socialism means justice and common decency. But what he does not grasp is that Socialism cannot be narrowed down to mere economic justice and that a reform of that magnitude is bound to work immense changes in our civilization and his own way of life. His vision of the Socialist future is a vision of present society with the worst abuses left out, and with interest centring round the same things as at present—family life, the pub, football, and local politics. As for the philosophic side of Marxism, the pea-and-thimble trick with those three mysterious entities, thesis, antithesis, and synthesis, I have never met a working man who had the faintest interest in it. It is of course true that plenty of people of working-class *origin* are Socialists of the theoretical bookish type. But they are never people who have *remained* working men; they don't work with their hands, that is. They belong either to the type I mentioned in the last chapter, the type who squirms into the middle class via the literary intelligentsia, or the type who becomes a Labour M.P. or a high-up trade union official. This last type is one of the most desolating spectacles the world contains. He has been picked out to fight for his mates, and all it means to him is a soft job and the chance of 'bettering' himself. Not merely while but *by* fighting the bourgeoisie he becomes a bourgeois himself. And meanwhile it is quite possible that he has remained an orthodox Marxist. But I have yet to meet a *working* miner, steel-worker, cotton-weaver, docker, navvy, or whatnot who was 'ideologically' sound.

One of the analogies between Communism and Roman Catholicism is that only the 'educated' are completely orthodox. The most imme-diately striking thing about the English Roman Catholics—I don't mean the real Catholics, I mean the converts: Ronald Knox, Arnold Lunn *et hoc genus*—is their intense self-consciousness. Apparently they never think, certainly they never write, about anything but the fact that they *are* Roman Catholics; this single fact and the self-praise resulting from it form the entire stock-in-trade of the Catholic liter-ary man. But the really interesting thing about these people is the way in which they have worked out the supposed implications of ortho-doxy until the tiniest details of life are involved. Even the liquids you drink, apparently, can be orthodox or heretical; hence the campaigns of Chesterton, 'Beachcomber', etc., against tea and in favour of beer. According to Chesterton, tea-drinking is 'pagan', while beer-drinking is 'Christian', and coffee is 'the puritan's opium'. It is unfortunate for this theory that Catholics abound in the 'Temperance' movement and the greatest tea-boozers in the world are the Catholic Irish; but what I am interested in here is the attitude of mind that can make even food and drink an occasion for religious intolerance. A working-class Catholic would never be so absurdly consistent as that. He does not spend his time in brooding on the fact that he is a Roman Catholic, and he is not particularly conscious of being different from his non-Catholic neighbours. Tell an Irish dock-labourer in the slums of Liverpool that his cup of tea is 'pagan', and he will call you a fool. And even in more serious matters he does not always grasp the implica-tions of his faith. In the Roman Catholic homes of Lancashire you see the crucifix on the wall and the *Daily Worker* on the table. It is only the 'educated' man, especially the literary man, who knows how to be a bigot. And, *mutatis mutandis*, it is the same with Communism. The creed is never found in its pure form in a genuine proletarian.

It may be said, however, that even if the theoretical book-trained Socialist is not a working man himself, at least he is actuated by a love of the working class. He is endeavouring to shed his bourgeois status and fight on the side of the proletariat—that, obviously, must be his motive.

But is it? Sometimes I look at a Socialist—the intellectual, tract-writing type of Socialist, with his pullover, his fuzzy hair, and his Marxian quotation—and wonder what the devil his motive really *is*. It is often difficult to believe that it is a love of anybody, especially of the working class, from whom he is of all people the furthest removed. The underlying motive of many Socialists, I believe, is simply a hyper-trophied sense of order. The present state of affairs offends them not because it causes misery, still less because it makes freedom impos-sible, but because it is untidy; what they desire, basically, is to reduce the world to something resembling a chessboard. Take the plays of a lifelong Socialist like Shaw.* How much understanding or even awareness of working-class life do they display? Shaw himself declares that you can only bring a working man on the stage 'as an object of compassion'; in practice he doesn't bring him on even as that, but merely as a sort of W. W. Jacobs figure of fun—the ready-made comic East Ender, like those in *Major Barbara* and *Captain Brassbound's Conversion*. At best his attitude to the working class is the sniggering *Punch* attitude, in more serious moments (consider, for instance, the young man who symbolizes the dispossessed classes in *Misalliance*) he finds them merely contemptible and disgusting. Poverty and, what is more, the habits of mind created by poverty, are something to be abolished *from above*, by violence if necessary; perhaps even prefer-ably by violence. Hence his worship of 'great' men and appetite for dictatorships, Fascist or Communist; for to him, apparently (*vide* his remarks apropos of the Italo-Abyssinian war and the Stalin–Wells conversations), Stalin and Mussolini are almost equivalent persons. You get the same thing in a more mealy-mouthed form in Mrs Sidney Webb's autobiography, which gives, unconsciously, a most revealing picture of the high-minded Socialist slum-visitor. The truth is that, to many people calling themselves Socialists, revolution does not mean a movement of the masses with which they hope to associate themselves; it means a set of reforms which 'we', the clever ones, are going to impose upon 'them', the Lower Orders. On the other hand, it would be a mistake to regard the book-trained Socialist as a bloodless creature entirely incapable of emotion. Though seldom giving much evidence of affection for the exploited, he is perfectly capable of displaying hatred—a sort of queer, theoretical, *in vacuo* hatred—against the exploiters. Hence the grand old Socialist sport of denouncing the bourgeoisie. It is strange how easily almost any Socialist writer can lash himself into frenzies of rage against the class to which, by birth or by adoption, he himself invariably belongs. Sometimes the hatred of bourgeois habits and 'ideology' is so far-reaching that it extends even to bourgeois characters in books. According to Henri Barbusse, the characters in the novels of Proust, Gide, etc., are 'characters whom one would dearly love to have at the other side of a barricade'. 'A barricade', you observe. Judging from *Le Feu*, I should have thought Barbusse's experience of barricades had left him with a distaste for them. But the imaginary bayoneting of 'bourgeois', who presumably don't hit back, is a bit different from the real article.

The best example of bourgeois-baiting literature that I have yet come across is Mirsky's *Intelligentsia of Great Britain*. This is a very interesting and ably-written book, and it should be read by everyone who wants to understand the rise of Fascism. Mirsky (formerly Prince Mirsky) was a White Russian *émigré* who came to England and was for some years a lecturer in Russian literature at London University. Later he was converted to Communism, returned to Russia, and produced his book as a sort of 'show-up' of the British intelligentsia from a Marxist standpoint. It is a viciously malignant book, with an unmistakable note of 'Now I'm out of your reach I can say what I like about you' running all through it, and apart from a general distortion it contains some quite definite and probably intentional misrepresentation: as, for instance, when Conrad is declared to be 'no less imperialist than Kipling', and D. H. Lawrence is described as writing 'bare-bodied pornography' and as having 'succeeded in erasing all clues to his proletarian origin'—as though Lawrence had been a pork-butcher climbing into the House of Lords! This kind of thing is very disquieting when one remembers that it is addressed to a Russian audience who have no means of checking its accuracy. But what I am thinking of at the moment is the effect of such a book on the English public. Here you have a literary man of aristocratic extraction, a man who had probably never in his life spoken to a working man on anything approaching equal terms, uttering venomous screams of libel against his 'bourgeois' colleagues.

Why? So far as appearances go, from pure malignity. He is battling *against* the British intelligentsia, but what is he battling *for*? Within the book itself there is no indication. Hence the net effect of books like this is to give outsiders the impression that there is nothing in Communism except *hatred*. And here once again you come upon that queer resemblance between Communism and (convert) Roman Catholicism. If you want to find a book as evil-spirited as *The Intelligentsia of Great Britain*, the likeliest place to look is among the popular Roman Catholic apologists. You will find there the same venom and the same dishonesty, though, to do the Catholic justice, you will not usually find the same bad manners. Queer that Comrade Mirsky's spiritual brother should be Father————! The Communist and the Catholic are not saying the same thing, in a sense they are even saying opposite things, and each would gladly boil the other in oil if circumstances permitted; but from the point of view of an outsider they are very much alike.

The fact is that Socialism, *in the form in which it is now presented*, appeals chiefly to unsatisfactory or even inhuman types. On the one hand you have the warm-hearted unthinking Socialist, the typical working-class Socialist, who only wants to abolish poverty and does not always grasp what this implies. On the other hand, you have the intellectual, book-trained Socialist, who understands that it is necessary to throw our present civilization down the sink and is quite willing to do so. And this type is drawn, to begin with, entirely from the middle class, and from a rootless town-bred section of the middle class at that. Still more unfortunately, it includes—so much so that to an outsider it even appears to be composed of—the kind of people I have been discussing; the foaming denouncers of the bourgeoisie, and the more-water-in-your-beer reformers of whom Shaw is the prototype, and the astute young social-literary climbers who are Communists now, as they will be Fascists five years hence, because it is all the go, and all that dreary tribe of high-minded women and sandal-wearers and bearded fruit-juice drinkers who come flocking towards the smell of 'progress' like bluebottles to a dead cat. The ordinary decent person, who is in sympathy with the *essential* aims of Socialism, is given the impression that there is no room for his kind in any Socialist party that means business. Worse, he is driven to the cynical conclusion that Socialism is a kind of doom which is probably coming but must be staved off as long as possible. Of course, as I have suggested already, it is not strictly fair to judge a movement by its adherents; but the point is that people invariably do so, and that the popular conception of Socialism is coloured by the conception of a Socialist as a dull or disagreeable person. 'Socialism' is pictured as a state of affairs in which our more vocal Socialists would feel thoroughly at home. This does great harm to the cause. The ordinary man may not flinch from a dictatorship of the proletariat, if you offer it tactfully; offer him a dictatorship of the prigs, and he gets ready to fight.

There is a widespread feeling that any civilization in which Socialism was a reality would bear the same relation to our own as a brand-new bottle of colonial burgundy bears to a few spoonfuls of first-class Beaujolais. We live, admittedly, amid the wreck of a civilization, but it has been a great civilization in its day, and in patches it still flourishes almost undisturbed. It still has its bouquet, so to speak; whereas the imagined Socialist future, like the colonial burgundy, tastes only of iron and water. Hence the fact, which is really a disastrous one, that artists of any consequence can never be persuaded into the Socialist fold. This is particularly the case with the writer whose political opinions are more directly and obviously connected with his work than those of, say, a painter. If one faces facts one must admit that nearly everything describable as Socialist literature is dull, tasteless, and bad. Consider the situation in England at the present moment. A whole generation has grown up more or less in familiarity with the idea of Socialism; and yet the higher-water mark, so to speak, of Socialist literature is W. H. Auden, a sort of gutless Kipling,* and the even feebler poets who are associated with him. Every writer of consequence and every book worth reading is on the other side. I am willing to believe that it is otherwise in Russia—about which I know nothing, however—for presumably in post-revolutionary Russia the mere violence of events would tend to throw up a vigorous literature of sorts. But it is certain that in Western Europe Socialism has produced no literature worth having. A little while ago, when the issues were less clear, there were writers of some vitality who called themselves Socialists, but they were using the word as a vague label. Thus, if Ibsen and Zola described themselves as Socialists, it did not mean much more than that they were 'progressives', while in the case of Anatole France it meant merely that he was an anticlerical. The real Socialist writers, the propagandist writers, have always been dull, empty windbags—Shaw, Barbusse, Upton Sinclair, William Morris, Waldo Frank, etc., etc. I am not, of course, suggesting that Socialism is to be condemned because literary gents don't like it; I am not even suggesting that it ought necessarily to produce literature on its own account, though I do think it a bad sign that it has produced no songs worth singing. I am merely pointing to the fact that writers of genuine talent are usually indifferent to Socialism, and sometimes actively and mischievously hostile. And this is a disaster, not only for the writers themselves, but for the cause of Socialism, which has great need of them.

This, then, is the superficial aspect of the ordinary man's recoil from Socialism. I know the whole dreary argument very thoroughly, because I know it from both sides. Everything that I say here I have both said to ardent Socialists who were trying to convert me, and had said to me by bored non-Socialists whom I was trying to convert. The whole thing amounts to a kind of *malaise* produced by dislike of individual Socialists, especially of the cocksure Marx-quoting type. Is it childish to be influenced by that kind of thing? Is it silly? Is it even contemptible? It is all that, but the point is that *it happens*, and therefore it is important to keep it in mind.

XII

However, there is a much more serious difficulty than the local and temporary objections which I discussed in the last chapter.

Faced by the fact that intelligent people are so often on the other side, the Socialist is apt to set it down to corrupt motives (conscious or unconscious), or to an ignorant belief that Socialism would not 'work', or to a mere dread of the horrors and discomforts of the revolutionary period before Socialism is established. Undoubtedly all these are important, but there are plenty of people who are influenced by none of them and are nevertheless hostile to Socialism. Their reason for recoiling from Socialism is spiritual, or 'ideological'. They object to it not on the ground that it would not 'work', but precisely because it would 'work' too well. What they are afraid of is not the things that are going to happen in their own lifetime, but the things that are going to happen in a remote future when Socialism is a reality.

I have very seldom met a convinced Socialist who could grasp that thinking people may be repelled by the *objective* towards which Socialism appears to be moving. The Marxist, especially, dismisses this kind of thing as bourgeois sentimentality. Marxists as a rule are not very good at reading the minds of their adversaries; if they were, the situation in Europe might be less desperate than it is at present. Possessing a technique which seems to explain everything, they do not often bother to discover what is going on inside other people's heads. Here, for instance, is an illustration of the kind of thing I mean. Discussing the widely held theory—which in one sense is certainly true—that Fascism is a product of Communism, Mr N. A. Holdaway, one of the ablest Marxist writers we possess, writes as follows:

The hoary legend of Communism leading to Fascism.... The element of truth in it is this: that the appearance of Communist activity warns the ruling class that democratic Labour Parties are no longer capable of holding the working class in check, and that capitalist dictatorship must assume another form if it is to survive.

You see here the defects of the method. Because he has detected the underlying economic cause of Fascism, he tacitly assumes that the spiritual side of it is of no importance. Fascism is written off as a manoeuvre of the 'ruling class', which at bottom it is. But this in itself would only explain why Fascism appeals to capitalists. What about the millions who are not capitalists, who in a material sense have nothing to gain from Fascism and are often aware of it, and who, nevertheless, are Fascists? Obviously their approach has been purely along the ideological line. They could only be stampeded into Fascism because Communism attacked or seemed to attack certain things (patriotism, religion, etc.) which lay deeper than the economic motive; and in *that* sense it is perfectly true that Communism leads to Fascism. It is a pity that Marxists nearly always concentrate on letting economic cats out of ideological bags; it does in one sense reveal the truth, but with this penalty, that most of their propaganda misses its mark. It is the spiritual recoil from Socialism, especially as it manifests itself in sensitive people, that I want to discuss in this chapter. I shall have to analyse it at some length, because it is very widespread, very powerful, and, among Socialists, almost completely ignored.

The first thing to notice is that the idea of Socialism is bound up, more or less inextricably, with the idea of machine-production. Socialism is essentially an *urban* creed. It grew up more or less concurrently with industrialism, it has always had its roots in the town proletariat and the town intellectual, and it is doubtful whether it could ever have arisen in any but an industrial society. Granted industrialism, the idea of Socialism presents itself naturally, because private ownership is only tolerable when every individual (or family or other unit) is at least moderately self-supporting; but the effect of industrialism is to make it impossible for anyone to be self-supporting even for a moment. Industrialism, once it rises above a fairly low level, *must* lead to some form of collectivism. Not necessarily to Socialism, of course; conceivably it might lead to the Slave-State of which Fascism is a kind of prophecy. And the converse is also true. Machine-production suggests Socialism, but Socialism as a world-system implies machine-production, because it demands certain things not compatible with a primitive way of life. It demands, for instance, constant intercommunication and exchange of goods between all parts of the earth; it demands some degree of centralized control; it demands an approximately equal standard of life for all human beings and probably a certain uniformity of education. We may take it, therefore, that any world in which Socialism was a reality would be at least as highly mechanized as the United States at this moment,

probably much more so. In any case, no Socialist would think of deny-
ing this. The Socialist world is always pictured as a completely mechanized, immensely organized world, depending on the machine as
the civilizations of antiquity depend on the slave.

So far so good, or so bad. Many, perhaps a majority, of thinking
people are not in love with machine-civilization, but everyone who is
not a fool knows that it is nonsense to talk at this moment about
scrapping the machine. But the unfortunate thing is that Socialism,
as usually presented, is bound up with the idea of mechanical progress, not merely as a necessary development but as an end in itself,
almost as a kind of religion. This idea is implicit in, for instance, most
of the propagandist stuff that is written about the rapid mechanical
advance in Soviet Russia (the Dneiper dam,* tractors, etc., etc.).
Karel Capek hits it off well enough in the horrible ending of *R.U.R.*,*
when the Robots, having slaughtered the last human being, announce
their intention to 'build many houses' (just for the sake of building
houses, you see). The kind of person who most readily accepts
Socialism is also the kind of person who views mechanical progress,
as such, with enthusiasm. And this is so much the case that Socialists
are often unable to grasp that the opposite opinion exists. As a rule
the most persuasive argument they can think of is to tell you that the
present mechanization of the world is as nothing to what we shall see
when Socialism is established. Where there is one aeroplane now, in
those days there will be fifty! All the work that is now done by hand
will then be done by machinery: everything that is now made of
leather, wood, or stone will be made of rubber, glass, or steel; there
will be no disorder, no loose ends, no wildernesses, no wild animals,
no weeds, no disease, no poverty, no pain—and so on and so forth.
The Socialist world is to be above all things an *ordered* world, an *efficient* world. But it is precisely from that vision of the future as a sort
of glittering Wells-world* that sensitive minds recoil. Please notice
that this essentially fat-bellied version of 'progress' is not an integral
part of Socialist doctrine; but it has come to be thought of as one,
with the result that the temperamental conservatism which is latent in
all kinds of people is easily mobilized against Socialism.

Every sensitive person has moments when he is suspicious of
machinery and to some extent of physical science. But it is important
to sort out the various motives, which have differed greatly at different times, for hostility to science and machinery, and to disregard the

jealousy of the modern literary gent who hates science because science has stolen literature's thunder. The earliest full-length attack on science and machinery that I am acquainted with is in the third part of *Gulliver's Travels*. But Swift's attack, though brilliant as a *tour de force*, is irrelevant and even silly, because it is written from the standpoint—perhaps this seems a queer thing to say of the author of *Gulliver's Travels*—of a man who lacked imagination. To Swift, science was merely a kind of futile muckraking and the machines were nonsensical contraptions that would never work. His standard was that of practical usefulness, and he lacked the vision to see that an experiment which is not demonstrably useful at the moment may yield results in the future. Elsewhere in the book he names it as the best of all achievements 'to make two blades of grass grow where one grew before'; not seeing, apparently, that this is just what the machine can do. A little later the despised machines began working, physical science increased its scope, and there came the celebrated conflict between religion and science which agitated our grandfathers. That conflict is over and both sides have retreated and claimed a victory, but an anti-scientific bias still lingers in the minds of most religious believers. All through the nineteenth century protesting voices were raised against science and machinery (see Dickens's *Hard Times*, for instance), but usually for the rather shallow reason that industrialism in its first stages was cruel and ugly. Samuel Butler's attack on the machine in the well-known chapter of *Erewhon* is a different matter. But Butler himself lives in a less desperate age than our own, an age in which it was still possible for a first-rate man to be a dilettante part of the time, and therefore the whole thing appeared to him as a kind of intellectual exercise. He saw clearly enough our abject dependence on the machine, but instead of bothering to work out its consequences he preferred to exaggerate it for the sake of what was not much more than a joke. It is only in our own age, when mechanization has finally triumphed, that we can actually *feel* the tendency of the machine to make a fully human life impossible. There is probably no one capable of thinking and feeling who has not occasionally looked at a gas-pipe chair and reflected that the machine is the enemy of life. As a rule, however, this feeling is instinctive rather than reasoned. People know that in some way or another 'progress' is a swindle, but they reach this conclusion by a kind of mental shorthand; my job here is to supply the logical steps that are usually left out. But first one must ask,

what is the function of the machine? Obviously its primary function
is to save work, and the type of person to whom machine-civilization
is entirely acceptable seldom sees any reason for looking further. Here
for instance is a person who claims, or rather screams, that he is thoroughly at home in the modern mechanized world. I am quoting from
World Without Faith, by Mr John Beevers. This is what he says:

It is plain lunacy to say that the average £2 10s. to £4 a week man of today
is a lower type than an eighteenth-century farm labourer. Or than the
labourer or peasant of any exclusively agricultural community now or in
the past. It just isn't true. It is so damn silly to cry out about the civilizing
effects of work in the fields and farmyards as against that done in a big
locomotive works or an automobile factory. Work is a nuisance. We work
because we have to and all work is done to provide us with leisure and the
means of spending that leisure as enjoyably as possible.

   And again:

Man is going to have time enough and power enough to hunt for his own
heaven on earth without worrying about the super-natural one. The earth
will be so pleasant a place that the priest and the parson won't be left with
much of a tale to tell. Half the stuffing is knocked out of them by one neat
blow. Etc., etc., etc.

   There is a whole chapter to this effect (Chapter 4 of Mr Beevers's
book), and it is of some interest as an exhibition of machine-worship
in its most completely vulgar, ignorant, and half-baked form. It is the
authentic voice of a large section of the modern world. Every aspirin-
eater in the outer suburbs would echo it fervently. Notice the shrill
wail of anger ('It just isn't troo-o-o!', etc.) with which Mr Beevers
meets the suggestion that his grandfather may have been a better man
than himself; and the still more horrible suggestion that if we returned
to a simpler way of life he might have to toughen his muscles with
a job of work. Work, you see, is done 'to provide us with leisure'.
Leisure for what? Leisure to become more like Mr Beevers, presumably. Though as a matter of fact, from that line of talk about 'heaven
on earth', you can make a fairly good guess at what he would like civilization to be; a sort of Lyons Corner House lasting *in saecula saecu-
lorum* and getting bigger and noisier all the time. And in any book by
anyone who feels at home in the machine-world—in any book by
H. G. Wells, for instance—you will find passages of the same kind.
How often have we not heard it, that glutinously uplifting stuff about

'the machines, our new race of slaves, which will set humanity free', etc., etc., etc. To these people, apparently, the only danger of the machine is its possible use for destructive purposes; as, for instance, aeroplanes are used in war. Barring wars and unforeseen disasters, the future is envisaged as an ever more rapid march of mechanical progress; machines to save work, machines to save thought, machines to save pain, hygiene, efficiency, organization, more hygiene, more efficiency, more organization, more machines—until finally you land up in the by now familiar Wellsian Utopia, aptly caricatured by Huxley in *Brave New World*, the paradise of little fat men. Of course in their day-dreams of the future the little fat men are neither fat nor little; they are Men Like Gods. But why should they be? All mechanical progress is towards greater and greater efficiency; ultimately, therefore, towards a world in which *nothing goes wrong*. But in a world in which nothing went wrong, many of the qualities which Mr Wells regards as 'godlike' would be no more valuable than the animal faculty of moving the ears. The beings in *Men Like Gods* and *The Dream* are represented, for example, as brave, generous, and physically strong. But in a world from which physical danger had been banished—and obviously mechanical progress tends to eliminate danger—would physical courage be likely to survive? *Could* it survive? And why should physical strength survive in a world where there was never the need for physical labour? As for such qualities as loyalty, generosity, etc., in a world where nothing went wrong, they would be not only irrelevant but probably unimaginable. The truth is that many of the qualities we admire in human beings can only function in opposition to some kind of disaster, pain, or difficulty; but the tendency of mechanical progress is to eliminate disaster, pain, and difficulty. In books like *The Dream* and *Men Like Gods* it is assumed that such qualities as strength, courage, generosity, etc., will be kept alive because they are comely qualities and necessary attributes of a full human being. Presumably, for instance, the inhabitants of Utopia would create artificial dangers in order to exercise their courage, and do dumb-bell exercises to harden muscles which they would never be obliged to use. And here you observe the huge contradiction which is usually present in the idea of progress. The tendency of mechanical progress is to make your environment safe and soft; and yet you are striving to keep yourself brave and hard. You are at the same moment furiously pressing forward and desperately holding back. It is as though a London stockbroker should go to his office in a suit of chain mail and insist on talking medieval Latin. So in the last analysis the champion of progress is also the champion of anachronisms.

Meanwhile I am assuming that the tendency of mechanical progress *is* to make life safe and soft. This may be disputed, because at any given moment the effect of some recent mechanical invention may appear to be the opposite. Take for instance the transition from horses to motor vehicles. At a first glance one might say, considering the enormous toll of road deaths, that the motor-car does not exactly tend to make life safer. Moreover it probably needs as much toughness to be a first-rate dirt-track rider as to be a broncho-buster or to ride in the Grand National. Nevertheless the *tendency* of all machinery is to become safer and easier to handle. The danger of accidents would disappear if we chose to tackle our road-planning problem seriously, as we shall do sooner or later; and meanwhile the motor-car has evolved to a point at which anyone who is not blind or paralytic can drive it after a few lessons. Even now it needs far less nerve and skill to drive a car ordinarily well than to ride a horse ordinarily well; in twenty years' time it may need no nerve or skill at all. Therefore, one must say that, taking society as a whole, the result of the transition from horses to cars has been an increase in human softness. Presently somebody comes along with another invention, the aeroplane for instance, which does not at first sight appear to make life safer. The first men who went up in aeroplanes were superlatively brave, and even today it must need an exceptionally good nerve to be a pilot. But the same tendency as before is at work. The aeroplane, like the motor-car, will be made foolproof; a million engineers are working, almost unconsciously, in that direction. Finally—this is the objective, though it may never quite be reached—you will get an aeroplane whose pilot needs no more skill or courage than a baby needs in its perambulator. And all mechanical progress is and must be in this direction. A machine evolves by becoming more efficient, that is, more foolproof; hence the objective of mechanical progress is a foolproof world—which may or may not mean a world inhabited by fools. Mr Wells would probably retort that the world can never become foolproof, because, however high a standard of efficiency you have reached, there is always some greater difficulty ahead. For example (this is Mr Wells's favourite idea—he has used it in goodness knows how many perorations), when you have got this planet of ours perfectly into trim, you start upon the enormous task of reaching and colonizing another. But this is merely to push the objective further into the future; the objective itself remains the same. Colonize another planet, and the game of mechanical progress begins anew; for the foolproof world you have substituted the foolproof solar system—the foolproof universe. In tying yourself to the ideal of mechanical efficiency, you tie yourself to the ideal of softness. But softness is repulsive; and thus all progress is seen to be a frantic struggle towards an objective which you hope and pray will never be reached. Now and again, but not often, you meet somebody who grasps that what is usually called progress also entails what is usually called degeneracy, and who is nevertheless in favour of progress. Hence the fact that in Mr Shaw's Utopia a statue was erected to Falstaff, as the first man who ever made a speech in favour of cowardice.

But the trouble goes immensely deeper than this. Hitherto I have only pointed out the absurdity of aiming at mechanical progress and also at the preservation of qualities which mechanical progress makes unnecessary. The question one has got to consider is whether there is *any* human activity which would not be maimed by the dominance of the machine.

The function of the machine is to save work. In a fully mechanized world all the dull drudgery will be done by machinery, leaving us free for more interesting pursuits. So expressed, this sounds splendid. It makes one sick to see half a dozen men sweating their guts out to dig a trench for a water-pipe, when some easily devised machine would scoop the earth out in a couple of minutes. Why not let the machine do the work and the men go and do something else. But presently the question arises, what else are they to do? Supposedly they are set free from 'work' in order that they may do something which is not 'work'. But what is work and what is not work? Is it work to dig, to carpenter, to plant trees, to fell trees, to ride, to fish, to hunt, to feed chickens, to play the piano, to take photographs, to build a house, to cook, to sew, to trim hats, to mend motor bicycles? All of these things are work to somebody, and all of them are play to somebody. There are in fact very few activities which cannot be classed either as work or play according as you choose to regard them. The labourer set free from digging may want to spend his leisure, or part of it, in playing the piano, while the professional pianist may be only too glad to get out and dig at the potato patch. Hence the antithesis between work, as something intolerably tedious, and not-work, as something desirable, is false. The truth is that when a human being is not eating, drinking, sleeping, making love, talking, playing games, or merely lounging about—and these things will not fill up a lifetime—he needs work and usually looks for it, though he may not call it work. Above the level of a third- or fourth-grade moron, life has got to be lived largely in terms of effort. For man is not, as the vulgarer hedonists seem to suppose, a kind of walking stomach; he has also got a hand, an eye, and a brain. Cease to use your hands, and you have lopped off a huge chunk of your consciousness. And now consider again those half-dozen men who were digging the trench for the water-pipe. A machine has set them free from digging, and they are going to amuse themselves with something else—carpentering, for instance. But whatever they want to do, they will find that another machine has set them free from *that*. For in a fully mechanized world there would be no more need to carpenter, to cook, to mend motor bicycles, etc., than there would be to dig. There is scarcely anything, from catching a whale to carving a cherry stone, that could not conceivably be done by machinery. The machine would even encroach upon the activities we now class as 'art'; it is doing so already, via the camera and the radio. Mechanize the world as fully as it might be mechanized, and whichever way you turn there will be some machine cutting you off from the chance of working—that is, of living.

At a first glance this might not seem to matter. Why should you not get on with your 'creative work' and disregard the machines that would do it for you? But it is not so simple as it sounds. Here am I, working eight hours a day in an insurance office; in my spare time I want to do something 'creative', so I choose to do a bit of carpentering—to make myself a table, for instance. Notice that from the very start there is a touch of artificiality about the whole business, for the factories can turn me out a far better table than I can make for myself. But even when I get to work on my table, it is not possible for me to feel towards it as the cabinet-maker of a hundred years ago felt towards his table, still less as Robinson Crusoe felt towards his. For before I start, most of the work has already been done for me by machinery. The tools I use demand the minimum of skill. I can get, for instance, planes which will cut out any moulding; the cabinet-maker of a hundred years ago would have had to do the work with chisel and gouge, which demanded real skill of eye and hand. The boards I buy are ready planed and the legs are ready turned by the lathe. I can even go to the wood-shop and buy all the parts of the table ready-made and only needing to be fitted together; my work being reduced to driving in a few pegs and using a piece of sandpaper. And if this is so at present, in the mechanized future it will be enormously more so. With the tools and materials available *then*, there will be no possibility of mistake, hence no room for skill. Making a table will be easier and duller than peeling a potato. In such circumstances it is nonsense to talk of 'creative work'. In any case the arts of the hand (which have got to be transmitted by apprenticeship) would long since have disappeared. Some of them have disappeared already, under the competition of the machine. Look round any country churchyard and see whether you can find a decently-cut tombstone later than 1820. The art, or rather the craft, of stonework has died out so completely that it would take centuries to revive it.

But it may be said, why not retain the machine *and* retain 'creative work'? Why not cultivate anachronisms as a spare-time hobby? Many people have played with this idea; it seems to solve with such beautiful ease the problems set by the machine. The citizen of Utopia, we are told, coming home from his daily two hours of turning a handle in the tomato-canning factory, will deliberately revert to a more primitive way of life and solace his creative instincts with a bit of fretwork, pottery-glazing, or handloom-weaving. And why is this picture an absurdity—as it is, of course? Because of a principle that is not always recognized, though always acted upon: that so long as the machine is *there*, one is under an obligation to use it. No one draws water from the well when he can turn on the tap. One sees a good illustration of this in the matter of travel. Everyone who has travelled by primitive methods in an undeveloped country knows that the difference between that kind of travel and modern travel in trains, cars, etc., is the difference between life and death. The nomad who walks or rides, with his baggage stowed on a camel or an ox-cart, may suffer every kind of discomfort, but at least he is living while he is travelling; whereas for the passenger in an express train or a luxury liner his journey is an interregnum, a kind of temporary death. And yet so long as the railways exist, one has got to travel by train—or by car or aeroplane. Here am I, forty miles from London. When I want to go up to London why do I not pack my luggage on to a mule and set out on foot, making a two days of it? Because, with the Green Line buses whizzing past me every ten minutes, such a journey would be intolerably irksome. In order that one may enjoy primitive methods of travel, it is necessary that no other method should be available. No human being ever wants to do anything in a more cumbrous way than is necessary. Hence the absurdity of that picture of Utopians saving their souls with fretwork. In a world where everything could be done by machinery, everything would be done by machinery. Deliberately to revert to primitive methods to use archaic tools, to put silly little difficulties in your own way, would be a piece of dilettantism, of pretty-pretty arty and craftiness. It would be like solemnly sitting down to eat your dinner with stone implements. Revert to handwork in a machine age, and you are back in Ye Olde Tea Shoppe or the Tudor villa with the sham beams tacked to the wall.

The tendency of mechanical progress, then, is to frustrate the human need for effort and creation. It makes unnecessary and even impossible the activities of the eye and the hand. The apostle of 'progress' will sometimes declare that this does not matter, but you can usually drive him into a corner by pointing out the horrible lengths to which the process can be carried. Why, for instance, use your hands at all—why use them even for blowing your nose or sharpening a pencil? Surely you could fix some kind of steel and rubber contraption to your shoulders and let your arms wither into stumps of skin and bone? And so with every organ and every faculty. There is really no reason why a human being should do more than eat, drink, sleep, breathe, and procreate; *everything* else could be done for him by machinery. Therefore the logical end of mechanical progress is to reduce the human being to something resembling a brain in a bottle. That is the goal towards which we are already moving, though, of course, we have no intention of getting there; just as a man who drinks a bottle of whisky a day does not actually intend to get cirrhosis of the liver. The implied objective of 'progress' is—not *exactly*, perhaps, the brain in the bottle, but at any rate some frightful sub-human depth of softness and helplessness. And the unfortunate thing is that at present the word 'progress' and the word 'Socialism' are linked inseparably in almost everyone's mind. The kind of person who hates machinery also takes it for granted to hate Socialism; the Socialist is always in favour of mechanization, rationalization, modernization—or at least thinks that he ought to be in favour of them. Quite recently, for instance, a prominent I.L.P.'er confessed to me with a sort of wistful shame—as though it were something faintly improper—that he was 'fond of horses'. Horses, you see, belong to the vanished agricultural past, and all sentiment for the past carries with it a vague smell of heresy. I do not believe that this need necessarily be so, but undoubtedly it is so. And in itself it is quite enough to explain the alienation of decent minds from Socialism.

A generation ago every intelligent person was in some sense a revolutionary; nowadays it would be nearer the mark to say that every intelligent person is a reactionary. In this connexion it is worth comparing H. G. Wells's *The Sleeper Awakes* with Aldous Huxley's *Brave New World*, written thirty years later. Each is a pessimistic Utopia, a vision of a sort of prig's paradise in which all the dreams of the 'progressive' person come true. Considered merely as a piece of imaginative construction *The Sleeper Awakes* is, I think, much superior, but it suffers from vast contradictions because of the fact that Wells, as the arch-priest of 'progress', cannot write with any conviction *against* 'progress'. He draws a picture of a glittering, strangely sinister world in which the privileged classes live a life of shallow gutless hedonism, and the workers, reduced to a state of utter slavery and sub-human ignorance, toil like troglodytes in caverns underground. As soon as one examines this idea—it is further developed in a splendid short story in *Stories of Space and Time*—one sees its inconsistency. For in the immensely mechanized world that Wells is imagining, why should the workers have to work harder than at present? Obviously the tendency of the machine is to eliminate work, not to increase it. In the machine-world the workers might be enslaved, ill-treated, and even underfed, but they certainly would not be condemned to ceaseless manual toil; because in that case what would be the function of the machine? You can have machines doing all the work or human beings doing all the work, but you can't have both. Those armies of underground workers, with their blue uniforms and their debased, half-human language, are only put in 'to make your flesh creep'. Wells wants to suggest that 'progress' might take a wrong turning; but the only evil he cares to imagine is inequality—one class grabbing all the wealth and power and oppressing the others, apparently out of pure spite. Give it quite a small twist, he seems to suggest, overthrow the privileged class—change over from world-capitalism to Socialism, in fact—and all will be well. The machine-civilization is to continue, but its products are to be shared out equally. The thought he dare not

face is that the machine itself may be the enemy. So in his more characteristic Utopias (*The Dream, Men Like Gods*, etc.), he returns to
optimism and to a vision of humanity, 'liberated' by the machine, as
a race of enlightened sunbathers whose sole topic of conversation is
their own superiority to their ancestors. *Brave New World* belongs to
a later time and to a generation which has seen through the swindle of
'progress'. It contains its own contradictions (the most important of
them is pointed out in Mr John Strachey's *The Coming Struggle for
Power*), but it is at least a memorable assault on the more fat-bellied
type of perfectionism. Allowing for the exaggerations of caricature, it
probably expresses what a majority of thinking people feel about
machine-civilization.

The sensitive person's hostility to the machine is in one sense
unrealistic, because of the obvious fact that the machine has come to
stay. But as an attitude of mind there is a great deal to be said for it.
The machine has got to be accepted, but it is probably better to accept
it rather as one accepts a drug—that is, grudgingly and suspiciously.
Like a drug, the machine is useful, dangerous, and habit-forming.
The oftener one surrenders to it the tighter its grip becomes. You
have only to look about you at this moment to realize with what sinister speed the machine is getting us into its power. To begin with, there
is the frightful debauchery of taste that has already been effected by
a century of mechanization. This is almost too obvious and too generally admitted to need pointing out. But as a single instance, take
taste in its narrowest sense—the taste for decent food. In the highly
mechanized countries, thanks to tinned food, cold storage, synthetic
flavouring matters, etc., the palate is almost a dead organ. As you can
see by looking at any greengrocer's shop, what the majority of English
people mean by an apple is a lump of highly-coloured cotton wool
from America or Australia; they will devour these things, apparently
with pleasure, and let the English apples rot under the trees. It is the
shiny, standardized, machine-made look of the American apple that
appeals to them; the superior taste of the English apple is something
they simply do not notice. Or look at the factory-made, foil-wrapped
cheese and 'blended' butter in any grocer's; look at the hideous rows
of tins which usurp more and more of the space in any food-shop,
even a dairy; look at a sixpenny Swiss roll or a twopenny ice-cream;
look at the filthy chemical by-product that people will pour down
their throats under the name of beer. Wherever you look you will see

some slick machine-made article triumphing over the old-fashioned article that still tastes of something other than sawdust. And what applies to food applies also to furniture, houses, clothes, books, amusements, and everything else that makes up our environment. There are now millions of people, and they are increasing every year, to whom the blaring of a radio is not only a more acceptable but a more *normal* background to their thoughts than the lowing of cattle or the song of birds. The mechanization of the world could never proceed very far while taste, even the taste-buds of the tongue, remained uncorrupted, because in that case most of the products of the machine would be simply unwanted. In a healthy world there would be no demand for tinned foods, aspirins, gramophones, gaspipe chairs, machine guns, daily newspapers, telephones, motor-cars, etc., etc.; and on the other hand there would be a constant demand for the things the machine cannot produce. But meanwhile the machine is here, and its corrupting effects are almost irresistible. One inveighs against it, but one goes on using it. Even a bare-arse savage, given the chance, will learn the vices of civilization within a few months. Mechanization leads to the decay of taste, the decay of taste leads to the demand for machine-made articles and hence to more mechanization, and so a vicious circle is established.

But in addition to this there is a tendency for the mechanization of the world to proceed as it were automatically, whether we want it or not. This is due to the fact that in modern Western man the faculty of mechanical invention has been fed and stimulated till it has reached almost the status of an instinct. People invent new machines and improve existing ones almost unconsciously, rather as a somnambulist will go on working in his sleep. In the past, when it was taken for granted that life on this planet is harsh or at any rate laborious, it seemed the natural fate to go on using the clumsy implements of your forefathers, and only a few eccentric persons, centuries apart, proposed innovations; hence throughout enormous ages such things as the ox-cart, the plough, the sickle, etc., remained radically unchanged. It is on record that screws have been in use since remote antiquity and yet that it was not till the middle of the nineteenth century that anyone thought of making screws with points on them; for several thousand years they remained flat-ended and holes had to be drilled for them before they could be inserted. In our own epoch such a thing would be unthinkable. For almost every modern Western man has his inventive faculty to some extent developed; the Western man invents machines as naturally as the Polynesian islander swims. Give a Western man a job of work and he immediately begins devising a machine that would do it for him; give him a machine and he thinks of ways of improving it. I understand this tendency well enough, for in an ineffectual sort of way I have that type of mind myself. I have not either the patience or the mechanical skill to devise any machine that would work, but I am perpetually seeing, as it were, the ghosts of possible machines that might save me the trouble of using my brain or muscles. A person with a more definite mechanical turn would probably construct some of them and put them into operation. But under our present economic system, whether he constructed them—or rather, whether anyone else had the benefit of them—would depend upon whether they were commercially valuable. The Socialists are right, therefore, when they claim that the rate of mechanical progress will be much more rapid once Socialism is established. Given a mechanical civilization the process of invention and improvement will always continue, but the tendency of capitalism is to slow it down, because under capitalism any invention which does not promise fairly immediate profits is neglected; some, indeed, which threaten to reduce profits are suppressed almost as ruthlessly as the flexible glass mentioned by Petronius.[1] Establish Socialism—remove the profit principle—and the inventor will have a free hand. The mechanization of the world, already rapid enough, would be or at any rate could be enormously accelerated.

And this prospect is a slightly sinister one, because it is obvious even now that the process of mechanization is out of control. It is happening merely because humanity has got the habit. A chemist perfects a new method of synthesizing rubber, or a mechanic devises a new pattern of gudgeonpin. Why? Not for any clearly understood purpose, but simply from the impulse to invent and improve, which has now become instinctive. Put a pacifist to work in a bomb-factory and in two months he will be devising a new type of bomb. Hence the appearance of such diabolical things as poison gases, which are not expected even by their inventors to be beneficial to humanity. Our attitude towards such things as poison gases *ought* to be the attitude

---

[1] For example: Some years ago someone invented a gramophone needle that would last for decades. One of the big gramophone companies bought up the patent rights, and that was the last that was ever heard of it.

of the king of Brobdingnag towards gunpowder; but because we live in a mechanical and scientific age we are infected with the notion that, whatever else happens, 'progress' must continue and knowledge must never be suppressed. Verbally, no doubt, we would agree that machinery is made for man and not man for machinery; in practice any attempt to check the development of the machine appears to us an attack on knowledge and therefore a kind of blasphemy. And even if the whole of humanity suddenly revolted against the machine and decided to escape to a simpler way of life, the escape would still be immensely difficult. It would not do, as in Butler's *Erewhon*, to smash every machine invented after a certain date; we should also have to smash the habit of mind that would, almost involuntarily, devise fresh machines as soon as the old ones were smashed. And in all of us there is at least a tinge of that habit of mind. In every country in the world the large army of scientists and technicians, with the rest of us panting at their heels, are marching along the road of 'progress' with the blind persistence of a column of ants. Comparatively few people want it to happen, plenty of people actively want it *not* to happen, and yet it is happening. The process of mechanization has itself become a machine, a huge glittering vehicle whirling us we are not certain where, but probably towards the padded Wells-world and the brain in the bottle.

This, then, is the case against the machine. Whether it is a sound or unsound case hardly matters. The point is that these or very similar arguments would be echoed by every person who is hostile to machine-civilization. And unfortunately, because of that nexus of thought, 'Socialism-progress-machinery-Russia-tractor-hygiene-machinery-progress', which exists in almost everyone's mind, it is usually the *same* person who is hostile to Socialism. The kind of person who hates central heating and gaspipe chairs is also the kind of person who, when you mention Socialism, murmurs something about 'beehive state' and moves away with a pained expression. So far as my observation goes, very few Socialists grasp why this is so, or even that it *is* so. Get the more vocal type of Socialist into a corner, repeat to him the substance of what I have said in this chapter, and see what kind of answer you get. As a matter of fact you will get several answers; I am so familiar with them that I know them almost by heart.

In the first place he will tell you that it is impossible to 'go back' (or to 'put back the hand of progress'—as though the hand of progress hadn't been pretty violently put back several times in human history!), and will then accuse you of being a medievalist and begin to descant upon the horrors of the Middle Ages, leprosy, the Inquisition, etc. As a matter of fact, most attacks upon the Middle Ages and the past generally by apologists of modernity are beside the point, because their essential trick is to project a modern man, with his squeamishness and his high standards of comfort, into an age when such things were unheard of. But notice that in any case this is not an answer. For a dislike of the mechanized future does not imply the smallest reverence for any period of the past. D. H. Lawrence, wiser than the medievalist, chose to idealize the Etruscans about whom we know conveniently little. But there is no need to idealize even the Etruscans or the Pelasgians, or the Aztecs, or the Sumerians, or any other vanished and romantic people. When one pictures a desirable civilization, one pictures it merely as an objective; there is no need to pretend that it has ever existed in space and time. Press this point home, explain that you wish to aim at making life simpler and harder instead of softer and more complex, and the Socialist will usually assume that you want to revert to a 'state of nature'—meaning some stinking palaeolithic cave: as though there were nothing between a flint scraper and the steel mills of Sheffield, or between a skin coracle and the *Queen Mary*!

Finally, however, you will get an answer which is rather more to the point and which runs roughly as follows: 'Yes, what you are saying is all very well in its way. No doubt it would be very noble to harden ourselves and do without aspirins and central heating and so forth. But the point is, you see, that nobody seriously wants it. It would mean going back to an agricultural way of life, which means beastly hard work and isn't at all the same thing as playing at gardening. I don't want hard work, you don't want hard work—nobody wants it who knows what it means. You only talk as you do because you've never done a day's work in your life,' etc., etc.

Now this in a sense is true. It amounts to saying, 'We're soft—for God's sake let's stay soft!' which at least is realistic. As I have pointed out already, the machine has got us in its grip and to escape will be immensely difficult. Nevertheless this answer is really an evasion, because it fails to make clear what we mean when we say that we 'want' this or that. I am a degenerate modern semi-intellectual who would die if I did not get my early morning cup of tea and my *New Statesman* every Friday. Clearly I do not, in a sense, 'want' to return to a simpler, harder, probably agricultural way of life. In the same sense I don't 'want' to cut down my drinking, to pay my debts, to take enough exercise, to be faithful to my wife, etc., etc. But in another and more permanent sense I do want these things, and perhaps in the same sense I want a civilization in which 'progress' is not definable as making the world safe for little fat men. These that I have outlined are practically the only arguments that I have been able to get from Socialists—thinking, book-trained Socialists—when I have tried to explain to them just *how* they are driving away possible adherents. Of course there is also the old argument that Socialism is going to arrive anyway, whether people like it or not, because of that trouble-saving thing, 'historic necessity'. But 'historic necessity', or rather the belief in it, has failed to survive Hitler.

Meanwhile the thinking person, by intellect usually left-wing but by temperament often right-wing, hovers at the gate of the Socialist fold. He is no doubt aware that he *ought* to be a Socialist. But he observes first the dullness of individual Socialists, then the apparent flabbiness of Socialist ideals, and veers away. Till quite recently it was natural to veer towards indifferentism. Ten years ago, even five years ago, the typical literary gent wrote books on baroque architecture and had a soul above politics. But that attitude is becoming difficult and even unfashionable. The times are growing harsher, the issues are clearer, the belief that nothing will ever change (i.e. that your dividends will always be safe) is less prevalent. The fence on which the literary gent sits, once as comfortable as the plush cushion of a cathedral stall, is now pinching his bottom intolerably; more and more he shows a disposition to drop off on one side or the other. It is interesting to notice how many of our leading writers, who a dozen years ago were art for art's saking for all they were worth and would have considered it too vulgar for words even to vote at a general election, are now taking a definite political standpoint; while most of the younger writers, at least those of them who are not mere footlers, have been 'political' from the start. I believe that when the pinch comes there is a terrible danger that the main movement of the intelligentsia will be towards Fascism. Just how soon the pinch will come it is difficult to say; it depends, probably, upon events in Europe; but it may be that within two years or even a year we shall have reached the decisive moment. That will also be the moment when every person with any brains or any decency will know in his bones that he ought to be on the Socialist side. But he will not necessarily come there of his own accord; there are too many ancient prejudices standing in the way. He will have to be persuaded, and by methods that imply an understanding of his viewpoint. Socialists cannot afford to waste any more time in preaching to the converted. Their job now is to make Socialists as rapidly as possible; instead of which, all too often, they are making Fascists.

When I speak of Fascism in England, I am not necessarily thinking of Mosley and his pimpled followers.* English Fascism, when it arrives, is likely to be of a sedate and subtle kind (presumably, at any rate at first, it won't be *called* Fascism), and it is doubtful whether a Gilbert and Sullivan heavy dragoon of Mosley's stamp would ever be much more than a joke to the majority of English people; though even Mosley will bear watching, for experience shows (*vide* the careers of Hitler, Napoleon III) that to a political climber it is sometimes an advantage not to be taken too seriously at the beginning of his career. But what I am thinking of at this moment is the Fascist attitude of mind, which beyond any doubt is gaining ground among people who ought to know better. Fascism as it appears in the intellectual is a sort of mirror-image—not actually of Socialism but of a plausible travesty of Socialism. It boils down to a determination to do the *opposite* of whatever the mythical Socialist does. If you present Socialism in a bad and misleading light—if you let people imagine that it does not mean much more than pouring European civilization down the sink at the command of Marxist prigs—you risk driving the intellectual into Fascism. You frighten him into a sort of angry defensive attitude in which he simply refuses to listen to the Socialist case. Some such attitude is already quite clearly discernible in writers like Pound, Wyndham Lewis, Roy Campbell, etc., in most of the Roman Catholic writers and many of the Douglas Credit group, in certain popular novelists, and even, if one looks below the surface, in so-superior conservative highbrows like Eliot and his countless followers. If you want some unmistakable illustrations of the growth of Fascist feeling in England, have a look at some of the innumerable letters that were written to the Press during the Abyssinian war, approving the Italian action, and also the howl of glee that went up from both Catholic and Anglican pulpits (see the *Daily Mail* of 17 August 1936) over the Fascist rising in Spain.

In order to combat Fascism it is necessary to understand it, which involves admitting that it contains some good as well as much evil.

In practice, of course, it is merely an infamous tyranny, and its methods of attaining and holding power are such that even its most ardent apologists prefer to talk about something else. But the underlying feeling of Fascism, the feeling that first draws people into the Fascist camp, may be less contemptible. It is not *always*, as the *Saturday Review* would lead one to suppose, a squealing terror of the Bolshevik bogey-man. Everyone who has given the movement so much as a glance knows that the rank-and-file Fascist is often quite a well-meaning person—quite genuinely anxious, for instance, to better the lot of the unemployed. But more important than this is the fact that Fascism draws its strength from the good as well as the bad varieties of conservatism. To anyone with a feeling for tradition and for discipline it comes with its appeal ready-made. Probably it is very easy, when you have had a bellyful of the more tactless kind of Socialist propaganda, to see Fascism as the last line defence of all that is good in European civilization. Even the Fascist bully at his symbolic worst, with rubber truncheon in one hand and castor oil bottle in the other, does not necessarily feel himself a bully; more probably he feels like Roland in the pass at Roncevaux,* defending Christendom against the barbarian. We have got to admit that if Fascism is everywhere advancing, this is largely the fault of Socialists themselves. Partly it is due to the mistaken Communist tactic of sabotaging democracy, i.e. sawing off the branch you are sitting on; but still more to the fact that Socialists have, so to speak, presented their case wrong side foremost. They have never made it sufficiently clear that the essential aims of Socialism are justice and liberty. With their eyes glued to economic facts, they have proceeded on the assumption that man has no soul, and explicitly or implicitly they have set up the goal of a materialistic Utopia. As a result Fascism has been able to play upon every instinct that revolts against hedonism and a cheap conception of 'progress'. It has been able to pose as the upholder of the European tradition, and to appeal to Christian belief, to patriotism, and to the military virtues. It is far worse than useless to write Fascism off as 'mass sadism', or some easy phrase of that kind. If you pretend that it is merely an aberration which will presently pass off of its own accord, you are dreaming a dream from which you will awake when somebody coshes you with a rubber truncheon. The only possible course is to examine the Fascist case, grasp that there is something to be said for it, and then make it clear to the world that whatever good Fascism contains is also implicit in Socialism.

At present the situation is desperate. Even if nothing worse befalls us, there are the conditions which I described in the earlier part of this book and which are not going to improve under our present economic system. Still more urgent is the danger of Fascist domination in Europe. And unless Socialist doctrine, in an effective form, can be diffused widely and very quickly, there is no certainty that Fascism will ever be overthrown. For Socialism is the only real enemy that Fascism has to face. The capitalist-imperialist governments, even though they themselves are about to be plundered, will not fight with any conviction against Fascism as such. Our rulers, those of them who understand the issue, would probably prefer to hand over every square inch of the British Empire to Italy, Germany, and Japan than to see Socialism triumphant. It was easy to laugh at Fascism when we imagined that it was based on hysterical nationalism, because it seemed obvious that the Fascist states, each regarding itself as the chosen people and patriotic *contra mundum*, would clash with one another. But nothing of the kind is happening. Fascism is now an international movement, which means not only that the Fascist nations can combine for purposes of loot, but that they are groping, perhaps only half consciously as yet, towards a world-system. For the vision of the totalitarian state there is being substituted the vision of the totalitarian world. As I pointed out earlier, the advance of machine-technique must lead ultimately to some form of collectivism, but that form need not necessarily be equalitarian; that is, it need not be Socialism. *Pace* the economists, it is quite easy to imagine a world-society, economically collectivist—that is, with the profit principle eliminated—but with all political, military, and educational power in the hands of a small caste of rulers and their bravos. That or something like it is the objective of Fascism. And that, of course, is the slave-state, or rather the slave-world; it would probably be a stable form of society, and the chances are, considering the enormous wealth of the world if scientifically exploited, that the slaves would be well-fed and contented. It is usual to speak of the Fascist objective as the 'beehive state', which does a grave injustice to bees. A world of rabbits ruled by stoats would be nearer the mark. It is against this beastly possibility that we have got to combine.

The only thing *for* which we can combine is the underlying ideal of Socialism; justice and liberty. But it is hardly strong enough to call this ideal 'underlying'. It is almost completely forgotten. It has been buried beneath layer after layer of doctrinaire priggishness, party squabbles, and half-baked 'progressivism' until it is like a diamond hidden under a mountain of dung. The job of the Socialist is to get it out again. Justice and liberty! *Those* are the words that have got to ring like a bugle across the world. For a long time past, certainly for the last ten years, the devil has had all the best tunes. We have reached a stage when the very word 'Socialism' calls up, on the one hand, a picture of aeroplanes, tractors, and huge glittering factories of glass and concrete; on the other, a picture of vegetarians with wilting beards, of Bolshevik commissars (half gangster, half gramophone), of earnest ladies in sandals, shock-headed Marxists chewing polysyllables, escaped Quakers, birth-control fanatics, and Labour Party backstairs-crawlers. Socialism, at least in this island, does not smell any longer of revolution and the overthrow of tyrants; it smells of crankishness, machine-worship, and the stupid cult of Russia. Unless you can remove that smell, and very rapidly, Fascism may win.

XIII

AND finally, is there anything one can do about it?

In the first part of this book I illustrated, by a few brief sidelights, the kind of mess we are in; in this second part I have been trying to explain why, in my opinion, so many normal decent people are repelled by the only remedy, namely by Socialism. Obviously the most urgent need of the next few years is to capture those normal decent ones before Fascism plays its trump card. I do not want to raise here the question of parties and political expedients. More important than any party label (though doubtless the mere menace of Fascism will presently bring some kind of Popular Front into existence) is the diffusion of Socialist doctrine in an effective form. People have got to be made ready to *act* as Socialists. There are, I believe, countless people who, without being aware of it, are in sympathy with the essential aims of Socialism, and who could be won over almost without a struggle if only one could find the word that would move them. Everyone who knows the meaning of poverty, everyone who has a genuine hatred of tyranny and war, is on the Socialist side, potentially. My job here, therefore, is to suggest—necessarily in very general terms—how a reconciliation might be effected between Socialism and its more intelligent enemies.

First, as to the enemies themselves—I mean all those people who grasp that capitalism is evil but who are conscious of a sort of queasy, shuddering sensation when Socialism is mentioned. As I have pointed out, this is traceable to two main causes. One is the personal inferiority of many individual Socialists; the other is the fact that Socialism is too often coupled with a fat-bellied, godless conception of 'progress' which revolts anyone with a feeling for tradition or the rudiments of an aesthetic sense. Let me take the second point first.

The distaste for 'progress' and machine-civilization which is so common among sensitive people is only defensible as an attitude of mind. It is not valid as a reason for rejecting Socialism, because it presupposes an alternative which does not exist. When you say, 'I object to mechanization and standardization—therefore I object to Socialism', you are saying in effect, 'I am free to do without the machine if I choose', which is nonsense. We are all dependent upon the machine, and if the machines stopped working most of us would die. You may hate the machine-civilization, probably you are right to hate it, but for the present there can be no question of accepting or rejecting it. The machine-civilization *is here*, and it can only be criticized from the inside, because all of us are inside it. It is only romantic fools who flatter themselves that they have escaped, like the literary gent in his Tudor cottage with bathroom h. and c., and the he-man who goes off to live a 'primitive' life in the jungle with a Mannlicher rifle and four wagon-loads of tinned food. And almost certainly the machine-civilization will continue to triumph. There is no reason to think that it will destroy itself or stop functioning of its own accord. For some time past it has been fashionable to say that war is presently going to 'wreck civilization' altogether; but, though the next full-sized war will certainly be horrible enough to make all previous ones seem a joke, it is immensely unlikely that it will put a stop to mechanical progress. It is true that a very vulnerable country like England, and perhaps the whole of western Europe, could be reduced to chaos by a few thousand well-placed bombs, but no war is at present thinkable which could wipe out industrialization in all countries simultaneously. We may take it that the return to a simpler, free, less mechanized way of life, however desirable it may be, is not going to happen. This is not fatalism, it is merely acceptance of facts. It is meaningless to oppose Socialism on the ground that you object to the beehive State, for the beehive State *is here*. The choice is not, as yet, between a human and an inhuman world. It is simply between Socialism and Fascism, which at its very best is Socialism with the virtues left out.

The job of the thinking person, therefore, is not to reject Socialism but to make up his mind to humanize it. Once Socialism is in a way to being established, those who can see through the swindle of 'progress' will probably find themselves resisting. In fact, it is their special function to do so. In the machine-world they have got to be a sort of permanent opposition, which is not the same thing as being an obstructionist or a traitor. But in this I am speaking of the future. For the moment the only possible course for any decent person, however much of a Tory or an anarchist by temperament, is to work for the establishment of Socialism. Nothing else can save us from the misery of the present or the nightmare of the future. To oppose Socialism *now*, when twenty million Englishmen are underfed and Fascism has conquered half Europe, is suicidal. It is like starting a civil war when the Goths are crossing the frontier.

Therefore it is all the more important to get rid of that mere nervous prejudice against Socialism which is not founded on any serious objection. As I have pointed out already, many people who are not repelled by Socialism are repelled by Socialists. Socialism, as now presented, is unattractive largely because it appears, at any rate from the outside, to be the plaything of cranks, doctrinaires, parlour Bolsheviks, and so forth. But it is worth remembering that this is only so because the cranks, doctrinaires, etc., have been allowed to get there first; if the movement were invaded by better brains and more common decency, the objectionable types would cease to dominate it. For the present one must just set one's teeth and ignore them; they will loom much smaller when the movement has been humanized. Besides, they are irrelevant. We have got to fight for justice and liberty, and Socialism does mean justice and liberty when the nonsense is stripped off it. It is only the essentials that are worth remembering. To recoil from Socialism because so many individual Socialists are inferior people is as absurd as refusing to travel by train because you dislike the ticket-collector's face.

And secondly, as to the Socialist himself—more especially the vocal, tract-writing type of Socialist.

We are at a moment when it is desperately necessary for left-wingers of all complexions to drop their differences and hang together. Indeed this is already happening to a small extent. Obviously, then, the more intransigent kind of Socialist has now got to ally himself with people who are not in perfect agreement with him. As a rule he is rightly unwilling to do so, because he sees the very real danger of watering the whole Socialist movement down to some kind of pale-pink humbug even more ineffectual than the parliamentary Labour Party. At the moment, for instance, there is great danger that the Popular Front which Fascism will presumably bring into existence will not be genuinely Socialist in character, but will simply be a manoeuvre against German and Italian (not English) Fascism. Thus the need to unite against Fascism might draw the Socialist into alliance with his very worst enemies. But the principle to go upon is this: that you are never in danger of allying yourself with the wrong people provided that you keep the essentials of your movement in the foreground. And what are the essentials of Socialism? What is the mark of a real Socialist? I suggest that the real Socialist is one who wishes—not merely conceives it as desirable, but actively wishes—to see tyranny overthrown. But I fancy that the majority of orthodox Marxists would not accept that definition, or would only accept it very grudgingly. Sometimes, when I listen to these people talking, and still more when I read their books, I get the impression that, to them, the whole Socialist movement is no more than a kind of exciting heresy-hunt—a leaping to and fro of frenzied witch-doctors to the beat of tom-toms and the tune of 'Fee fi, fo, fum, I smell the blood of a right-wing deviationist!' It is because of this kind of thing that it is so much easier to feel yourself a Socialist when you are among working-class people. The working-class Socialist, like the working-class Catholic, is weak on doctrine and can hardly open his mouth without uttering a heresy, but he has the heart of the matter in him. He does grasp the central fact that Socialism means the overthrow of tyranny, and the 'Marseillaise', if it were translated for his benefit, would appeal to him more deeply than any learned treatise on dialectical materialism. At this moment it is waste of time to insist that acceptance of Socialism means acceptance of the philosophic side of Marxism, plus adulation of Russia. The Socialist movement has not time to be a league of dialectical materialists; it has got to be a league of the oppressed against the oppressors. You have got to attract the man who means business, and you have got to drive away the mealy-mouthed Liberal who wants foreign Fascism destroyed in order that he may go on drawing his dividends peacefully—the type of humbug who passes resolutions 'against Fascism and Communism', i.e. against rats and rat-poison. Socialism means the overthrow of tyranny, at home as well as abroad. So long as you keep *that* fact well to the front, you will never be in much doubt as to who are your real supporters. As for minor differences—and the profoundest philosophical difference is unimportant compared with saving the twenty million Englishmen whose bones are rotting from malnutrition—the time to argue about them is afterwards.

I do not think the Socialist need make any sacrifice of essentials, but certainly he will have to make a great sacrifice of externals. It would help enormously, for instance, if the smell of crankishness which still clings to the Socialist movement could be dispelled. If only the sandals and the pistachio-coloured shirts could be put in a pile and burnt, and every vegetarian, teetotaller, and creeping Jesus sent home to Welwyn Garden City to do his yoga exercises quietly!

But that, I am afraid, is not going to happen. What *is* possible, however, is for the more intelligent kind of Socialist to stop alienating possible supporters in silly and quite irrelevant ways. There are so many minor priggishnesses which could so easily be dropped. Take for instance the dreary attitude of the typical Marxist towards literature. Out of the many that come into my mind, I will give just one example. It sounds trivial, but it isn't. In the old *Worker's Weekly* (one of the forerunners of the *Daily Worker*) there used to be a column of literary chat of the 'Books on the Editor's Table' type. For several weeks running there had been a certain amount of talk about Shakespeare; whereupon an incensed reader wrote to say, 'Dear Comrade, we don't want to hear about these bourgeois writers like Shakespeare. Can't you give us something a bit more proletarian?' etc., etc. The editor's reply was simple. 'If you will turn to the index of Marx's *Capital*,' he wrote, 'you will find that Shakespeare is mentioned several times.' And please notice that this was enough to silence the objector. Once Shakespeare had received the benediction of Marx, he became respectable. *That* is the mentality that drives ordinary sensible people away from the Socialist movement. You do not need to care about Shakespeare to be repelled by that kind of thing. Again, there is the horrible jargon that nearly all Socialists think it necessary to employ. When the ordinary person hears phrases like 'bourgeois ideology' and 'proletarian solidarity' and 'expropriation of the expropriators', he is not inspired by them, he is merely disgusted. Even the single word 'Comrade' has done its dirty little bit towards discrediting the Socialist movement. How many a waverer has halted on the brink, gone perhaps to some public meeting and watched self-conscious Socialists dutifully addressing one another as 'Comrade', and then slid away, disillusioned, into the nearest four-ale bar! And his instinct is sound; for where is the sense of sticking on to yourself a ridiculous label which even after long practice can hardly be mentioned without a gulp of shame? It is fatal to let the ordinary inquirer get away with the idea that being a Socialist means wearing sandals and burbling about dialectical materialism. You have got to make it clear that there is room in the Socialist movement for human beings, or the game is up.

And this raises a great difficulty. It means that the issue of class, as distinct from mere economic status, has got to be faced more realistically than it is being faced at present.

I devoted three chapters to discussing the class-difficulty. The principal fact that will have emerged, I think, is that though the English class-system has outlived its usefulness, it *has* outlived it and shows no signs of dying. It greatly confuses the issue to assume, as the orthodox Marxist so often does (see for instance Mr Alec Brown's in some ways interesting book, *The Fate of the Middle Classes*), that social status is determined solely by income. Economically, no doubt, there are only two classes, the rich and the poor, but socially there is a whole hierarchy of classes, and the manners and traditions learned by each class in childhood are not only very different but—this is the essential point—generally persist from birth to death. Hence the anomalous individuals that you find in every class of society. You find writers like Wells and Bennett who have grown immensely rich and have yet preserved intact their lower-middle-class Nonconformist prejudices; you find millionaires who cannot pronounce their aitches; you find petty shopkeepers whose income is far lower than that of the bricklayer and who, nevertheless, consider themselves (and are considered) the bricklayer's social superiors; you find board-school boys ruling Indian provinces and public-school men touting vacuum cleaners. If social stratification corresponded precisely to economic stratification, the public-school man would assume a cockney accent the day his income dropped below £200 a year. But does he? On the contrary, he immediately becomes twenty times more Public School than before. He clings to the Old School Tie as to a lifeline. And even the aitchless millionaire, though sometimes he goes to an elocutionist and learns a B.B.C. accent, seldom succeeds in disguising himself as completely as he would like to. It is in fact very difficult to escape, culturally, from the class into which you have been born.

As prosperity declines, social anomalies grow commoner. You don't get more aitchless millionaires, but you do get more and more public-school men touting vacuum cleaners and more and more small shopkeepers driven into the workhouse. Large sections of the middle class are being gradually proletarianized; but the important point is that they do not, at any rate in the first generation, adopt a proletarian outlook. Here am I, for instance, with a bourgeois upbringing and a working-class income. Which class do I belong to? Economically I belong to the working class, but it is almost impossible for me to think of myself as anything but a member of the bourgeoisie. And supposing I had to take sides, whom should I side with, the upper class which is trying to squeeze me out of existence, or the working class whose manners are not my manners? It is probable that I personally, in any important issue, would side with the working class. But what about the tens or hundreds of thousands of others who are in approximately the same position? And what about that far larger class, running into millions this time—the office-workers and black-coated employees of all kinds—whose traditions are less definitely middle class but who would certainly not thank you if you called them proletarians? All of these people have the same interests and the same enemies as the working class. All are being robbed and bullied by the same system. Yet how many of them realize it? When the pinch came nearly all of them would side with their oppressors and against those who ought to be their allies. It is quite easy to imagine a middle class crushed down to the worst depths of poverty and still remaining bitterly anti-working-class in sentiment; this being, of course, a ready-made Fascist Party.

Obviously the Socialist movement has got to capture the exploited middle class before it is too late; above all it must capture the office-workers, who are so numerous and, if they knew how to combine, so powerful. Equally obviously it has so far failed to do so. The very last person in whom you can hope to find revolutionary opinions is a clerk or a commercial traveller. Why? Very largely, I think, because of the 'proletarian' cant with which Socialist propaganda is mixed up. In order to symbolize the class war, there has been set up the more or less mythical figure of a 'proletarian', a muscular but downtrodden man in greasy overalls, in contradistinction to a 'capitalist', a fat, wicked man in a top hat and fur coat. It is tacitly assumed that there is no one in between; the truth being, of course, that in a country like England about a quarter of the population is in between. If you are going to harp on the 'dictatorship of the proletariat', it is an elementary precaution to start by explaining who the proletariat *are*. But because of the Socialist tendency to idealize the manual worker as such, this has never been made sufficiently clear. How many of the wretched shivering army of clerks and shopwalkers, who in some ways are actually worse off than a miner or a dock-hand, think of themselves as proletarians? A proletarian—so they have been taught to think—means a man without a collar. So that when you try to move them by talking about 'class war', you only succeed in scaring them; they forget their incomes and remember their accents, and fly to the defence of the class that is exploiting them.

Socialists have a big job ahead of them here. They have got to demonstrate, beyond possibility of doubt, just where the line of cleavage between exploiter and exploited comes. Once again it is a question of sticking to essentials; and the essential point here is that all people with small, insecure incomes are in the same boat and ought to be fighting on the same side. Probably we could do with a little less talk about 'capitalist' and 'proletarian' and a little more about the robbers and the robbed. But at any rate we must drop that misleading habit of pretending that the only proletarians are manual labourers. It has got to be brought home to the clerk, the engineer, the commercial traveller, the middle-class man who has 'come down in the world', the village grocer, the lower-grade civil servant, and all other doubtful cases that they *are* the proletariat, and that Socialism means a fair deal for them as well as for the navvy and the factory-hand. They must not be allowed to think that the battle is between those who pronounce their aitches and those who don't; for if they think that, they will join in on the side of the aitches.

I am implying that different classes must be persuaded to act together without, for the moment, being asked to drop their class-differences. And that sounds dangerous. It sounds rather too like the Duke of York's summer camp and that dismal line of talk about class-cooperation and putting our shoulders to the wheel, which is eyewash or Fascism, or both. There can be no cooperation between classes whose real interests are opposed. The capitalist cannot cooperate with the proletarian. The cat cannot cooperate with the mouse; and if the cat does suggest cooperation and the mouse is fool enough to agree, in a very little while the mouse will be disappearing down the cat's throat. But it is always possible to cooperate so long as it is upon a basis of common interests. The people who have got to act together are all those who cringe to the boss and all those who shudder when they think of the rent. This means that the small-holder has got to ally himself with the factory-hand, the typist with the coal-miner, the schoolmaster with the garage mechanic. There is some hope of getting them to do so if they can be made to understand where their interest lies. But this will not happen if their social prejudices, which in some of them are at least as strong as any economic consideration, are needlessly irritated. There is, after all, a real difference of manners and traditions between a bank clerk and a dock labourer, and the bank clerk's feeling of superiority is very deeply rooted. Later on he will have to get rid of it, but this is not a good moment for asking him to do so. Therefore it would be a very great advantage if that rather meaningless and mechanical bourgeois-baiting, which is a part of nearly all Socialist propaganda, could be dropped for the time being. Throughout left-wing thought and writing—and the whole way through it, from the leading articles in the *Daily Worker* to the comic columns in the *News Chronicle*—there runs an anti-genteel tradition, a persistent and often very stupid gibing at genteel mannerisms and genteel loyalties (or, in Communist jargon, 'bourgeois values'). It is largely humbug, coming as it does from bourgeois-baiters who are bourgeois themselves, but it does great harm, because it allows a minor issue to block a major one. It directs attention away from the central fact that poverty is poverty, whether the tool you work with is a pick-axe or a fountainpen.

Once again, here am I, with my middle-class origins and my income of about three pounds a week from all sources. For what I am worth it would be better to get me in on the Socialist side than to turn me into a Fascist. But if you are constantly bullying me about my 'bourgeois ideology', if you give me to understand that in some subtle way I am an inferior person because I have never worked with my hands, you will only succeed in antagonizing me. For you are telling me either that I am inherently useless or that I ought to alter myself in some way that is beyond my power. I cannot proletarianize my accent or certain of my tastes and beliefs, and I would not if I could. Why should I? I don't ask anybody else to speak my dialect; why should anybody else ask me to speak his? It would be far better to take those miserable class-stigmata for granted and emphasize them as little as possible. They are comparable to a race-difference, and experience shows that one *can* cooperate with foreigners, even with foreigners whom one dislikes, when it is really necessary. Economically, I am in the same boat with the miner, the navvy, and the farm-hand; remind me of that and I will fight at their side. But culturally I am different from the miner, the navvy, and the farm-hand: lay the emphasis on that and you may arm me against them. If I were a solitary anomaly I should not matter, but what is true of myself is true of countless others. Every bank clerk dreaming of the sack, every shopkeeper teetering on the brink of bankruptcy, is in essentially the same position. These are the sinking middle class, and most of them are clinging to their gentility under the impression that it keeps them afloat. It is not good policy to *start* by telling them to throw away the life-belt. There is a quite obvious danger that in the next few years large sections of the middle class will make a sudden and violent swing to the Right. In doing so they may become formidable. The weakness of the middle class hitherto has lain in the fact that they have never learned to combine; but if you frighten them into combining *against* you, you may find that you have raised up a devil. We had a brief glimpse of this possibility in the General Strike.

To sum up: There is no chance of righting the conditions I described in the earlier chapters of this book, or of saving England from Fascism, unless we can bring an effective Socialist party into existence. It will have to be a party with genuinely revolutionary intentions, and it will have to be numerically strong enough to act. We can only get it if we offer an objective which fairly ordinary people will recognize as desirable. Beyond all else, therefore, we need intelligent propaganda. Less about 'class consciousness', 'expropriation of the expropriators', 'bourgeois ideology', and 'proletarian solidarity', not to mention the sacred sisters, thesis, antithesis, and synthesis; and more about justice, liberty, and the plight of the unemployed. And less about mechanical progress, tractors, the Dnieper dam, and the latest salmon-canning factory in Moscow; that kind of thing is not an integral part of Socialist doctrine, and it drives away many people whom the Socialist cause needs, including most of those who can hold a pen. All that is needed is to hammer two facts home into the public consciousness. One, that the interests of all exploited people are the same; the other, that Socialism is compatible with common decency.

As for the terribly difficult issue of class-distinctions, the only possible policy for the moment is to go easy and not frighten more people than can be helped. And above all, no more of those muscular-curate efforts at class-breaking.* If you belong to the bourgeoisie, don't be too eager to bound forward and embrace your proletarian brothers; they may not like it, and if they show that they don't like it you will probably find that your class-prejudices are not so dead as you imagined. And if you belong to the proletariat, by birth or in the sight of God, don't sneer too automatically at the Old School Tie; it covers loyalties which can be useful to you if you know how to handle them.

Yet I believe there is some hope that when Socialism is a living issue, a thing that large numbers of Englishmen genuinely care about, the class-difficulty may solve itself more rapidly than now seems thinkable. In the next few years we shall either get that effective Socialist party that we need, or we shall not get it. If we do not get it, then Fascism is coming; probably a slimy Anglicized form of Fascism, with cultured policemen instead of Nazi gorillas and the lion and the unicorn instead of the swastika. But if we do get it there will be a struggle, conceivably a physical one, for our plutocracy will not sit quiet under a genuinely revolutionary government. And when the widely separate classes who, necessarily, would form any real Socialist party have fought side by side, they may feel differently about one another. And then perhaps this misery of class-prejudice will fade away, and we of the sinking middle class—the private schoolmaster, the half-starved free-lance journalist, the colonel's spinster daughter with £75 a year, the jobless Cambridge graduate, the ship's officer without a ship, the clerks, the civil servants, the commercial travellers, and the thrice-bankrupt drapers in the country towns—may sink without further struggles into the working class where we belong, and probably when we get there it will not be so dreadful as we feared, for, after all, we have nothing to lose but our aitches.

APPENDIX
PHOTOGRAPHS

THE original edition of *The Road to Wigan Pier* was illustrated with a section of thirty-two plates, twenty-eight of which are reproduced in this volume. The quality is compromised because they have had to be reproduced from the plates used in the original edition. Nevertheless, the photographs are worthy of inclusion because they were a highly significant feature of the first edition, and noted as such by several reviewers. They shaped readers' understanding of the book's intention and conclusions. Four illustrations are not included due to high resolution files not being available.

The illustrations appear to have been the idea of Victor Gollancz and the architect Clough Williams Ellis. On 21 December 1936 they met George Orwell and agreed to have forty-eight plates in the book. Williams Ellis appears to have suggested names of those who might provide them. Ultimately only thirty-two plates were included. Victor Gollancz was keen to ensure that the book was published as quickly as possible, so the search for photographs was limited.

The thirty-two plates depict Welsh coal miners and poor housing across Britain. Their geographic range supports the point Orwell made repeatedly in *The Road to Wigan Pier*: that the problems he examined were endemic to working-class life, not confined to particular neighbourhoods or to the poorest regions. The importance of housing conditions in shaping people's lives was emphasized in the photographs of London as well as in Orwell's text.

In several important ways the photographs echo Orwell's own narrative and perspective. The significance of the photographs in giving a human face to unemployment and poverty was remarked upon by reviewers in the *Times Literary Supplement* and the *Manchester Guardian*. The photographic sequence offers no sense of progression; neither does Orwell's prose (except with regard to his own development). Most of the figures in the photographs are static: they bear witness to their conditions but cannot change them. Only rarely do they face the camera lens. The viewer is invited to observe and judge their conditions, while those in the photograph simply bear them. We are encouraged to admire but also to pity their stoicism. The photographs suggest that only the actions of those behind the camera—such as the viewers and readers themselves—can enact reform.

The conspicuousness of miners in the photographs emphasizes their iconic place in Orwell's version of working-class life. Missing are those elements of working-class life neglected in Orwell's own text that were in fact so distinctive to the 1930s. These include the signs of new affluence in south-east England, where the Depression was coming to an end: cinema queues and production lines in new factories were beyond the remit of Orwell's book. But the photographs also miss the NUWM rallies, hunger marches, and Workers' Educational Association classes that were part of working-class life in northern England. Orwell conspicuously avoided evidence that his subjects were hungry to change their own circumstances and had ideas about how to do so.

In other respects, the photographs differ from Orwell's authorial intention. The photographs corroborate Gollancz's conviction that the first part of *Wigan Pier*—Orwell's representation of the facts, figures, and human face of working-class life—was the most powerful part of the book. In this way, the inclusion of the photographs subtly shifts the balance of the book towards Part One, although in fact Part Two is just as long and, for Orwell, at least as significant.

'Limehouse' on page 172 © Mary Evans Picture Library.

All other illustrations © Mary Evans/Peter Higginbotham Collection.

Coal-searchers

South Wales: Miners of the Fernhill Colliery come to the surface after a stay-in strike of nearly two weeks underground

Cilfynydd, Pontypridd, South Wales: Unemployed miners watching the buckets tipping slag in the hope that some coal may fall

Nine Mile Point Colliery, Newport: Relatives and friends waiting at the pit-head for news of the miners, who are conducting a stay-in strike below

A row of undermined houses in Blaenavon, Monmouthshire

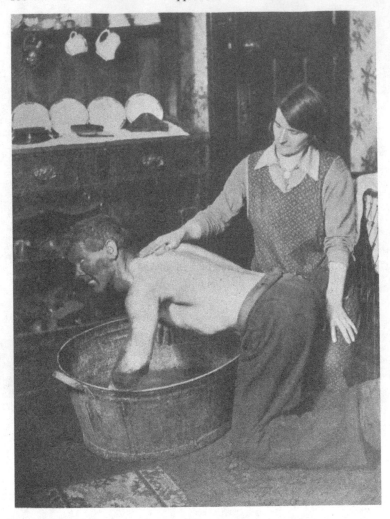

A South Wales miner takes his bath

Miners' cottages

Outside Newcastle: Whole families of miners live in these tiny and insanitary dwellings, for which a rent of seven shillings is charged

Miners' cottages at Coatbridge

Miners' cottages at Blantyre

Blaina, Wales: Rotting interior of a slum dwelling

House near Swansea threatened by slag-heap

Blaina, Wales

Gap by a window of a school in Wales

Limehouse

Limehouse

Scullery in Limehouse

Bethnal Green

Bethnal Green

Bethnal Green

Stepney: Shadwell district

Stepney: Shadwell district

Stepney

Dinner on the table in Poplar

St. Pancras: Before the slum clearance

Poplar

Caravan-dwellers near Durham quarry

Overcrowding

EXPLANATORY NOTES

3 *The first sound . . . cobbled street*: like some of the other most memorable lines in *The Road to Wigan Pier*, Orwell developed this one from a diary entry he made while on his travels. On 18 February 1936 he wrote: 'In the early morning the mill girls clumping down the cobbled street, all in clogs, make a curiously formidable sound, like an army hurrying into battle' (George Orwell, *Diary*, Orwell Foundation, https://theroadtowiganpier. wordpress.com/2011/02/18/18-2-36/).

the house had been an ordinary dwelling-house . . . tripe-shop and lodging-house: Orwell moved to these lodgings, above a tripe shop, on 15 February 1936. Prior to this he had lodged with Mr and Mrs Hornby at Warrington Lane, but left because Mrs Hornby was taken ill and had to go into hospital.

5 *The old-age pensioners had . . . been driven from their homes by the Means Test*: the household means test was introduced by Britain's Conservative-dominated National Government in 1931. Anyone seeking to claim unemployment benefit had to submit to having their household means-tested by the local Public Assistance Committee (PAC). Those considered to have property that was surplus to requirements, to be feckless spenders, or to have relatives bringing in an income considered sufficient to support the unemployed were denied benefit. As the assessors considered people could live on an extremely small income, this often led to unemployed men being obliged to rely on their teenage children's low earnings or their resident parents' old-age pensions. As a result, wage-earning children and pensioners often had to leave their homes to find lodgings elsewhere, or risk the entire household facing penury, inability to pay the rent, and ultimately homelessness.

8 *Mr Brooker was dodging the Means Test and drawing an allowance from the P.A.C.*: in 1929 the newly elected Labour government abolished the Poor Law, under which those in poverty had been forced to enter the local work-house unless they could convince the Board of Guardians (a body usually staffed by some elected councillors and local dignitaries such as Justices of the Peace, landed gentry, or large employers) that they should be given so-called 'outdoor relief'. The process of applying for poor relief was humiliating. Public Assistance Committees were intended to be more democratic in their composition and were given responsibility for set-ting the level of benefit that the poor could receive but in practice were often filled by those who had previously been guardians. Those in pov-erty or ill health could apply to the PAC for financial help. Mr Brooker may have been considered too sick to work and thus escaped the means test, which only applied to claimants of unemployment benefit (although PACs could and did interrogate those applying for other sorts of financial assistance).

12 *a young woman was kneeling . . . poking a stick up a foul drain-pipe*: in Orwell's diary this encounter occurs on 15 February and in rather different circumstances. He writes: 'Passing up a horrible squalid side-alley, saw a woman, youngish but very pale and with the usual draggled exhausted look, kneeling by the gutter outside a house and poking a stick up the leaden waste-pipe, which was blocked. I thought how dreadful a destiny it was to be kneeling in the gutter in a back-alley in Wigan, in the bitter cold, prodding a stick up a blocked drain. At that moment she looked up and caught my eye, and her expression was as desolate as I have ever seen; it struck me that she was thinking just the same thing as I was' (George Orwell, Diary, 15 February 1936, Orwell Foundation, https://theroadtowiganpier. wordpress.com/2011/02/15/15-2-36-2/).

13 *rooks treading*: in his diary Orwell wrote 'rooks copulating' and retained this description in the manuscript of *Wigan Pier* that he sent to Moore in December 1936. Orwell and Gollancz subsequently changed this to 'rooks courting'. In January 1927, at Orwell's request, his wife, Eileen, asked Gollancz to change this to 'rooks treading' because he considered 'rooks courting' to be an over-used phrase. Gollancz agreed. (Peter Davison, 'Note on *The Road to Wigan Pier*', Orwell Foundation, https:// www.orwellfoundation.com/the-orwell-foundation/orwell/library/ eileen-blair-to-miss-perriam-17-january-1937/).

14 *pace Chesterton*: Orwell is referring to the conservative Catholic author G. K. (Gilbert Keith) Chesterton (1874–1936). Chesterton wrote that 'civilisation is founded upon abstractions' in an essay entitled 'Tragedy of a Twopence', in *Tremendous Trifles* (New York: Dodd, Mead, 1913), 191. In 1928 Chesterton took part in a debate with George Bernard Shaw about whether to nationalize the coal mines (Shaw supported this idea, Chesterton opposed it).

16 *you have to go down several coal-mines*: Orwell went down Bryn Hall Colliery (known locally as Crippens Pit) in the Wigan coalfield, and Wentworth Pit and Grimethorpe Pit in the Barnsley coalfield, in that order.

25 *Miners' Welfare Fund*: the Miners' Welfare Fund was established by the Mining Industry Act of 1920, and funded by a levy on employers. It was administered by local committees that included employers' and miners' representatives and paid for university scholarships, healthcare, libraries, baths, and institutes. This followed a tradition of miners raising funds themselves to pay for such amenities.

55 *a 'Mary Ann'*: slang for a male homosexual.

58 *I had gone to Burma when I was still a boy*: Orwell joined the Indian Imperial Police in 1922 and served in Burma for five years.

93 *member of the C.P.G.B.*: the CPGB (the Communist Party of Great Britain) was founded in 1920. While Orwell focused on its wealthier members, the CPGB was strongest in mining and textile districts and increased its membership during the Depression, due in large part to the work of

Wal Hannington and other CPGB members in establishing the National Unemployed Workers' Movement (NUWM). After Adolph Hitler became Chancellor of Germany in 1933, all European Communist parties championed the idea of a Popular Front against Fascism. This meant that the CPGB sought to form alliances with the Independent Labour Party (ILP) and Labour activists and trade unionists. This did not prevent the CPGB standing candidates against Labour in elections, and in 1935 Willie Gallacher was elected MP for West Fife, the first Communist MP to be elected for six years, and the first ever to be elected against a Labour competitor.

108 *John Galsworthy*: John Galsworthy (1867–1933) was an English novelist and playwright, who wrote about class tensions and sex inequality within marriage.

112 *I.L.P.'er*: the ILP was established in 1893 with particular strength in Lancashire and Yorkshire. In 1931 the ILP disaffiliated from the Labour Party because members opposed Ramsay MacDonald's decision to form a National Government with the Conservative and Liberal parties. Its membership fell from 16,773 in 1932 to 4,392 by 1935, but most of those who remained were highly politically active, and many were young. In 1937 Orwell travelled to Spain as part of an ILP contingent to fight alongside Republican forces.

114 *Left Review*: this periodical was established in 1934 by writers with Communist sympathies. It attracted contributions from a wide range of left-wing authors, including W. H. Auden and Winifred Holtby. It ceased publication in 1938.

120 *Daily Worker*: the *Daily Worker* was founded in 1930 by the CPGB.

123 *Shaw*: George Bernard Shaw (1856–1950) was an Irish playwright, critic, and political activist, who lived in London for most of his life.

126 *W. H. Auden, a sort of gutless Kipling*: 'Orwell somewhat retracted this remark later. See "Inside the Whale", in *England Your England*, 120 (Secker & Warburg Collected Edition)' [Note added to the 1959 Secker & Warburg Uniform Edition].

130 *Dneiper dam*: Orwell misspells the name of the massive Dnieper Hydroelectric Station dam, constructed in Ukraine between 1921 and 1941.

Karel Capek . . . R.U.R.: Karel Capek (1890–1938) was a Czech writer, playwright, and critic. His play *R.U.R* (1920) introduced the word 'robot'. He was strongly opposed to both Fascism and Communism.

Wells-world: Orwell is referring to H. G. Wells (1866–1946), the author of futuristic science fiction novels, including *War of the Worlds* (1897), in which Martians colonize the earth.

146 *Mosley and his pimpled followers*: Sir Oswald Mosley (1896–1980) founded the British Union of Fascists (BUF) in 1932. He had entered Parliament as a Conservative MP in 1918, but joined the Labour Party

in 1924. In 1926 he became Labour MP for Smethwick. In 1931, dissatisfied with Labour, he founded the New Party, which increasingly inclined to Fascist politics. After the New Party failed to gain any seats in the 1931 general election, Mosley visited the Fascist leader of Italy, Benito Mussolini. He founded the BUF shortly after his return, and quickly attracted 50,000 members and the support of the *Daily Mail* and its wealthy proprietor, Lord Rothermere. By 1936 the BUF was losing many supporters, due to its violent suppression of protest and opposition at its rallies and growing concern about Fascism (the *Daily Mail*, which had initially supported the BUF, withdrew its support in 1934 after the BUF's Olympia Rally, at which BUF stewards brutally attacked hecklers). On 4 October 1936, while Orwell was writing *Wigan Pier*, 1,900 Fascists were prevented from marching through London's East End by 100,000 anti-Fascist trade unionists, Socialists, and local residents in the Battle of Cable Street. Orwell's dismissal of Mosley's followers as adolescent boys refers to the young unemployed men who were among the BUF's members. Mosley did succeed in attracting older, middle-class supporters, though their numbers were falling by 1936. Orwell went to see Mosley speak in Barnsley on 16 March 1936. He describes the meeting in his diary:

Last night to hear Mosley speak at the Public Hall, which is in structure a theatre. It was quite full—about 700 people I should say. About 100 Blackshirts on duty, with two or three exceptions weedy-looking specimens, and girls selling *Action* etc. Mosley spoke for an hour and a half and to my dismay seemed to have the meeting mainly with him. He was booed at the start but loudly clapped at the end. Several men who tried at the beginning to interject questions were thrown out, one of them—who as far as I could see was only trying to get a question answered—with quite unnecessary violence, several Blackshirts throwing themselves upon him and raining blows on him while he was still sitting down and had not attempted any violence. M. is a very good speaker. His speech was the usual claptrap—Empire free trade, down with the Jew and the foreigner, higher wages and shorter hours all round etc. etc. After the preliminary booing the (mainly) working-class audience was easily bamboozled by M. speaking from as it were a Socialist angle, condemning the treachery of successive governments towards the workers. (Orwell, Diary, Orwell Foundation, https://theroadtowiganpier. wordpress.com/2011/03/16/16-3-36/)

147 *Roland in the pass at Roncevaux*: Roland (d. 778) was a prefect of the Breton March, responsible for defending Francia against the Bretons. He was killed by Basques at the Battle of Roncevaux Pass in 778, an episode later romanticized in *chansons de gestes* such as the Song of Roland.

159 *muscular-curate efforts at class-breaking*: Orwell refers to the university settlement movement that developed in Britain and the United States in

the late nineteenth century and was still popular in the 1930s. Christian volunteers established 'settlement houses' in poor urban areas, where settlement workers lived and tried to educate and alleviate the poverty of their neighbours. Clergymen and university students were among those who staffed the settlements.

The Oxford World's Classics Website

www.worldsclassics.co.uk

- Browse the full range of Oxford World's Classics online

- Sign up for our monthly e-alert to receive information on new titles

- Read extracts from the Introductions

- Listen to our editors and translators talk about the world's greatest literature with our Oxford World's Classics audio guides

- Join the conversation, follow us on Twitter at OWC_Oxford

- Teachers and lecturers can order inspection copies quickly and simply via our website

www.worldsclassics.co.uk

American Literature

British and Irish Literature

Children's Literature

Classics and Ancient Literature

Colonial Literature

Eastern Literature

European Literature

Gothic Literature

History

Medieval Literature

Oxford English Drama

Philosophy

Poetry

Politics

Religion

The Oxford Shakespeare

A complete list of Oxford World's Classics, including Authors in Context, Oxford English Drama, and the Oxford Shakespeare, is available in the UK from the Marketing Services Department, Oxford University Press, Great Clarendon Street, Oxford OX2 6DP, or visit the website at www.oup.com/uk/worldsclassics.

In the USA, visit www.oup.com/us/owc for a complete title list.

Oxford World's Classics are available from all good bookshops. In case of difficulty, customers in the UK should contact Oxford University Press Bookshop, 116 High Street, Oxford OX1 4BR.

	Late Victorian Gothic Tales
	Literature and Science in the Nineteenth Century
JANE AUSTEN	Emma
	Mansfield Park
	Persuasion
	Pride and Prejudice
	Selected Letters
	Sense and Sensibility
MRS BEETON	Book of Household Management
MARY ELIZABETH BRADDON	Lady Audley's Secret
ANNE BRONTË	The Tenant of Wildfell Hall
CHARLOTTE BRONTË	Jane Eyre
	Shirley
	Villette
EMILY BRONTË	Wuthering Heights
ROBERT BROWNING	The Major Works
JOHN CLARE	The Major Works
SAMUEL TAYLOR COLERIDGE	The Major Works
WILKIE COLLINS	The Moonstone
	No Name
	The Woman in White
CHARLES DARWIN	The Origin of Species
THOMAS DE QUINCEY	The Confessions of an English Opium-Eater
	On Murder
CHARLES DICKENS	The Adventures of Oliver Twist
	Barnaby Rudge
	Bleak House
	David Copperfield
	Great Expectations
	Nicholas Nickleby

ANTHONY TROLLOPE

The American Senator
An Autobiography
Barchester Towers
Can You Forgive Her?
Cousin Henry
Doctor Thorne
The Duke's Children
The Eustace Diamonds
Framley Parsonage
He Knew He Was Right
Lady Anna
The Last Chronicle of Barset
Orley Farm
Phineas Finn
Phineas Redux
The Prime Minister
Rachel Ray
The Small House at Allington
The Warden
The Way We Live Now

	Travel Writing 1700–1830
	Women's Writing 1778–1838
WILLIAM BECKFORD	Vathek
JAMES BOSWELL	Life of Johnson
FRANCES BURNEY	Camilla
	Cecilia
	Evelina
ROBERT BURNS	Selected Poems and Songs
LORD CHESTERFIELD	Lord Chesterfield's Letters
JOHN CLELAND	Memoirs of a Woman of Pleasure
DANIEL DEFOE	A Journal of the Plague Year
	Moll Flanders
	Robinson Crusoe
	Roxana
HENRY FIELDING	Jonathan Wild
	Joseph Andrews and Shamela
	Tom Jones
JOHN GAY	The Beggar's Opera and Polly
WILLIAM GODWIN	Caleb Williams
OLIVER GOLDSMITH	The Vicar of Wakefield
MARY HAYS	Memoirs of Emma Courtney
ELIZABETH INCHBALD	A Simple Story
SAMUEL JOHNSON	The History of Rasselas
	Lives of the Poets
	The Major Works
CHARLOTTE LENNOX	The Female Quixote
MATTHEW LEWIS	The Monk